COURAGE
WAS MY
ONLY OPTION

COURAGE WAS MY ONLY OPTION

THE AUTOBIOGRAPHY OF ROMAN KENT

With a Foreword by Lawrence Eagleburger,
Former U.S. Secretary of State

VANTAGE PRESS
New York

Descriptions of Photographs on Front of Jacket

Upper Part of Cover (Left to Right): Featured in *Changing Times*, May, 1991, photo by Ken Shung—mirror image of Roman Kent depicts a lion, the Dreyfus Fund logo, after his "David vs. Goliath" victory against Dreyfus Fund; a young Roman Kent aboard the *Marine Perch* on his voyage to America in 1946; cover of children's book by Roman Kent entitled *My Dog Lala* published in 2006.

Lower Part of Cover (Left to Right): Roman and Hannah Kent visiting Auschwitz Concentration Camp in 1979 during filming of award-winning documentary "Children of the Holocaust"; Roman Kent speaking before the General Assembly of the United Nations in January, 2006 at International Day of Holocaust Commemoration.

FIRST EDITION

Copyright © 2008 by Roman Kent

Published by Vantage Press, Inc.
419 Park Ave. South, New York, NY 10016

Manufactured in the United States of America
ISBN: 978-0-533-15653-5

Library of Congress Catalog Card No.: 2006909086

0 9 8 7 6 5 4 3 2 1

Contents

Selected Speeches

Foreword

Reader's Digest used to have an item it ran regularly entitled "The Most Unforgettable Character I Ever Met." As one goes through life one meets many "characters," most of them eminently forgettable. To meet someone who strikes such a chord as to become positively "unforgettable" truly signifies someone of heady attributes, usually entwined with morality, stature, and principle. Roman Kent would be one of very few people I would include in such a list were I to search through the some fifty years of people I have known in and out of government.

To me, Roman ranks high on my "unforgettable" list for a host of reasons. As you will see as you read through this volume, he has lived a remarkable life—a life from concentration camp to refugee, from refugee to young immigrant to the U.S., and from there to successful businessman and leader of the Jewish community in the U.S. and internationally. Throughout his remarkably full life he has always maintained his kindness and his decency.

This is apparent in the way he has lived his life. His book is easily divided into four different "chapters." It begins, as all biographies do, with the story of his family and an introduction to Lala, his wonderful little dog. This puppy's impact on his life became a lesson of love and loyalty, tolerance and loss, that is a valuable teaching tool—and leads one to understand the sterling values that drive my friend Roman.

His travails in the ghettoes and camps did not destroy his dignity and honor. Even in times of horrendous adversity, he sought to choose life, savoring a bit of optimism, as he and his brother found ways to maintain the family togetherness. Despite the loss of his beloved father and Lala, he and his brother used ingenuity to maintain a little vegetable plot in the ghetto so he could feed his mother and sisters until that, too, was destroyed. In Auschwitz and beyond, he tried to maintain a shred of dignity, caring for his brother and daring to do, sometimes, what others could not.

Arriving in America in the aftermath and to discover himself in Atlanta was a cultural shock. Yet he was determined to make things work, honestly and decently. He and his brother began to live the American dream—working and toiling to lift themselves out of "charity," to create productive and happy lives. Roman became a successful businessman—starting out of the trunk of his car, selling dry goods to sharecropper families—until he reached the Empire State Building and QVC's shopping channel on TV. His success in business did not stop him from being actively involved in many charitable organizations. His brother continued his studies and became a successful neurosurgeon.

When Roman was semi-retired, he expanded his role as a community activist and public figure. When he became active in Jewish life, he discovered his new mission: caring for fellow Holocaust survivors less fortunate than he and teaching children to stop the hate, any hate.

It is at this fourth stage in his life that I met this incredibly decent man, one who has devoted himself to teaching people some of the important lessons he learned through experience. I see in him a man who does what he can to make this world a little bit better than the way he found it.

Roman Kent doesn't have a mean bone in his body. If he, as a Holocaust survivor, harbors any hatred toward the sons and daughters of the perpetrators, I have yet to encounter it. If he seeks vengeance for those crimes, I have not seen it. What I have seen is a man searching for justice, for Roman's heart and soul have been devoted to a decades-long struggle to provide economic and psychological support for Holocaust survivors and their heirs from those who destroyed their families and stole the best years of their lives. One of his key motivations was forcing the German government to take moral responsibility for its crimes. He holds those responsible for the Holocaust in contempt, and is devoted to the memory of the Six Million.

My relationship with Roman intensified when I was appointed Chairman of the International Commission on Holocaust Era Insurance Claims (ICHEIC). Roman, as one of the Commissioners representing the Jewish participating organizations, has been a driving force in our efforts to find potential beneficiaries of unpaid insurance policies written on Holocaust victims and survivors. He has been unstinting in his pursuit of errant insurance companies that have failed to meet their commitments to their insured for over five decades.

Despite their "strictly business" approach to the claims of beneficiaries, their bureaucratic and often heartless attempts to stonewall and avoid their fiduciary obligations, he has never engaged in vicious or *ad hominem* attacks on those companies; rather, his command of the facts, his tenacity, and his persuasive advocacy have brought the companies to a far more cooperative stance than could be achieved by constant confrontation (although he has been a master of confrontation when necessary). I believe that whatever success ICHEIC has had is in large part a consequence of Roman's consummate diplomacy and unyielding determination.

And so, as you read through this volume, you can see the diplomatic Mr. Kent describe his life experiences, often sweet, often bitter, but without the vitriol one might find in a person who has encountered life's challenges and injustices—challenges and injustices with which few of us are ever faced—and managed to persevere and, in fact, successfully overcome them. Yet underneath his reasoned narrative, one can visualize the turmoil of a man persecuted for his faith and almost killed; a man discriminated against by his own people when he came to America in search of freedom; a man who founded a successful business, only to be cheated by the partner he trusted; a man who undertook a mission to seek justice for his brothers and sisters who survived the Holocaust and those who did not and to constantly face not only the slings and arrows of the perpetrators but of his fellow Jews who, with their own agendas, hamper the process of obtaining that justice; a man who, in the face of personal tragedy, continues to fight a battle that may never see resolution in his lifetime. And yet, this gentle man fights on with a will of steel.

Roman Kent has become a truly "unforgettable" character in

my lifetime, and will become one to those who read this book. Others who will read it may be inspired to continue Roman's mission—finding "Truth, Justice, and the American Way," a more fitting way of guiding one's life than doing "strictly business."

Lawrence Eagleburger
Former Secretary of State
Washington, D.C.
2005

Acknowledgments

It took many years for me to compile my life's story into a meaningful, condensed version for the reading public. Being unfamiliar with the modern world of computers, I dictated each and every page to my devoted secretary, Irene Schechter, who lovingly and painstakingly typed and fine-tuned the dictation page by page. After reviewing, I made appropriate changes, and the text was retyped into a more stimulating, engaging narrative. Reaching this juncture, I then spent countless hours with Jeanette Friedman, whose editorial skills helped to improve and enhance its contents even further. Without their imput and devotion, my saga might never have been completed.

In a way, the final momentum to complete my autobiography was affectionately, but forcefully, provided by former Secretary of State, The Honorable Lawrence Eagleburger. After writing a touching Foreword on my behalf, he stated ". . . now that you have the Foreword, it is time for you to complete the book." Obviously, his words inspired me to finish the project without further delay.

There are many individuals, exemplified by my cherished father, who greatly influenced my life and commitments. To all of them I owe a debt of gratitude, and I say a collective "Thank You." My story was written as an historical and personal remembrance for my family and the community at large. Since the publication of this book coincides with my 50th Wedding Anniversary, it is also a "love letter" to my wife, Hannah.

COURAGE
WAS MY
ONLY OPTION

Prologue:
From the Holocaust
to a New Life

How does one write about a life when it consists of three separate, distinct, and unique stories? Why should that life story be told at all? Sixty years after the Holocaust, why should a single survivor bother writing about his personal experiences? The shortest and most obvious answer would be, "Why not?"

Yet that answer is too effortless for someone who came through the attempted genocide of the Jews that saw 6,000,000—4.5 million adults and 1.5 million children—destroyed in sadistic and venal ways. That number of victims is so large—considering the sheer mass of the destruction—it is humanly incomprehensible. I believe that no one can be expected to understand such mammoth destruction.

As one of the minuscule number of children who escaped annihilation, I am compelled to give a better and more painstaking answer than, "Why not?" I am writing my memoirs because I have concluded that producing this chronicle is a sacred duty and testament to those who perished and those who survived.

A survivor writes his or her memoirs because—while the Holocaust is a collective disaster, each innocent Jewish life affected by the atrocities of the Holocaust has its own specific story. Our stories are like little survival kits that contain the essentials to keep civilization civil and hatred at bay.

Our story is not just for telling. We write so that the details of our experience are documented and never forgotten. We write to remember so that others might learn.

As writers, we hope that our children—our readers—will take positive knowledge from what happened to us, so that our pain and loss will not be forgotten; that it will not disappear like smoke on a windy day. We write about what we learned from our

1

own complacency and powerlessness, and hope that others take it to heart.

We ask a great deal from our readers. We sound a warning to our children, imploring them to pay attention to injustice whenever and wherever it rears its ugly head. Our stories tell of the hazards of apathy, of isolation, of silence. Silence does, indeed, equal death.

With the passage of time, precise dates and specific names have evaporated from my consciousness. Time does take its toll—another lesson learned. While tiny details escape me, what I saw, heard, and felt is firmly planted in my brain. What I witnessed will speak for itself.

I write my story for my children, Susan and Jeffrey, for my grandchildren, Dara, Eryn, and Sean, and for future generations.

For years, Susan and Jeffrey encouraged me to write about my life in all its incarnations—before, during, and after the Holocaust. I've managed to tell them bits and pieces here and there, but I have not, until now, been able to sit down and offer a comprehensive account. The perspective that time offers is priceless. It becomes the enabler, allowing us to confront the past by softening the pain and agony.

My children expressed their need for me to do this work in eloquent ways. When we came back from the American Gathering of Jewish Holocaust Survivors in Washington, D.C. in 1983, Susan wrote me and her mother, Hannah—also a survivor—a letter.

July 9, 1983

Dear Mom and Dad:

I'm lying here right now reading the commemoration book put together by the Washington Post. Again the tears are flowing as they so often do when I think of all the atrocities and pain you went through during the war and have relived since.

I wonder how you or anyone could have survived and be living now, with a new life, an outward appearance that is unscathed by the horrors once lived, no, not once but many times over. My heart breaks every time I think of your childhood years.

Childhood, a time that is supposed to be carefree and fun-filled. Yes, yours were filled with excitement, but an excitement of such a kind the world should never have allowed.

The family I never knew; all perished without a trace. There were the people you lived with, who raised you, who you grew up with, who you played with but who never survived. They are all gone. The world never knowing what each one of them had to offer. Why? Nothing makes sense.

How could all this have happened? How can all those who survived live new lives while a part of them must have died a long time ago? How can and do you, the survivors, have the will and strength to get through each passing day?

I want to know and understand how you felt and how you feel now. Yet, I know that this is an impossibility. How can anyone, not having gone through it first-hand ever expect to really know? Yet, let us hope that even without that knowledge, we never forget what did take place in that land not so very far away in distance, nor in time.

Love, Susan

My son Jeffrey gave a presentation at the General Assembly at that same American Gathering. Among the things he said:

". . . World War II brings to mind many whys: Why did it happen? Why to me? Why should I remember? Why must I remember? Why don't I understand?

"All survivors have been through the inferno and none were left untouched. That which cannot be seen, heard, felt, or done exists within each one. They are separate from us—the non-survivors. They are separate from life itself. They are special. Soon there will be no survivors. Their generation will be gone and there will be no witnesses to tell the tale.

"To do them justice is not to glorify them, for their story is not one of glory. It is a story of the worst horrors of life—the dark side of man, the shadow. The story is not told to elicit pity, respect or love. It is told because it happened and we must remember. Though we will never understand why or how, we must know when and what.

"There are no superheroes in this story—only men, women, and children. Some maybe were more fortunate, some maybe less. There is no one ultimate survivor. Each and every one is an ultimate survivor and each one has a tale that should be heard, not so that we will understand better, but so that we have more to remember so less will be forgotten. But remembering is not enough—not without applying the remembering to the present. We cannot contradict it. We must maintain ourselves, the tolerance we preach, and so very much wish existed in 1939."

My children have the right to know—this alone is reason enough to write.

But there is more, much more. Prejudice, hatred, hunger, wars, and atrocities in the name of religion and political ideologies rage across the planet. In Chechnya, school children are murdered just as they were in Maalot, Israel, decades ago, by the same kinds of Islamic terrorism responsible for the destruction of the World Trade Center in New York City on 9/11.

We have witnessed eleven years of ethnic cleansing in the Balkans; genocides in Sudan, East Timor, Rwanda; religious killings in Somalia, Ireland, and Afghanistan. Everywhere we look, blood still soaks the ground—and for what?

Still, the Holocaust stands alone, a singular event among the genocides committed by civilizations run amuck.

I was a child who lived through a devastating reality created by human beings. As a parent and grandparent, I know from bitter experience what it feels like to watch a child be injured or damaged in any way. To know that any child was tortured and murdered because I could not prevent it from happening shatters my heart and soul.

How do we prevent other Holocausts? How do we prevent more genocides and senseless wars? In a nuclear age, it may very well be impossible. Jewish tradition, however, implores us to do all we can, under the tenet of Tikkun Olam, repairing the world. And while we didn't start this work, and we may not finish it, it is incumbent upon us to toil away and try to make the world safer and more just.

The key to our success is education. Knowing about the consequences of apathy and hate, the effects of the abuse of power, about corruption in big business and politics, how economies are manipulated; understanding how media is used to transmit propaganda and lies about "the other"—putting together the big picture in a classroom and learning how to confront the evils in our lives—that is what Holocaust education is all about.

Forgiveness can only be granted by the 6,000,000 who perished and are no longer with us; whose voices have been silenced forever. Forget? We refuse. If we forget, we bury the conscience of mankind together with the 6,000,000.

How alone we were during the Holocaust! If we, the survivors, become bystanders of our own stories, our morality and ethics will be buried and laid to rest alongside our 6,000,000.

Survivors cannot be bystanders; we must be involved. Our obligation is to tell the story and be a moral force, by example and deed. That would be the greatest legacy to leave for posterity.

One
A Happy Childhood in Lodz

"In the beginning . . ."

My name is Roman Kent (born Kniker, pronounced Knicker with a hard K) and I come from Lodz, the second largest city in Poland and capital of its textile industry. Before the Second World War broke out in September 1939, the population of the city was about 600,000; approximately one-third were Polish nationals, one-third was German in origin, and one-third was Jewish. By and large it was not a beautiful city—it was an industrial town, a working man's city.

It was also a city full of contrasts. Factories with high brick chimneys that belched smoke adorned the skyline; tenement houses lined the streets. It was a city of mansions and a city of slums. There were some buildings with elevators and more were walk-up tenements, three and four stories high. There were places with indoor plumbing and some that had no running water with outhouses in their backyards. Some streets were paved with asphalt, some with cobblestones. Out in the country there were streets of clay that turned to mud whenever it rained.

Beautifully dressed men and women walked past beggars in rags, and while people from every economic level lived in Lodz, most of them were poor. This was the city of my birth in 1925.

I was the first-born son and the third child of the family. My parents were Emanuel and Sonia; my two older sisters were Dasza and Renia. As I understand it, after two girls, there was great rejoicing when I arrived. Of course, I had no clue at the time, but being a first-born son—the one entrusted to carry on the family name—was going to bring me a number of privileges, including traveling with my father on business.

A year-and-a-half later, the family celebrated the birth of

7

my brother, Leon. The family was then almost complete—a few years later another family member came along—but for the moment, we were two parents, two boys, and two girls, perfectly balanced.

I have precious few memories of our family life from very early times, and some are not particularly good. Around the time I turned three, my father was struck with a rare type of eczema and he and my mother left Poland to seek medical treatment for him in Austria, Germany, and Italy. I am sure the treatment my father received, and the expense of traveling all over Europe to get it, must have been costly, but our family had evidently been able to bear it.

During the more than eighteen months they spent looking for a cure, my siblings and I were farmed out to various relatives. I was taken to an aunt who lived nearby, but I don't remember the time I spent at her house. I am sure my early childhood memories are faint because of this traumatic disruption, and it's remarkable that even now, in my later years, I seem to have trouble remembering things that must have made an indelible impression on me in my childhood. I seem to have erased whatever I obviously did not want to remember.

When my parents returned from their medical pilgrimage, we all moved back to our comfortable apartment at 38 Srodmiejska Street, an apartment building right next door to the Poznanski Palace, where one of the richest men in the city lived. It was not by chance that we lived at this address, for directly across the street, at 35-37, was the textile factory my father owned ever since I could remember, where he manufactured all sorts of woven and knitted fabrics. The 35-37 represented two separate entrances, one to the factories and the other to a yard that contained a separate building. We were what you might call conservative and well-to-do, and my life was centered around my family, extended family, and school friends.

The factory was a major part of my growing-up years. My schoolmates and I spent hours there each week, playing soccer or hide-and-seek and other games in the courtyard. We were no different from other children our age and every now and then, and fairly frequently, we managed to shatter a window or two.

It was never a problem. Our sporty transgressions were quickly hidden by Kazimierz, our Polish-Catholic factory superintendent. Kazimierz, in his late thirties, was tall and well-built, with blond hair. He often took pity on us and repaired any damage we caused before my father could notice. He also taught me to ride small animals. He was raising a pig in a small pen in the factory yard, and sometimes took it out to let me ride it like a horse—actually more like a small pony. In fact, Kazimierz had named the pig Hitler, a name that meant nothing to me at the time, but now, in retrospect, strikes me as an odd act of courage.

When I'd learned to marshal the pig, Kazimierz took me to the outskirts of the city to teach me to ride my bicycle. I didn't know it at the time, but I realize now that he was my bodyguard, assigned by my father (whom I lovingly called Tatush) to protect me from anti-Semitic attacks. At that tender age, I had yet to be exposed to anti-Semitism.

My father's factory fascinated me because it was in perpetual motion. I watched as individual threads mysteriously combined to form beautiful pieces of cloth. Some of the machines twirled; others shuttled back and forth. I never knew any of the machine's names, but I came to recognize what they did. Some machines had hundreds of little needles, and if even one broke, or a thread would break, everything would come to an instant halt. As soon as that would happen, the "meisters" (the mechanics) would converge on the trouble spot and make the repairs.

My favorite part of hanging around the factory was being allowed to start up a machine. Normally, because the process was complicated, I could only do so under supervision. But one day, thinking I had had enough supervision and experience, I sneaked in to start a machine on my own, and I did a bang-up job. I managed to break every single needle on that particular machine, a much tougher problem for the mechanics to solve than fixing a broken windowpane. They managed to fix it before Tatush found out, or I and the meister would have had hell to pay! One would think I'd have learned my lesson from that experience. But for how long? It was no time before I would get into new kinds of mischief.

My father had no siblings in Lodz, but he did have an aging, invalid mother who lived in the apartment below us. Confined to her bed, we made it our business to visit her regularly. She wasn't at all like the grandmothers of the 21st century and died long before the war began. Leon and I weren't allowed to attend the funeral because we were too young.

Mamma had two brothers and two sisters who lived in town with their families. Her oldest sister, Clara, and her husband, Anatol, had a pharmacy that was very different from pharmacies today. It was a gem of a place. I loved to visit on weekends or holidays because of the shop's distinct and pleasing aromas, and because I was allowed to play with hundreds of little bottles of medicines and herbs that lined the shelves.

Aunt Clara's children were her son, Izio, who studied medicine abroad because the Jewish quotas in Polish medical schools were filled, and her daughter, Dasza, a divorcée who lived in Warsaw. We didn't see either of them very much. Since people didn't talk about things like divorce in those days, when they did talk about it, they did so in hushed voices so the children wouldn't hear. That's why we never got to know much about Dasza.

Every family has a character who stands out from the rest. Aunt Clara was the one who stood out in ours. She was the most religious person in Mamma's family and in her house, after sundown on Friday, all work stopped and Shabbat was observed, strictly and by the rules (except when Anatol took care of sick people, if he had to).

But Aunt Clara had a weakness that caused her to suffer from a severe conflict of interest. She loved to play cards. Poor Aunt Clara faced the horns of a dilemma every week. Friday night was the best time to play cards because it was the end of the long work-week and was supposed to be an evening of rest. But how can you play cards on Shabbat when it is expressly forbidden to do so?

Not to worry. Aunt Clara found a way around the law by devising a system of card-playing "by proxy." The housekeeper sat down in Aunt Clara's chair, was dealt a hand of cards, and Aunt Clara would stand behind her for the rest of the game whispering instructions. It was a sight to see. Aunt Clara felt she did nothing wrong, since technically she absolutely wasn't the one playing cards on Shabbat!

Mamma's older brother, Leon, was married to Olga. Unfortunately, my siblings and I never met him because he and their child both died before any of us were born. As a consequence of her sad circumstances, Aunt Olga devoted a great deal of her time to the local orphanage, the same orphanage where Chaim Rumkowski—later head of the Jüdenrat in the Lodz ghetto—was in charge.

Although we weren't a particularly observant family, we held to most Jewish traditions, and we also had very strong Zionist roots. I recall a little blue tin box, a *pushka,* where we dropped in coins that went to support the settlements in Palestine, the *Yishuv.* Tatush was so dedicated, he donated office space in his factory to Hanoar Hazioni, a Jewish organization devoted to life in Israel. My older sisters participated in their meetings, but Leon and I were both too young to do so.

Tatush always regretted being unable to speak Hebrew, but his Zionism manifested itself when he purchased property in Palestine, in a region that is today part of the industrial area on the outskirts of Haifa. Although he never visited his land, it was his intention to eventually sell all of our property in Lodz and build a factory in Israel.

Sometimes I wonder what might have happened if we'd left Poland right after Tatush purchased the land—as he had wanted to. Mamma held him back because she didn't want to uproot her children at such an early age. She thought it best to wait until we received our diplomas before leaving—which would take at least ten years—and then we could go.

We kept kosher at home, though Tatush sometimes "cheated" and did occasionally eat non-kosher foods outside; when Mamma wasn't with us, sometimes we would also indulge. Mamma was more observant than my father and she followed Shabbat rituals more strictly.

We were all sent to a private school, the Jewish Gymnasium, where we studied Hebrew and became well-versed in our religious traditions. As a rule, our family did not attend Friday or Saturday services, but we did go to synagogue on all religious holidays. Tatush, Leon, and I attended services in a big beautiful synagogue where the men stayed in the main sanctuary on the first floor and the women were separate and above us in the balcony. Mamma preferred to take my sisters to a smaller, more Orthodox synagogue. Today, when I close my eyes, I can still visualize the men of the family sitting together in the house of worship in Lodz, listening to the beautiful voices of the large boys' choir. I regret I wasn't ever able to find a similar service and choir in any temple I ever visited in America.

In those days, we prayed entirely in Hebrew, though most of the congregation did not understand the meaning of what they were saying. At every opportunity, Leon and I would try to sneak out to meet our friends and play little games behind the building. Coming home after services, we were always greeted by my mother and sisters, whose services ended earlier, giving them time to prepare our meals.

When I had my bar mitzvah in the spring of 1938, we had a ceremony in the synagogue where I conducted the entire service in *shul,* and was called to the Torah in front of my family and family friends. We had a big reception later for my friends at our home, which Mamma prepared. I remember her filling the bathtub with fresh carp that swam around until she was ready to cook them!

At our house, as in most others in those days, roles were clearly defined. A man was a man and a woman was a woman (whatever that meant!). As a boy child, I was always intrigued by what the females were doing, so I would sneak into women's territory, into the kitchen, to see what was going on. Whenever Tatush caught me snooping around there, he would give me a stern look and say, "Roman, have you ever seen me examining the pots and sifting through the dishes? Your place is here," and he would point at the dining room table.

Mamma spent more time with us than Tatush did. She would get up early every morning to prepare our hearty breakfasts and proper lunches for us to take to school. Then, at the end of the school day, she would be waiting for us at home with a snack—to make sure we completed our homework before we went out to play.

Tatush got up later than we did and didn't eat breakfast with us. He was almost always there for our main meal of the day, a supper served shortly after we returned from school. Sometimes, though, he was even too busy for that, and Mamma would send the housekeeper across the street with his meal. Every night before we were sent to bed, Mamma would serve us a light snack. It was a wonderful, carefree life.

When my parents wanted to communicate with each other and didn't want us to understand, they spoke in Russian. Yiddish was seldom heard at our house, though both my parents were fluent in it, and Tatush read the daily Yiddish newspaper as well as the Polish one. We spoke Polish all the time at home and in school our day was bi-lingual. We used Polish for our secular studies and Hebrew for our Jewish studies.

My fondest memories of home come from the time I spent in our formal dining room. The room played an important part in our lives, especially during Chanukah and even more so at Passover, when we used it for the *sedarim,* our most festive annual meals. Those special meals, served in that room, were spiritually charged by the reading of the Haggadah—the telling of the Passover story—and the singing of Hebrew songs. Tatush loved to listen to us until well after midnight, and his face would glow with pride as he listened to our young voices singing in Hebrew.

The real fun at the Seder would begin when the children were allowed to run wild, playing hide-and-seek and searching for the Afikoman. I can still remember, year after year, the triumphant pose struck by the child who found the middle matzoh and sold it off to the highest bidder—the bid being the best toy we could demand from the grown-ups.

The dining room itself consisted of lovely, ornate furniture, around a rectangular wood table. It was all hand-carved by a Jewish Russian master craftsman who had escaped during the Russian Revolution and landed in Lodz. When the Russian first arrived, Tatush gave him an apartment in the house in the factory yard, where he was able to live and practice his craft.

The dining room also had a great glass-doored breakfront that displayed beautiful crystal objects in every color imaginable. At the base of one of them there were two large compartments that held a Russian encyclopedia. The pages were of the finest paper and the bindings were made of richly tooled leather. The books were filled with multi-colored pictures and photographs. Of course, I couldn't read Russian, but I spent hours and hours admiring the images of fish, birds, animals, flowers, and whatever else caught my fancy.

I remember the dining room for another reason, too. During the winter, when it was too cold to go outside and play, Leon and I used the dining room as a miniature cycling rink. We closed the doors and squeezed the chairs as close as possible to the table; when this was accomplished, we would climb on our bicycles and ride around in ovals as fast as we could, hoping not to break anything.

Obviously, Mamma was never pleased about our indoor racetrack. As soon as she found out about it, she ordered us to stop immediately. Generally, we were having lots of fun, so we rarely listened. But when she resorted to the threat, "If you don't stop at once, I will have to call your father!" we would worry there would be hell to pay! Deep down, we knew that Mamma didn't really want to call him, but we could tell from the tone of her voice when she meant it, and only then would we stop.

During the winter, our apartment was heated by a built-in coal-burning stove of ceramic tile. When we'd come in from making snowmen and throwing snowballs at each other, it kept us warm. But when it was too cold to go outside, and we were sure Tatush was at the factory and Mamma was not home, Leon and I played a special game.

We had a very long hallway running the length of the apartment, and one of our favorite things to do was hang a target at one end of it, close all the doors on both sides of the hall, and then tell our sisters and their visiting friends not to pass through or open any of its doors. Then Leon and I set ourselves up at the opposite end of the hall and faced the target. Using an air gun, we would proceed to aim darts at the target from quite a distance away. It's funny that almost fifty years later one of my sister's friends reminded me of this very game, which I had forgotten. She recalled the details and the memories flooded back. Then she commented on how much I had grown up since using the long hallway as a shooting gallery.

When I think back to those years, there is one object d'art we owned that has always remained in my thoughts. It is a portrait of Mamma as a bride that my father commissioned to celebrate their tenth wedding anniversary. It hung in their bedroom, and I remember it now as vividly as I saw it then. Mamma's bridal veil had been pulled away from her face and her hands, palms touching as if in prayer, rested in front of her. Mamma was beautiful, and made a stunning bride, and my feeling was that her portrait completely caught her essence. We adored the painting, and Mamma considered it her most precious possession.

The painting sticks in my memory for another reason, too. The invading German Army confiscated our apartment, forcing us to leave, empty-handed, immediately. The apartment, with its entire contents, was given to a *Volksdeutsche* (a Polish person of German origin), and we were prohibited from entering it. Tatush contacted one of his factory workers, also a *Volksdeutsche,* and asked him to negotiate with the person who had our apartment. The *Volksdeutsche,* who now possessed every single thing we owned, from our toothbrushes to our silverware, also had this treasured painting. But the factory worker came back empty-handed, and told him what the *Volksdeutsche* had said: "I would rather burn the painting than give it to a Jew."

As the oldest son, I was sometimes allowed to accompany my father on business trips to Warsaw. The trips I took, the businessmen I met, and the way I saw my father do business, had a lasting effect on me. I remember that most of his business was done by word and handshakes, without the need for formal contracts or lawyers. Tatush taught me that my word is my bond.

My other contact with the business world at this early stage of life consisted of visiting the small loft factories leasing space from my father. One of these was a soap factory owned by a man named Mr. First. As a good friend of the family, Mr. First allowed Leon and me to wander around the premises and watch them make soap. We had a great time there, but there was something even better. It was paradise—a chocolate factory. And what could possibly be better than that, especially when we were allowed to scrape out and enjoy the chocolate residue at the bottom of the kettles? I have had a sweet tooth ever since those days.

Today, when I reflect on the past, I realize how special and exceptional my father really was. He never said a harsh word about anyone, he was always soft-spoken, and everyone he knew trusted him. My wife, Hannah, and I met Kazimierz, Tatush's old super, many years after the war and all he wanted to talk about was my father and what he meant to him. He wanted Hannah to understand who my father was.

"Mr. Kniker was a rich man; I was a poor man," he told us. "Mr. Kniker was a capitalist; I was a socialist. It never mattered to him in the least. He would visit my home, play with my child, and he always brought him toys. How many people did things like that? To me, he was a real human being, and I loved him and respected him for that."

Maybe it is because Tatush possessed such special qualities that I cannot remember a single fight, or even a quarrel, ever taking place between my parents. Mamma didn't want to burden him with household details or problems with us. She knew how hard he worked and didn't want to add more pressure. It may have also helped that Mamma had a beautiful voice, and when any of us were sick with the usual childhood illnesses, Mamma would sing to us to make us forget our aches and pains.

Tatush, on the other hand, did not have a good voice, but he loved listening to my mother sing. He also enjoyed hearing music on the radio, and could be found many evenings adjusting the knobs in order to pull in operas and Russian music that were being transmitted from Russia.

My parents were fairly well-educated and, because they experienced uprooting and persecution of Jews in Poland and Russia, they understood the crucial importance of education. They told us, "Whatever might happen to you, wherever you might go or be taken, you can never lose what you have learned." That is why, from first grade on, we were sent to the Jewish Gymnasium, one of the finest schools in Lodz.

My school, located at 21 Magistracka Street, was under the directorship of Dr. Perelman. The school was really three separate buildings, two different schools for boys on one street and one for girls at a different location, with different directors in each unit, all of them under the supervision of Dr. Braude.

Two-thirds of our time was spent studying languages, math, physics, world history, and the humanities, in Polish. The rest of the time we spent studying Hebrew and Jewish-related subjects like history, religion, and the study and interpretation of Torah, in Hebrew.

School was in session six days a week (every day except Saturday), from eight o'clock in the morning until three o'clock in the afternoon, with five-minute breaks between fifty-five-minute periods, and one long break for lunch. There were no more than twenty-three students in a class; we would stay in our "homeroom" all day, and the teachers would come to us.

I had very little to do with girls during my school years. We boys considered them nuisances worth teasing, and not people to take seriously. After all, girls didn't play soccer and they were never any good at other sports, either. Besides, the way our school was structured, we couldn't fraternize with the opposite sex, even if we wanted to, because the girls were in a different building.

The teaching at the Jewish school was first-rate. Each and every one of our teachers, even those who taught us in the early grades, held either a doctorate or a professor's degree or both. As a rule, teachers taught subjects in their own areas of expertise. Of course, boys being boys, we had nicknames for most of them. Dr. Zylberbogen, our biology professor, for instance, was called Baldy. Dr. Taube, who taught us Latin, was Sardine; Dr. Luboszycki, our Torah and Hebrew teacher, was Fritz, and our English and German instructor, Dr. Pinkus, was called Redhead. Some of the names, like Baldy or Redhead, were obvious choices. But I don't remember how we came to name our Latin teacher Sardine.

Our parents held our teachers in high esteem and believed that they were always right. No questions asked. Understandably, some teachers left more of a mark on me than others. They never had to use corporal punishment since they could do with words what other teachers did with rulers. But we still risked punishment when playing the occasional prank.

As a rule, when Dr. Taube taught, you could hear a pin drop. We studied our Latin and knew our subject. It is for this reason I considered our act against Dr. Taube to be doubly courageous.

I do remember, for example, the day we drew a caricature of Dr. Taube on the blackboard, his head blown up and the rest of his body in the shape of a sardine. But do not underestimate the tremendous amount of respect we had for our teachers in those days. As soon as a teacher entered the classroom, we automatically got to our feet and remained standing until the teacher took his seat and told us we could sit. Therefore, drawing a caricature of Dr. Taube on the chalkboard was quite scandalous and, I like to think, way ahead of its time.

On that day Dr. Taube entered the classroom, looked at the blackboard, and did not utter a word. He erased our little masterpiece and then sat down. He took out the roll book and slowly called aloud the name of every student from A to Z. He asked each of us a question or two, and the questions were so tough, none of us knew the answers. When he was done with the roll call, he calmly looked at each of us and said, "It is unfortunate that you all have not sufficiently prepared for the assignment, considering that you had enough time to draw a sardine on the blackboard. Each person in this class can now be proud to have earned a zero."

Another noteworthy classroom incident took place many years later, when I was a student at Emory University in Atlanta, Georgia. It involved Professor Blitch, who taught chemistry. His voice was so monotonous I often dozed off during his lectures. At the end of one of his classes, I once approached him to ask a question. After responding, he looked at me and politely asked if I had enjoyed my nap. I asked how, in a class of 100 students, he happened to notice me, since I thought I had disguised myself quite well. He explained that basically he paid attention to two types of students: the exceptionally good and the exceptionally bad . . . which brings me back to Lodz and my music teacher there.

Professor Fajwyszycz was my favorite teacher. I was so bad at music that he once told me, "You can be excused anytime you like." On the one hand it was nice to be given such freedom; on the other, it is a sad state of affairs when your teacher feels there is no hope for you.

There was only one teacher we took advantage of almost to the point of abuse because we could get away with it. Dr. Luboszycki was my Hebrew and religion teacher. He was fond of saying that nobody deserves an A because receiving an A meant you knew everything, and the only one who knows everything is God. We got even with his proclaimed philosophy by misbehaving in a variety of ways: we talked loudly to each other while he was teaching and we threw paper at each other, especially paper balls and airplanes. We moved stealthily from seat to seat behind his back, and once we did something and then realized, ourselves, that we had gone too far. Today, the little devices we used that day are known as cherry bombs. We placed these round, paper-wrapped mini-explosives under the legs of his chair, because we knew that when he really got upset, he would slam his chair down hard on the floor and yell, "That's enough!"

Carefully we manipulated him to the boiling point, awaiting his "That's enough!" He lifted the chair, high in the air, and when it came down, the explosives detonated. Even though we knew what to expect, we were still shocked by the resulting sound. He just stood there, stunned and speechless, and so were we.

During my school years, children did not have the luxury of school buses or private cars to take them to and from school. We used our feet, and my walk to school was a good thirty to forty minutes each way. On days when the weather was extremely bad—if there was a downpour or if it was extremely cold or snowing heavily—we hired a *droshky,* a horse and buggy, from the corner near our apartment to take us.

On one particularly rainy day, I was comfortably seated in the back when the wagon hit a very deep hole in the road and I flew out and landed in a puddle of water. Mamma was concerned for my safety, but when she saw I was fine, she let me have it. Of course, it had to be my fault because I wasn't paying proper attention, and I was most likely fooling around and not holding the handle firmly enough. And, of course, Mamma, as usual, was not completely wrong about that.

Once in a while I would encounter a different kind of obstacle on the way to school. In order to get to the Jewish Gymnasium, we had to pass a public school attended by non-Jewish boys. Normally, when walking to school, we went in small groups—this made the time pass quicker and made it less likely for the boys at the public school to pick fights with us.

It was always easy to tell that we were the kids who went to the Jewish Gymnasium; our school uniforms were different from theirs, and that made us stand out.

Skirmishes rarely happened, but when they did, we usually escaped without any major injuries. Generally, the worst that would come of it would be a bloody nose, a couple of bruises, or some torn clothes. When this occurred, our teachers stepped in and dealt directly with the administrators of the other school.

In the long run, my encounters with the non-Jewish boys proved beneficial because they helped me develop running and fighting skills that I put to good use in my various sporting endeavors. At school, everyone, without exception, had to participate in gym classes and in soccer, basketball, and volleyball games. We were divided into teams and, in due course, had to play against each other. There were also inter-school tournaments where there were usually more participants than spectators. Cheerleaders, alas, were unknown. Swimming was one of our favorite sports, but there were few swimming pools around the city, and those were located in public places and private clubs. These were restricted and Jewish students had to leave Lodz to swim.

Every so often, high-ranking officials from the Board of Education would come to the Gymnasium to hold inspections—more like a "show & tell" for our teachers that would give them a chance to showcase their students.

One of my classmates, Sochaczewski, was strangely talented. He had the uncanny ability to do complicated 10- to 12-digit multiplication in his head, and then quickly write the long numeric response on the blackboard. Our teachers would always bring the inspector to my class and put Sochaczewski on display. The inspectors would give him the problem, Sochaczewski's lips would move as if he was mumbling, and in seconds the answer would appear on the blackboard.

The inspectors were often skeptical, so they were given a pencil and piece of paper, the fastest method of calculation available to them, to see if they could keep up with him. Of course, they couldn't. And it turned into real fun whenever they had different answers. Then Sochaczewski and the rest of us would watch the inspectors work out the problem on the blackboard. The amazing thing was my classmate was never wrong, but in every other way he was as average as the rest of us, and he could never explain how he managed this extraordinary feat.

My life as a child was normal and carefree. I played, I studied, I was full of mischief. Some might even venture to say I was spoiled. My life was filled with the love of family and friends, a love that prepared me for so many things. My parents gave me an appreciation for learning; a sense of respect for others and for myself; they imbued me with high ethical standards and taught me to shoulder my responsibilities.

These values became a part of my life, and were guidelines that helped me survive during the Holocaust and shape my future.

Two
Golden Summers

"Summertime, and the livin' is easy."

Thank heaven for summertime! (Though I liked school very much, I liked it even better when it was closed.) We waited for summer's golden days with longing and anticipation, becoming happier and livelier as the days grew brighter and warmer. Long before the school year officially ended, our appetites for vacation would be whetted when Mamma began to prepare for one of her major annual undertakings—moving us to our summer house.

My parents owned a large villa in a village called Podębie, about thirty miles from Lodz—two hours travel time by train from the city. Getting settled in Podębie for the season was no easy task and involved planning and logistics.

Everything we needed for the summer months—clothing, linens, pots and pans, whatever Mamma thought necessary—was transported in the only vehicle large enough to take everything at once, a huge horse-drawn wagon. It was always an adventure for me to ride in the wagon, because you never knew what could happen on the road. There were few asphalt highways, and mostly cobblestones and graveled roads led from one place to another. The last few miles from the main road to our villa, for instance, dissolved into sand and the wagon wheels often sank deeply into its softness—and then refused to budge. Unless the two horses we'd hired in the city were very strong (and they usually weren't), we would have to hire and hitch another pair to the wagon to get our things to the villa.

Naturally, I preferred to ride in the wagon and, of course, if I could manage it, I would ride up front with the wagon driver. Mamma, of course, objected. Most of the time, she insisted that I stay with the family and travel to the villa by train.

Leon, my sisters, and I were also expected to prepare for the summer, a very involved process. Before we would leave Lodz, we boys would visit a leather-goods factory owned by my father's friend, who manufactured sporting equipment. Leon and I were given free reign to select anything we deemed essential for the summer activities we enjoyed—soccer, volleyball, and basketball were our favorites. We needed lots of equipment because, in many ways, our villa in Podębie was a center for many youngsters also on vacation.

Podębie was not a shtetl, it was a resort located in a beautiful forest dotted with lakes and meadows. The wooden villas of different sizes were owned and/or rented by many Jews from Lodz, who came for the summer months to enjoy the fresh air.

The normal layout of a European village was usually centered around the market square in front of the town's most important church. Podębie had no marketplace, no church, and no shul, but there were a few specialty shops scattered around, none of them concentrated in any particular area. They had a small general store where you could buy necessities—from flour to dresses. We would buy live chickens there and then take them to a local *schoichet* (ritual slaughterer).

My family's villa sat on a huge piece of property that was so vast, it went as far as the eye could see and beyond. We were surrounded by enough land to provide all the kids in the neighborhood with a grass basketball court, a full-sized soccer field, and a volleyball court, which is why they would all gather at our place—especially since we had all the equipment as well.

Because the "sports" facilities were at my personal disposal, I often had the opportunity to be as demanding as I wanted to be. For instance, when my sisters' older boyfriends wanted to play ball without me, I told them in no uncertain terms that if I couldn't play with them, I wouldn't give them the ball. At last, having older sisters paid off; I could enjoy playing a good ballgame with older, better players, and it was fun to "pull rank."

There was one particular youngster, a few years older than us, who truly loved to play soccer. Whenever he showed up during a game he would try to sell us his special blueberry buns, which he carried in a large metal platter on the top of his head.

With the platter full of buns still on his head, he would run onto the field and go after the soccer ball. It was amazing that he never lost his balance and never dropped a single bun!

Our villa was very large and had six or eight apartments on two floors with private entrances, verandas, and kitchens. Tatush rented three or four apartments to different families, and the rest were filled with our extended family members. There were, of course, no modern conveniences, but the spring water we pumped from the well near the house was pure, crystal clear, and sweet. Every room conveniently had its own kerosene lamp, but we didn't have a toilet—we had a privy, an outhouse, that was more than three hundred feet away, off to the side. When the weather was fine, there were no real problems, but when it rained, especially when it was stormy, it was no fun and a major inconvenience to have to go, especially for the girls and women!

Opposite the outhouse was a small cottage where there lived a tenant farmer who looked after the property all year long. The vegetable garden he maintained brought joy to my father, who came to Podębie on weekends and relished picking his own corn, radishes, cucumbers, and beets. The farmer, there all year long, planted the fields with potatoes, corn, and wheat that he would sell.

The main access road behind our villa was wide and sandy. On the other side of the road was a beautiful pine forest that I still remember and long for. After the warm summer rains, as the scent of the pine would come wafting across the road, a group of us would go deep into the woods to collect mushrooms. The baskets full of fresh fungus had to pass a thorough expert inspection from Mamma and, more importantly, our farmer, so that we wouldn't eat any poisonous ones.

We knew the weekend was approaching whenever the sweet aroma of baking cookies permeated the villa. The scent of cinnamon and vanilla heralded Tatush's arrival from the city. We all missed him, of course, but we also had an ulterior motive for anxiously awaiting his visit. Whenever he came to Podębie after spending a long, hard-working, and lonely week in Lodz, he was laden with gifts—usually board games or more sporting equipment. On Friday afternoons, our routine was to walk to the train station, about fifteen to twenty minutes away, to greet him and keep him company.

We never had to check the clock to see when we needed to leave for the station. For some unexplained reason, our dog, Lala, a spitz, could sense his imminent arrival and knew exactly when we needed to get moving. Dear Lala conveyed her message by barking loudly and gripping our pant legs or other piece of clothing, if necessary, to drag each of us out the front door.

Maybe Lala instinctively knew when Tatush was coming home because he was her favorite human. It was uncanny how she knew the precise instant to advise us so that we could be there to greet him on time. She may have had a built-in alarm clock and calendar, but that was just one of her special talents. In fact, Lala, who adored us, deserves her own chapter, and perhaps even her own book.

Whenever my father arrived at the villa for the weekend, life changed—if only for two days. On Saturday and Sunday mornings, I would accompany him to the vegetable garden where our farmer would join us. I loved to hear him give us the update on the state of the vegetable garden, and how the different varieties were doing. He would show us what was ripe for picking, what needed more time on the vine, which vegetables were in abundance, and which were not doing so well that season. We would open an ear of corn to see if it was ripe and scrutinize the color and size of the kernels. The radishes, if they were ready, would protrude from the surface of the earth, and you could feel the ground around them to estimate their size. The same would hold true for carrots and onions. We also had strawberries, and I still can taste them, tart and fresh, filling my mouth with a juicy flavor that I haven't found in any other strawberries, anywhere!

After the farmer gave us our weekly seminar, my father, my brother, and I would pick the vegetables needed for that day's meal. More than half a century later, I do not ever remember eating vegetables as fresh or as delicious and tender as those grown in the garden of our villa. Compared to the flavors of those organically grown, hand-farmed vegetables, today's produce tastes like paper.

After Saturday's lunch, Tatush would take us horseback riding, a great treat Leon and I waited for all week long. Mamma made sure we wore our special sailor suits for that purpose, navy blue with white trim and wide collars. We rode through the meadows and forests around the villa, stopping from time to time for short rests. My sisters were not particularly fond of horses and Tatush didn't take them with us because he felt it wasn't a woman's place to go horseback riding. As for Mamma, she was afraid of horses and dared not come close, touching them was entirely out of the question. She was not particularly pleased that Leon and I indulged in such a dangerous pastime.

On one occasion, my mother's fears were justified. One Saturday afternoon, the horse I was riding lost its saddle while we were trotting along at a fast clip. Apparently, the saddle hadn't been properly fastened before we left. I realized too late what was happening, and could do nothing except hold on tight until the saddle finally slipped off the horse's back altogether. Luckily, I maintained my balance by grabbing the horse's neck with all my might, preventing me from being thrown.

(Life does repeat itself. My daughter, Susan, acquired my love of horses very early on and my wife, Hannah, fears them as much as my mother did. I applaud my daughter for the great accomplishment of successfully tricking her mother into once touching a horse. It was a sight to behold. We had gone to visit Susan at summer camp, and she was showing off her equestrian talents. Susie asked her mother to hold the reins so that she could get off, and Hannah touched the horse's nose with her hand extended as far as her arm could go—staying as far away as possible from the creature, her body stiff with fright. She never did it again, but we can no longer say that she never touched a horse.)

On the long summer weekends, the grown-ups liked to play cards, which gave us kids an opportunity to engage in our own entertainments. One such amusement was to build a campfire and sit around it baking potatoes and singing. There is an old Yiddish song, "Arum dem fire singen mir leider" (around the fire we sing songs), that describes an idyllic scenario. Many of our summer nights were exactly like that old Yiddish song. My brother, my sisters, my cousins, and my friends all baked our potatoes in the ashes of the fire and sang songs. Of course, there was no reference in the songs about "borrowing" the potatoes from our neighbors' farms!

After feasting on potatoes, we roasted marshmallows over the open fire. This was a co-ed event because the girls did most of the baking and cooking, while the boys collected dry wood to keep the fire going. It was such a delight, with the only unpleasant result being that our hands and faces were covered with soot from the charred, roasted potatoes and the crispy blackened marshmallows that melted in our mouths.

One of the advantages of being a boy was having my own bicycle. Father believed that there were things boys did and things girls did and riding a bike was not something a girl did. My sisters, of course, resented this and complained that Leon and I got everything and they got nothing.

Those precious months in the country provided me with large swaths of land on which to practice my bike-riding skills and tricks. Of course, I'm not talking about professional tricks—my bicycle was just a simple piece of machinery. It was a far cry from a ten-speed mountain bike or the hi-tech equipment in use today. My brother and I rode our bikes whenever and wherever we could and, because there were no repair shops near us, we became expert mechanics. Our favorite stunts were to ride without using our hands, riding while standing on the frame and/or the saddle and riding backwards jetting down the steepest hills at the highest speeds possible in order to test our expertise and the capabilities of our bicycles.

I felt bad about girls not being allowed to ride bikes that, one summer, I made the unfortunate decision to let my cousin join me—if she heeded my instructions. Aunt Olga and Uncle Izio, and their daughters, Danusia and Irena, had come to stay in one of the apartments, and on one particularly beautiful afternoon, Cousin Irena insisted on joining me while I was riding my bike. Initially, I gave her a resounding "no," but after being nagged for hours, with no end in sight, I relented and said she could sit on the frame while I pedaled and steered. I warned her emphatically to keep her feet away from the chain to avoid getting hurt and she promised to sit perfectly still and keep her feet high up, away from the chain—a promise that lasted only five minutes.

Then, bingo, she let her feet drop and her big toe got caught in the chain. Her screams could be heard throughout the entire village, and there was blood all over the place. We rushed her to the doctor and discovered she had lost a small part of her big toe. In the long run, it proved to be much more serious for me than it was for her.

When her parents found out, I received a stern lecture that fully blamed me. For two weeks I could only look at, not ride, my precious bicycle. This, to me, was just another incident to convince me that girls were definitely a nuisance. (I have since changed my mind about that.)

At least once during the last few summers in Podębie, I accompanied Tatush back to Lodz for a few days. As soon as he opened the door to our apartment, I discovered that our living quarters had been converted into a small, first-rate winery. (So that was what he did while we played in the meadows!) Mamma's beautiful furniture was loosely covered with white sheets, making it difficult to find a place to sit down. Tatush had purchased a huge quantity of grapes and other fresh fruits at the market and bottles containing different fruits, sugar, and other ingredients used in winemaking. In most of the rooms he had set up contraptions of huge bottles connected by tubing. It was amazing to watch them in action. Drop after drop fell from one bottle to another through myriad tubes and filters, ending up as a delicious, potent liquid that he bottled, labeled, and carefully stored in the factory cellar.

Before we came home in the fall, Tatush disassembled his winemaking equipment and stored it in the factory for safekeeping and re-use the following year. Each summer, he experimented with miscellaneous fruits and concoctions to come up with different flavors, and ultimately he became quite a winemaster.

My boyhood summers were filled with an abundance of joy, laughter, and good times. At the end of each season I was always shocked at how fast the weeks had gone by and how nice it would be if summer could last forever. I had no idea that my carefree existence was rapidly coming to an end, and that the summer of 1939 would be our last in Podębie.

Three
Winds of War

"In the midst of it all, we hoped for the best."

The year 1939 was a particularly difficult one for Jews in Poland. As children, we did not fully understand the significance of the events that had been unfolding in Germany since the 1920s. It was in 1939, for the very first time, that we directly felt the despair of the Jewish community in Germany when the German government expelled many Jews and dumped them on the Polish border.

When the Polish Jews realized the gravity of the situation, they organized themselves to come to the assistance of their evicted brethren. My father was engaged in rescue operations, and I could see how bewildered he was by the unbelievable events taking place. The Polish Jewish community's plan was to disperse the German-Jewish families throughout the various communities in the larger cities, including Lodz. Committees were formed and employment strategies devised to provide the uprooted with sustenance.

By the spring and summer of 1939, Polish patriotic slogans filled the air in anticipation of the approaching "skirmish" with Germany. The prevailing sentiment in the country was, "Who's afraid of the Germans?" The politicians and military leaders who spoke on the radio and were quoted in the newspapers constantly reassured the population that all would be well. According to Polish sources, the Polish Armed Forces, under the leadership of General Smigly Rydz, were invincible. Germany could never defeat us.

Of course, there was no actual basis for this optimism and history has proven that none of this was realistic. For generations, Poland had been a divided country, dominated alternately

by Germany, Austria, and Russia. It was unified only after the
First World War. But history or no history, most of us felt secure
in Poland; we believed in the might of our great military.

Then, on the morning of September 1, a screaming headline
appeared in the daily newspaper: "Germany attacks Poland!"
Patriotic songs blasted from the radio, interrupted by instructions for mobilization of our troops. In no time, we read and
heard about the Polish Army's numerous victories over the Germans.

On that infamous day, we were at the villa in Podębie finishing up our summer vacation. School was postponed because of
the war, and Tatush decided we should stay in the country because the city would be in a state of chaos and we would be safer
where we were.

Most of the population was on the go—even in our little village we witnessed the daily movement of thousands of people,
seemingly scrambling in different directions. Some walked;
many drove loaded horse-drawn wagons that carried the sum of
their possessions. We also saw thousands of foot soldiers, some
cavalry, and rarely, motorized units of the Polish Armed Forces.
I later learned that these foot soldiers were sent to fight German
tanks.

As children, we were blithely ignorant of the magnitude of
the events taking place around us. We didn't worry at all about
the drastic consequences that were about to hit us. We lived quietly in the villa and our favorite pastime was to look up in the sky
for planes and traces of anti-aircraft fire. Every now and then we
would see a flash of light in the sky and watch a plane plummet
to the ground in a blaze of smoke and fire. It was exciting to
guess which plane might fall out of the sky next. To me, it was
like watching a movie.

Except for these unusual diversions, life in the country was
basically pleasant and unchanged. For the youngsters, this was
an extended holiday. Although we were usually anxious to get
back to school after the long summer break, I couldn't say we
minded the prospect of an indefinite postponement.

A few days after the war began, our dog Lala began behaving very strangely. For no apparent reason, she began running

out into the yard to howl—not her normal bark, but a sound I had never before heard her make. We took her back into the house, but as soon as we left her unattended, she would make her way outside again to make her keening sounds. We were puzzled by her behavior. What could make such a peaceful dog force her way outside at every opportunity to howl in the dark?

Soon enough we got the answer when our neighbor, his family in tow, came running to our doorstep. Out of breath, he told us to get out of the village as soon as possible: the Germans were only a few kilometers away.

I remember Mamma was stunned; we were all dumbfounded. How was this possible? What had happened to our invincible Polish army? There was no time to ponder. The neighbors were hurrying to catch the next train to Lodz and advised us to do the same. Otherwise, they warned, we would surely be stranded and overrun by the Germans.

This was beyond comprehension. My mother quickly decided that we should return to Lodz. There was no time to lose; we left all our possessions in trust of the villa's caretaker. We even left our beloved Lala behind, thinking Tatush would be back in a few days to retrieve her, close up the house, and make the appropriate arrangements to bring our stuff to town.

In the middle of the night, we joined the maddening rush to the train station. The closer we got, the larger the crowds became. As we approached the main highway, all we could see was a mass of humanity, pressing toward the same destination.

The change was sudden: the population of our quiet country village was in a frenzied mass exodus. The highway was filled with wall-to-wall people, and milling among the crowd were thousands of Polish soldiers, the same Polish soldiers who had, just a few days earlier, been marching proudly to the front lines, singing patriotic songs, convinced they would beat the Germans in no time. Now, with weapons abandoned, they were fleeing as fast as they could. At the station we overheard some soldiers saying that the Germans were right behind us. This scared us even more.

Finally, the train arrived. A sea of humanity rushed to fill its spaces—every square inch. People stood on steps, rode between cars, hung out the doors—anywhere they could find a handhold or foothold. It was a miracle that the five of us were able to stay together, as we were literally thrown into one of the cars.

As the train started moving, Mamma instructed us to hold onto each other so that we wouldn't be separated. We didn't need her advice. Our fear had already caused us to clutch each other with all our might.

As our anxiety increased, the uncertainty of our fate made the trip seem endless. Adding to our tension, the train stopped continually, often halting inexplicably in the middle of nowhere. The sense of dread was amplified by the darkness outside and the almost complete darkness inside. We were standing so close together it made us feel like sardines in a can.

Suddenly, I felt something brush against my leg. I jumped reflexively and looked down. Unbelievably, it was Lala! Only God knows how she found us in the midst of all that tumult! Lala was the one bright spot on our return to Lodz that fateful evening.

Arriving in Lodz in the middle of the night, we were surprised to find the streets alive with masses of people. The chaos surrounding us was an unusual contrast to the peace that generally reigned at that late hour. When we finally reached home, Tatush was surprised but relieved to see us all.

Shortly after our return, the Germans arrived in Lodz. Our parents became very nervous as they looked out the window and watched column after column of German troops. As they poured into the city in trucks, motorcycles, cars, and tanks, the streets were filled with the hearty cheers of the boisterous local German population. German banners flew everywhere, decorated with the *hakenkroutz,* (the swastika). The Volksdeutscher Poles, one-third of the city's residents, welcomed their conquerors, rejoicing in their takeover. There were so many banners, it seemed to me they must have been prepared in anticipation of this momentous occasion. The "fatherland" had finally reclaimed the city.

As soon as the German administration was in place, they confiscated the city's most prestigious buildings, using them for military and civilian purposes. Ironically, in 1939, the Jewish

Gymnasium we attended (the three separate buildings) had just been consolidated into a beautiful new building with the most modern amenities. The new school was to open officially with an elaborate ceremony, but this never took place because the elegant structure was commandeered by the Germans.

As the celebration of the city's takeover continued, Tatush, somehow, got caught up in the revelry when three of his factory supervisors, all Germans who greatly respected him, asked him to join them in toasting this momentous victory. There was no way he could refuse to participate. I remember a hushed discussion taking place between my parents before he left the house that night, but I was too young to fully understand his words of comfort to my mother. He was attempting to explain that he had no choice in the matter and assured her that since the men were his friends and employees, everything would be all right. He told her not to worry or be afraid, and instructed her not to wait up for him, as he did not know when the "festivities" would be over.

Despite his assurances, Mamma was agitated. When I went to sleep, she was wide awake. When I woke in the middle of the night, I found her pacing back and forth as she waited for him. Finally, in the wee hours of the morning, he returned. Still in one piece, Tatush was nevertheless in a frightful condition. He was, for the first time in his life, thoroughly inebriated. The entire family helped put him to bed. He was so deeply under the influence that he fell dead asleep as soon as his head hit the pillow.

A few days later, school reopened in our old buildings. The teachers tried their best to stay calm, but we could see they were merely going through the motions and we reacted by going through the motions ourselves. We pretended to learn and study.

We came home from school one day and tried to enter by the front door, as usual, but it was locked. There was a large seal on the door: BESHLAGNAMT "This property has been taken over by the German government." Later, I learned that Mamma was not home during the takeover and that Tatush was in the factory when it happened.

My father found out about it when our housekeeper came running to him, screaming that the Germans were taking over the apartment. Unfortunately, in spite of the intervention of his

German employees at the factory, there was nothing that could prevent the appropriation of our property. His workers did all they could to persuade the newly arrived German authorities to stop, but to no avail.

In the blink of an eye, all our worldly possessions were gone. The next day, a local *volksdeutscher* inhabited our apartment, still filled with all of our belongings. We were left with nothing but the clothes on our backs.

We soon learned that the same thing was happening to the other well-to-do Jewish families in Lodz. Jews were thrown out of their homes without warning and not allowed to take anything with them. Their homes were given over, "lock, stock, and barrel," to the *volksdeutschers.*

In the midst of this upheaval, we were luckier than most. The factory was right across the street with an additional small building, the one we used for Hanoar Hazioni and the woodworker from Russia. The red brick building had four floors, and we occupied a few unfurnished rooms on one of them.

This "apartment" was certainly not the comfortable home we left behind, but we considered ourselves lucky to have a roof over our heads. Many did not. My parents managed to buy some articles of clothing, cooking utensils, and a few inexpensive pieces of furniture.

We continued at school, as Tatush continued to supervise the factory. But it wasn't long before the first *befehls,* orders regarding new rules and regulations imposed on Jews, were posted in the streets. As bad as things seemed then, it was truly a blessing that we did not know what would happen next.

Soon the Germans confiscated the factory, but they needed someone with my father's vast knowledge and expertise to operate it—so they allowed him to continue working. They did make sure to bring in a German to oversee his work, a *troyhandler* who, in effect, became the new owner of the factory.

The situation for the Jews in Lodz became increasingly desperate. Every Jew was required to wear a yellow Star of David so that Germans and Poles could immediately recognize who was Jewish. My mother cut out the Star of David from yellow material, but I don't remember whether the word Jüde was written on it. I do recall that many people had the star sewn onto the front and back of their clothing, but I had it prominently displayed only on the front of my jackets and shirts.

Without realizing the consequences of disobeying the order, every now and then I ventured out on the street without wearing my yellow mark of Cain. I was not the only one doing so and, eventually, some children were caught and badly beaten; a few slightly older than me were executed on the spot. Bearing that in mind, I stopped venturing out without my yellow star.

New *befehls* were issued on a daily basis. For example, signs that read *Jüden eintritt verboten and Hund unt Jüden eintritt verboten* (Jews, Entry Forbidden and For Dogs and Jews, Entry Forbidden), were posted at hotels and restaurants—increasing the misery in our lives.

Then the Germans began burning our synagogues. To our horror, our beautiful old *shul,* the largest in Lodz, was set ablaze. I went to see the fire myself—it was one of the times I sneaked out without the star—but my father did not come. This form of arson was a public spectacle, and as our houses of worship and study went up in flames, the Germans and Poles stood by and laughed.

The *Volksdeutsche* (local Germans) and German soldiers took advantage of every opportunity to flex their muscles and terrorize any Jew crossing their paths. Beatings were popular, and soldiers gleefully forced Jewish men to bend down on their hands and knees to lick their boots. I watched as German officers took photographs to document this new form of entertainment. Religious Jews were caught and held down while their beards were cut off. Sometimes, the Germans cut off only one side to increase their amusement. This process of dehumanizing the Jewish population was deliberate and methodical. My father, a kind, decent individual, could never understand such ruthless behavior on the part of so-called civilized people.

Some Germans, those who worked at the factory for instance, eased their consciences by telling him he was somehow different from the rest of the Jewish people. "You are a different Jew," they would say. It is true that Tatush was special, but even at that age, I understood my father was a wonderful man and it had nothing to do with being a Jew or a Gentile. Even then I believed you do not equate the character of a person with his religion.

The Germans had by then taken over the entire city and renamed it Litzmannstadt. Their plan was to evacuate all Jews from the city, forcing them to move into a ghetto. They callously chose the poorest and most dilapidated part of town for that. While still living in the cramped quarters in the confines of the factory, we slowly but surely reached the conclusion that our departure was imminent. With dread, we waited for the inevitable and hoped for the best.

Four
My Dog Lala, a Child's Best Friend

"A dog is a child's best friend."

Relationships between people and their pets, especially children and their dogs, are very special. So I need to digress. In my later years in America, when I had children of my own, every now and then, as all children do, they would ask me to tell them a bedtime story about my life before, during, or right after the war. Their favorite, even as grown-ups, is the story of Lala, the same Lala who found her way onto the train back to Lodz from Podębie.

It is a story about children and their beloved dog, but above all . . . in the mind of a child who happened to be me, the story of Lala was a living miracle.

We dreamed about "it" constantly, we talked and talked about "it," and we yearned for "it," but we dared not think "it" would become reality. The truth was that at the ripe old ages of eleven, nine, seven, and six, the four of us despaired of ever owning a dog. It couldn't possibly happen. And yet, one afternoon in the early 1930s when we got home from school, there had mysteriously appeared, in Mamma's immaculate apartment, an adorable golden fluff-ball of a puppy. What a glorious day in our lives! We all immediately agreed to call her Lala, which means doll in Polish.

I still have not figured out exactly what kind of a dog she was, but she had a long, two-toned golden bushy tail, furry, not hairy, like a squirrel's. Her face was like a collie's, but her snout was shorter and she had pointy ears and a stout little body. The breed that most looked like our Lala was the Finnish Spitz, but we had no idea what kind of dog she was. We didn't care. We knew we wanted her and we loved her, and that was all that mattered.

37

From the moment I first saw her I adored her and was over-whelmed with joy. I spent countless hours filled with the plea-sure of just looking at her. Playing with her and running around the house with her was sheer heaven. However, the idyll did not last long. It took only a few days before Mamma became upset. Lala was messing up her carpets.

None of us had stopped to think that dogs, like people, have to be properly trained when it comes to their bodily functions, and that such training required a great deal of time and effort. It takes a year or two before toddlers get toilet-trained, but dogs are different—instruction needs to commence almost immedi-ately after they are born. In our excitement, we overlooked this detail and failed to take it into consideration. As a result, Mamma was very annoyed.

A few days later, I came home from school full of happy an-ticipation, looking for my wonderful, magical Lala. I was expect-ing to find Lala at the door, jumping in circles like an ice skater, barking, tail wagging, thrilled to see me, all ready to play. But on this day there was no Lala. I asked Mamma if Lala was across the street at the factory, but no, she was not. Mamma's answer devastated me. I could feel my heart sink into my feet, my throat tightened and tears filled my eyes. "Where was she?" I wailed. Mamma had given Lala back to her previous owner, because Lala was too much of a mess and she didn't want to deal with car-ing for her.

Every one of my siblings was devastated, so we planned a course of action. Being a young child, I did not fully comprehend the meaning of the word strike, so the idea had to come from one of my sisters, because Leon, younger than me, could not have come up with it. Without much deliberation, the four of us real-ized that unified action would be required to get Lala back. With this common goal in mind, we proceeded with our supposedly foolproof strategy and hoped that it would not fail.

It was rare for all of us to be of one mind, joining together to achieve a single goal. But our puppy was worth it. Holding on to our united front was the only hope we had to win our quest for Lala's return.

We nagged, we whined, we were stubborn, we cried, we

stamped our feet, in concert and as solos. We did not stop. We refused to do our homework. And we went on a hunger strike. No after school snack, no dinner. We followed Mamma around the apartment. All she could hear was Lala, Lala, Lala, and please, please, please, please.

It would make for a better story if I could say our strike was a long, protracted one, but with the four of us in top form, how could Mamma, or any mother, withstand such a calculated barrage of nagging negativity from all of her children simultaneously? For Mamma, there was no escape. For her, our strike must have seemed to last an eternity.

In reality, it took us approximately four hours to get Mamma to relent and ask the housekeeper to fetch Lala and bring her back. Deep in my heart I believe that the reason she caved in was that she wanted to spare Tatush the horror of arriving home and finding a house in chaos.

To reward Mamma for her kindness and generosity, we promised to play an active role in Lala's training. I am sure Mamma was pleased by what she heard, but in her heart she knew full well that the task would ultimately fall upon her and the housekeeper because we were in school most of the day.

Lala came home that night, carried in the arms of our housekeeper. As soon as the door opened, she jumped out of her arms, and the four of us chased her around the apartment because we all wanted to snuggle her. From that moment, she became a full-fledged member of our family, something my siblings and I understood from day one. It took my parents, particularly my mother, longer to be won over by our puppy, but soon her appealing warmth and charm could not be resisted. Lala captivated all of us and made us aware that Tatush was the boss. He was, indubitably, her favorite human. It was amazing how that little animal became so attached to us and changed our lives.

On every school day, she would wait for us on the balcony, her golden fur glinting in the sun. Her nose twitched in anticipation, her body braced for action, ears up to catch our sounds, her tail curved up over her back. The moment she knew we were headed in her direction, she would bark and dash to the door to greet us, jumping high in the air, spinning around, trying to hug us, licking our faces and hands, and then jumping around some more as she yipped with delight. And slowly, but surely, Lala was trained. Finally Mamma accepted her completely.

Lala was often more important to me than my brother and sisters. She earned this privileged position by her patience, understanding, and sympathy. I could snuggle her up against me and she was always there to listen to my various complaints about my siblings, parents, and classmates. She would console me by licking my hands and face and by wagging her bushy tail. Could anyone else in my family do that for me?

Over the years it became clear that Lala's peers cherished her as much as we did. Lala was never spayed, and so there was annual proof positive of how much she was adored when she gave birth to a litter at the end of each summer. She generally had four to six beautiful little pups that looked just like her.

The first time it happened, of course, we wanted to keep all her puppies in the apartment. But Mamma put her foot down and insisted that as long as Lala had to have her little puppies with her, they must all stay at Tatush's factory. This did not pose a problem for clever little Lala, who chose to go back and forth, to and from the factory, so she could be with both of her families.

And Lala was even smarter than that! When she realized she had a very small puppy in the litter who did not get enough milk from her because it could not compete with the larger puppies, she did something incredible. When the others were done, Lala would use her jaws to pick up the runt of the litter by the scruff of his neck and carry it to our apartment, where it could suckle in peace and get some quality time with its mommy. Then, when the baby was finished nursing, Lala would pick it up and carry it back across the street to its sisters and brothers. How Lala understood that she needed to do this was one of the miracles of motherhood. How did she know this child needed its mommy more than the rest? What she didn't realize is that every time she brought the puppy to our house or took it back to the factory, she stopped all traffic. Everyone would stop in their tracks, dumbfounded at the sight of this precious dog carrying a tiny puppy in its mouth. Of course, it wasn't as if she was stopping traffic in Times Square. We still used horses and buggies and there were no cars to speak of, but Lala caused traffic jams none-theless. It was truly a remarkable sight.

Lala had no trouble adjusting to city life in Lodz and country life in Podębie every summer. The years passed quickly. Then, when the war started and we were evicted and lived in the building adjacent to the factory, I liked to imagine that Lala preferred it to our old apartment because, from her point of view, it was co-zier and she no longer had to go back and forth from her annual litter to us.

I don't remember exactly how long it took, but finally the day came when even the factory was no longer safe, as the Germans ordered us to the ghetto in the northern part of the city. We were now all teenagers and we had to think about what to do with Lala, since we were all forced to live in the ghetto.

We had returned from the country a few months earlier, and Lala had given birth to her new litter—four golden puppies. But bringing five animals to the ghetto was out of the question. Tatush and Mamma remained steadfast, though the four of us wanted to take them. As a result, Lala and her puppies were left in the care of Kazimierz, the same factory superintendent who taught me to ride a bicycle and fixed the factory windows when I broke them. We hoped he would find a way to smuggle her into the ghetto, but we had no idea what was waiting for us.

We tried, but we could not postpone our move any longer. The winter was over. After a certain date the ghetto would be closed, and if we were caught outside, we'd find ourselves at the mercy of the Germans. Reluctantly, we trekked to the ghetto.

The miserable March weather was typical of a Polish spring—all four seasons rolled into one—and I can remember walking several kilometers through freezing rain, falling sleet, and many mud puddles until we came to our destination: the ghetto gate. We could not imagine what would happen next and thought only about what we were forced to leave behind. Tired, wet, and shocked by the unfamiliar surroundings, the six of us huddled together in the two rooms we managed to find.

That night we were too nervous to sleep. While our parents were talking to their friends in subdued voices about our options and possible fate, the four of us stayed awake and tried to figure out how to smuggle Lala into the ghetto. In due course, exhaustion overcame us and we fell asleep without a plan.

Then, in the dead of night, in the deep silence and thickly dense blackness of our room, we were wakened by sounds that seemed to emanate from the front door. Our parents froze, expecting the worst. Jolted from bed by the noise, an unlikely positive thought crossed my mind. I jumped to my feet and yelled, "It's Lala. Lala is here!"

Four of us rushed to the door to let her in. She was a sight to behold. Her long golden fur was soaked and covered with clumps of snow and mud. She was trembling like a leaf, and we could see how very tired she was. But the moment she looked up at us, her tail started to wag. Shortly thereafter, her tongue joined in as she began licking our faces.

How could a dog with no idea of where we were travel such a far distance to find us in a place where we had never been before? To us, a simple explanation came to mind: it was a miracle.

In the morning, Lala left us; we knew she went back to the factory to see her babies. All day long, there was only one thought in my mind and in the minds of my siblings: will Lala come back again to see us at night?

For the next few weeks, we experienced a phenomenon of nature. Sometimes in the middle of the night, after we had been sleeping for hours, we would hear Lala scratching at the door, asking to be let in. In the morning, the same process took place in reverse; she left for the factory to tend to her newborn puppies.

Obviously, she had created a way of dividing time between her natural family and her adopted one. That little dog showed us that love is stronger than hate, and no guns, no barbed wire, and no German guards could stop her from proving it.

Love . . . Lala was the first to teach me the true meaning and understanding of this word. It never mattered to Lala if we were in our beautiful apartment, in our cramped quarters at the factory, or in our dismal room in the ghetto. All she cared about was being with us. After a couple of months, when her puppies had grown and could be given away, Lala came to the ghetto and stayed with us. She didn't mind the tight living quarters and the lack of her favorite food. We shared whatever we had with her and she was satisfied and never complained. We took her for walks and played with her in the streets. Just as before, when we left her alone in our room and returned, she greeted us with the same kind of enthusiasm she'd always shown. Geography was not important to our Lala . . . she still jumped up, licked our faces, and wagged her tail.

It was not long before the Germans felt compelled to be cruel not only to us, but to everything and anything associated with Jews. Each day they found new and different ways to demean us, to make our lives even more miserable. To our great sorrow, one day a notice appeared that all "Jewish dogs" had to be handed over to the Germans.

My siblings and I, as well as my parents, looked at this official proclamation in disbelief and with great resentment and anger. We could not believe it. How could it be possible? What could they have against our adorable little animal? In hushed voices, our family and some of our friends who had beloved pets discussed the matter to see what we could do. We couldn't smuggle her to the factory. The Germans had the names of everyone who owned dogs because the Germans had the lists from the Lodz city hall. Though Lala had sneaked into the ghetto, there was no way to deny that we owned the dog—they could simply look up the records. Penalties for non-compliance with the proclamation were severe. Slowly but surely the day of reckoning arrived, and Lala had to leave us forever.

Normally, Lala loved to go for walks. Whatever the time of day, all we had to do was call her name and shout, "Let's go for a walk." Automatically she would bring her leash to us, go to the door, and we would begin our journey. On this fateful day, it did not happen.

Lala instinctively knew something was wrong. She hid under the bed in the furthest corner, and no amount of prodding could cajole her into coming out of her hiding place. I looked under the bed and saw she was in the fetal position, trembling as she had on the first night she came to us in the ghetto. We had to move the entire bed to get to her, and she refused to stand up and walk by herself. We had to pick her up and carry her in our arms to the designated place.

I have tried very hard to recall what actually happened once we left the house to surrender Lala to our enemy. I do not remember handing her over to the Germans or any of the details once we were in the street. This was obviously so painful for me, and still is, that I have not been able to remember the rest of that day, even as I write this down.

In spite of the unusual and terrible times in which I lived, this was the first personal misfortune to deeply affect me. The loss of our home and the move to the ghetto were losses of material things. Losing Lala was the same as losing a member of our family. We never saw our precious Lala again, yet she still lives on in my heart, in the hearts of my children and grandchildren, and I hope she will live in the hearts of all who read this story.

Five
Moving to the Ghetto

"Our misery was visible to all . . ."

I once heard that the difference between God and historians is that God can't change the past but He can foresee the future. The historian can change the past and can't foresee the future. Thank God we could not predict what would happen next. And even if we could escape our immediate surroundings, where could we go?

My father had thought it through. He assumed that with the Germans caught between the British and the French, the war would not last very long and that we would be going home soon enough. He decided it was better for us to move into the ghetto than it would be for us to leave for places unknown.

The weather was appropriately abysmal when we left the factory in March, carrying with us what we could. As we trudged in silence, huddled close for warmth, the sky above was a leaden gray, heavy and gloomy. Cold and rainy, there was even some sleet to bedevil our march. The streets, filled with icy mud, froze our feet, while the wind bit frostily and painfully at our ears and noses.

The ghetto was in Baluty, the oldest part of the city, in the north, an area of about four square kilometers, with an eleven kilometer perimeter. This was Lodz's slum, formerly home to the impoverished and crooked, thieves and unsavory cutthroats.

Since this part of the city was totally foreign to me, I didn't know what to expect. When we got to the ghetto, the barbed wire fence was about eight feet high. The buildings were mostly of wood and were packed closely together, few of them higher than four stories. There were roughly 32,000 apartments there, most of them consisting only of one room. About three percent of the apartments had running water and toilets and the majority had limited electricity. These small spaces now had to absorb the 240,000 Jews still in Lodz.

The purpose of ghettoizing the Jews was to bring them to one confined place. The rich and poor, the Orthodox and secular, the Zionists and the Bundists, the young and the old, the healthy and the infirm, and even those who thought they had long left their Judaism behind them—all of us were living together under wretched conditions. Not one of us could replicate our normal routines and be who we had been just months before. The ghetto was the great equalizer—there, whether we wanted to be or not, we were all Jews.

Slowly, we made our way to our new residence, secured for us with great difficulty by my father's connections. Our new address was Spacerowa 13a, apartment 4. We were on the first floor of a two-story wooden building that contained three more apartments, one like ours and two single rooms. The "luxurious accommodations," built of wood, contained a kitchen with a table and chairs and one additional room, with running water and a toilet. We managed to find some extra beds and slept in one room. The wood-burning kitchen stove also served as our heater.

Spacerowa was a small and narrow dead-end street lined with similarly unappealing structures. We were located quite close to the ghetto center but our area was not as densely populated. Our apartment had good and bad features, most of them bad. The room was dilapidated, paint was peeling from the walls and falling from the ceiling, and there were cracks everywhere. The electric light was insufficient for reading or anything else—people in the slums had low wattage to avoid high electricity costs—but at least we had some light. Above all, we had indoor plumbing, which was very important. By ghetto standards, our apartment with its amenities was considered quite a good find. This now became our home and we remained there until the ghetto was liquidated in 1944.

Amazingly, there was a streetcar track that ran right down the middle of the ghetto. To prevent us from contacting anyone on the outside, the Germans fenced both sides with barbed wire at least twelve feet high and built an overpass to connect the two sides of the ghetto so the inhabitants could move from one side to the other. This way the non-Jews and freight could pass through the ghetto and its inhabitants would still be isolated.

Every day, the residents of Lodz passed through the ghetto in the streetcars as they went about their business. Our misery was visible to all of them. For those of us behind the fences, the streetcar was a reminder of how we were "hermetically" sealed from the outside world.

Looking back, two elements of life in the ghetto struck me and underscored the trauma we endured during those years. The first is the way we were systematically starved and the second was the constant deportations. My concerns about starvation and deportation became self-evident after the ghetto was permanently locked on May 1, 1940.

Two things were happening: the elderly, sick, and young were almost certainly being killed off, while the dissenters and volunteers—the people of good health—were being sent off to work for the Germans. To perpetuate the hearsay about those being sent to work camps, there were people in the ghetto who received postcards from "deportees" notifying friends and family that they were well and working.

The starvation of the Jews in the ghetto was a visual as well as physical trauma. As the years progressed, I watched as hundreds of people deteriorated before my eyes to become skin and bones. Many grew so weak they just lay down in their beds and never woke up, while others simply died in the streets. I watched as the dead were transported to the cemeteries located on the northeastern side of the ghetto. Most of the time people, in lieu of horses, pulled those wagons. The mark left on me by this horror is indelible; there was no way to avoid seeing death all around me.

The constant deportations created equal distress in those of us who were managing to "live," but it was more of a psychological nature. The pressure of not knowing when and where you would be taken further stressed our fragile states. The deportations may have seemed haphazard, but I noticed an obvious method to the Germans' madness. Deporting one family member eroded the stability of the entire family unit, so the Germans did that whenever they could.

The deportations did not discriminate against class or stature, cutting across all distinctions—people who came from other cities and even other countries; people who did not have a secure place in the ghetto workforce; people who were sick, particularly those who were hospitalized; dissenters, so-called volunteers, the elderly—and most agonizing of all, the young children. All of them were deported, seemingly at random, by the German authorities. There were, of course, some exceptions: families of policeman, high administration officials, and individuals with *protexia*—those who had connections to the ghetto leaders—also fell into this category.

So there we were, locked behind gates, Lala gone, our possessions gone, with nothing but ourselves to keep us going. We were deliberately starved and tortured, physically and mentally. Rumors of where the deportees were being taken and what would happen next were in the air around us, at home and in the streets—like a sick miasma tainted with fear.

Real news and hard facts were scarce commodities in the Lodz ghetto. Outside newspapers were prohibited, and we hadn't been able to establish an underground press of our own. Communication with the external "Aryan" side was verboten on pain of death, so there was no information coming in that way. As time passed, even those who smuggled food into the ghetto were able to provide less and less news—their numbers dwindled as they were caught and executed or caught in roundups for deportation. As a result, the rumor mill was our major news source.

Frankly, those were not my worries. My major concern, eclipsing all others, was for my family and keeping us intact, under one roof. Despite the horrendous deportations and terrible happenings going on around us daily, the one thing that kept our spirits up and our hope alive was that we loved each other and had each other to hold onto.

As time inexorably pressed forward, conditions in the ghetto steadily deteriorated. Whenever we thought we had hit bottom, there were additional humiliations, degradations, and ever-deepening despair.

After the initial shock of adjusting to ghetto life, Tatush made an important decision. Because he believed the war would not last long, and because he didn't give up on education and its importance, he insisted that the four of us continue with our schooling. He also did not want us hanging around doing nothing. So he hired a tutor and we continued with our studies privately, but not with the same intensity we had before the war. Our teacher, a woman, was one of the teachers from the Jewish Gymnasium who, like many others in the ghetto, had no means of support. Tatush managed to smuggle some money into the ghetto and was able to pay whatever he could. She taught us in secular subjects like mathematics and Polish history, but at this point, we did not continue with our Hebrew studies.

As long as our money lasted, our situation was better than it was for most. We were able to buy food on the black market smuggled into the ghetto or stolen from warehouses.

We were also lucky because three of my father's former workers, the same Germans who celebrated the arrival of the troops with him in September 1939, brought food into the ghetto for us. Now that they were big shots in the local German organization, they would visit my father at our little place. Whenever they came to Spacerowa, other Jews would disperse in fear and leave the streets deserted. They had no idea that these men were endangering their own lives. If these Gentiles had been caught in the ghetto socializing with us and bringing us food, they would have been severely punished and charged with *rassenshande*—disgracing the German race.

Mamma lived in a constant state of fear because of the political discussions Tatush had with these Germans. She would become particularly afraid whenever my father would make his by-now famous gesture—one of his favorites—repeatedly pointing to his palm and telling them the Germans would win the war only when hair grew there. The Germans took it all in stride, and I took that as a sign of the respect and admiration they accorded my father. These three men were willing to risk punishment and disgrace in order to help my father, their Jewish former boss. What is even more astonishing was that they smuggled Tatush out of the ghetto to a German firm specializing in dyeing textiles.

My father had done business with the owners for many years and had developed a solid friendship with them. At the start of the war, Tatush made arrangements with them to hold his goods until he was able to retrieve them. But now that we were imprisoned in the ghetto and the factory had been confiscated, my father knew there would be no way for him to make a living for the foreseeable future. He thought it might be prudent to sell his merchandise to the German fabric finishers, and let them pay him whatever they thought the goods were worth.

This may have sounded very simple, but in practice it was quite risky. For the Germans to come to the ghetto to see Tatush was dangerous. To smuggle him out of the ghetto was illegal, and if caught, they would have been arrested and my father summarily executed. And so, to make it work, there were many obstacles to overcome. First, we had to make Tatush "invisible," because he had no papers to allow him out of the ghetto. The Germans planned to take him out in a fancy *droshky* (horse and buggy), crouching inconspicuously between them. But they also needed to cross the no-man's land created by the Germans after the ghetto was built, an area immediately surrounding us and carefully watched. Any suspicious person quickly became a victim of the Nazi's "shoot now, ask questions later" policy.

Though we were children and had no idea of what was really happening, we knew something risky was going on. Mother was nervous and anxious, and spoke to Tatush in a subdued voice. We could hear her asking him if he really had to be smuggled out to sell the fabric. We had no idea when Tatush would return. He left in the morning, on a beautiful day, hidden in the *droshky*. The hours passed agonizingly slowly.

When dusk fell, we became anxious and more and more upset. Mamma paced back and forth across the small room, back and forth, back and forth, mumbling all the while that she never should have let him go. When the *droshky* finally pulled up with Tatush in it, the relief was like a physical shock, as if a rock had literally been lifted off our hearts. I could never understand how these righteous Germans had managed to get in and out of the ghetto in order to help my father.

At first I couldn't understand why Tatush would have taken

such a risk. But it soon became obvious that if he hadn't taken on this dangerous mission, we would have died of gradual starvation. In fact, life would have been easier for us if Tatush had consented to accept any of the high-ranking positions in the ghetto administration that were offered to him by Chaim Rumkowski, the notorious *alteste* (Elder) of the ghetto.

My father was constantly urged, especially by his good friend Dr. Josef Klementynowski, to accept an important position, to be the director of either the leather or the sewing factory. My father's response was always the same. "If I took such a job," he would say, "I would not be able to look people in the eye after the war."

At the time, I was too young to fully understand what he meant. As I grew older, the meaning of this philosophy became more and more clear to me, and that was just one example of why my father was so respected by each and every person he met. He would never compromise his convictions for temporary gain.

In order to understand what took place in the Lodz ghetto, you need to know something about the individual primarily responsible for its daily operation. He was Chaim Mordecai Rumkowski, and the Germans selected him as the Elder of the Jews. Under his direction, key departments were established and functioned during the transition period. He put police, fire, economic, and social welfare departments in place and had the responsibility for overseeing the transfer of the Jews from Lodz to the ghetto before it was officially closed to the outside world.

Later on, Rumkowski also added an Archives Department, a Department of Statistics, a Department of Vital Statistics, a Registration Bureau, and a Rabbinical Council. All of these agencies were organized and headed by Henryk Naftalin, a Rumkowski confidante.

Finally, Rumkowski established the "Chronicle Department" under the leadership of the same Dr. Klementynowski, who tried to convince my father to take an important position. The chronicle was published almost daily, and supposedly reflected all statistics garnered the day before. But these superficial accounts did not account for, or report, the suffering of the ghetto population. The information regarding resettlement and deportation was untrustworthy, since the chroniclers knew nothing about the whereabouts of the individuals they were counting.

The Chronicle Department, like everything else in the ghetto, was under the watchful eye of Rumkowski. Since he controlled the announcements and declarations, he obviously made sure nothing derogatory was ever written about him personally. Over time, he crafted his own legacy—one filled with superlatives describing an infallible leader working for the good of his people.

In addition to controlling the press, Rumkowski also controlled the distribution of food, the police, the courts, the prisons, the managers of ghetto workshops, and the supply of Lodz ghetto currency. In truth, he was in charge of all of the inner workings of the ghetto. Basically, he was a dictator who refused to understand that he served solely at the whim of the Germans. It was forbidden to protest against his policies. The strikes called by the workers because they were hungry and because their workloads were onerous were blamed on "irresponsible elements" (i.e., the Bundists and the Communists). Despite the constant deaths and deportations of thousands of ghetto inmates, the production quotas in the ghetto workshops were constantly rising. In the words of Rumkowski himself, "The Lodz ghetto is running like a clock," and this sentiment was emblazoned on all official proclamations.

The German-appointed Council of Elders was powerless, a rubber stamp for German policy. It finally became obvious that whatever noble intentions Rumkowski may have had—the most important of them being his desire to save the children—almost all his efforts on behalf of the residents of the ghetto were in vain. In the end, Rumkowski succeeded in proving the old axiom that power corrupts, absolute power corrupts absolutely. He had become the self-proclaimed King of the Jews, and no dissension was possible.

Created in 1939, the Lodz ghetto was one of the first ghettos to be established; in 1944, it became the last ghetto to be liquidated. Despite all the disadvantages we experienced in the ghetto, statistically more of us survived there than in the concentration camps. Though we were forced to live in a confined area

isolated from the outside world, we were not as constantly subjected to the caprices of thousands of German officers and guards
in the camps, who indiscriminately persecuted, killed, and tortured Jews in any way they could. At least in the ghetto we still
lived as a family unit. This in itself was maybe the most important factor in our long-term survival as individuals, because it
gave us an inner strength and will to survive anything.

Whether Rumkowski realized how important it was for families to remain intact in the quest for survival will never be
known. His power, though quite dictatorial, was strictly limited
to the internal affairs of the ghetto and even that power was limited. Absolute power to rule the ghetto belonged to Hans Biebow,
the German overseer, and to Biebow's superiors in Berlin.

Rumkowski's long-range strategy for the survival of the
Jews in Lodz was to keep them working at top speed. "Only one
thing can save us, a collective acceptance of productive life," he
would say, determined to make the Jewish work force in the
ghetto indispensable to the Germans and a plentiful source for
manufactured items needed by the German armed forces.

By 1941, about 40,000 Jews were employed in various factories in the ghetto, all of them producing goods for the Germans.
Though Rumkowski's goal was to save tens of thousands of Jews,
Biebow, his willing partner in this endeavor, was plainly motivated by greed. He was only interested in making money, lots
and lots of money. Though Rumkowski and his advisors had noble goals, in effect they became the de facto enforcers of German
decrees, and you might say, did the dirty work for their "bosses."

To consolidate his power over the population, especially the
Orthodox Jews, Rumkowski abolished the Rabbinical Council
and performed marriage ceremonies himself. He imposed economic control by printing ghetto currency—which displayed his
image.

Had the war ended sooner, Rumkowski would have been
considered a hero for saving many Jewish lives. But because the
ghetto was completely liquidated, many see Rumkowski as a vil-
lain—a power-hungry dictator. I believe that the only true historical conclusion we can reach is that Chaim Mordecai
Rumkowski was, is, and always will be an extremely controver-

sial figure, who originally tried to save children until he was caught in a trap of his own making and had to surrender those he tried to protect.

My family had known Rumkowski before we were put into the ghetto. My Aunt Olga, in particular, knew him well. After she was widowed and had lost her child at a young age, she dedicated her life to volunteering at the orphanage in Helenowiek, on the outskirts of Lodz. The orphanage was run by Rumkowski and Aunt Olga provided them with significant financial resources.

As for the members of our extended family, they left the ghetto almost immediately, but were soon caught and sent back. They stayed with us for a while, before leaving for Warsaw. I never saw any of them again, except for Danka, my only cousin to survive the war.

Six

Ghetto Life

"Loss becomes much more personal."

Soon after the ghetto was locked in May 1940, after things stabilized a bit, Rumkowski set up a school in Marysin, south of Baluty. As the former head of an orphanage, he was more than qualified to establish such an institution.

Besides providing us with secular and Hebrew studies, the school was an important place for the children because they were able to get an extra ration of food on school days. Each day, at lunchtime, we were all provided with a cup of hot soup. While it may have been an "extra" ration for some of us, for others it was the only food they got, and so, by going to school, many children managed to stay alive.

Rumkowski's school was pretty much fashioned the same way as our Jewish Gymnasium had been. Classes were divided according to age. We would sit in the classroom and our teachers, some of them from our old school, would go from room to room for course changes. The difference was that all children were in our classes, not just children who came from well-to-do or middle-class families.

The intensity of study at the Rumkowski school, however, was not the same as the Gymnasium's and the level of learning was somewhat lower than it was before the war. That's because hungry kids have a hard time studying.

The school was located quite a distance from Spacerowa, in a semi-suburban section of the ghetto. The long walk to classes took me past some trees and fields, which was a welcome diversion, since I was quickly losing the innocence of my childhood. By now I was fourteen years old. School was very important to me because it gave my day routine and structure, helping me to forget the everyday miseries that plagued us.

The Germans, however, always trying to demoralize us, closed the school after just one year. Though I remember a great deal about my experiences, I have only two photographs from my childhood. One is a family portrait taken before the war and given to me by Kazimierz, the factory superintendent, many years later. The other is a class photo from the school in the ghetto found in a diary kept by one of my classmates, David Sierakowiak. David perished in the ghetto, and his diary, hidden in a buried can, was discovered years after the war ended. The diary was first published in Polish and later translated into English and is a most personal and emotional contemporary account of life in the Lodz ghetto. As I read his words, I re-lived the daily pain, hunger, and despair of ghetto life, as David expressed the tremendous upheaval, turmoil, and evil, the physical and emotional trauma, that ultimately caused his death.

In the meantime, Tatush, so smart and resourceful, always thought in the long-term. When we first came to the ghetto, Rumkowski's administration subdivided empty lots and assigned them to families to grow their own food. The assigned plots were in large fields in Marysin that were designated for cultivation and divided between the families. Each little piece of property was called a *dzialki* (about 20' x 20').

My father, who so loved his garden in Podębie, took a plot to farm. Most of the people in the ghetto did not seize on this idea because farming in the city never occurred to them, so some of them gave Tatush their lots. Others applied for lots when my father paid them a small fee, and then turned them over to him. He understood the vital importance of what he accomplished, even before the Germans continually decreased our rations. The garden that was almost a philosophical symbol of life in Podębie became the key to life in the Lodz ghetto. By caring for the lots properly, we had a source of food that would save our rapidly dwindling finances.

Once the plots were marked off, the real work began. Never having been farmed before, the land seemed to have more stones than soil, so it first had to be cleared to prepare it for planting.

This was a backbreaking job. We had no proper tools, except for shovels, so we had to do everything by hand. Leon, now thirteen, and I worked on the *dzialki* from dawn to dusk. The tedious work reminded us of the biblical verse: "By the sweat of your brow shall you earn your bread." It took us weeks to finish the clearing job.

After we tilled and raked the dirt with anything we could find, we planted cabbages, lettuce, carrots, beets, cucumbers, and radishes, because those were the seeds available to us. We wanted to plant potatoes, but to do that you need potatoes, and planting what you could actually eat was a luxury no one could afford. How could you plant a potato and wait for the months it took to grow while you starved?

Tatush, of course, had the solution. We would take a few of the potatoes we were supposed to eat when the right time came to plant them. We would pick those with the most eyes, because each eye became a seedling, and in this way we could get ten to fifteen seedlings from a single potato. Eventually, each seedling would grow into a potato bush.

Once everything was sown, we had to "irrigate" our "crops." This presented a problem because the only source of water was a well some distance away. Having no choice, and doing the best we could with what we had, we carried individual buckets of water back and forth to water our plants.

As time went on, Leon and I impatiently waited for tiny pale green leaves to sprout from the ground. When they began to push through, we realized that we had begun to accomplish our goal. The little seeds and potato eyes planted only a few weeks earlier were springing to life. And, as it had been since we got to the ghetto, we were now faced with a new challenge. Now that we'd gotten our vegetables to grow—and they were becoming visible to anyone who walked by—we had to devise a system to protect our crop from theft. The terrible hunger people suffered in the ghetto made our little garden a prime target for robbery. Day and night watches had to be organized, so we banded together with the other *dzialki* owners and set up a schedule to guard the lots day and night.

Of course, there were those with special connections, who

could get more of everything. Our neighbor in the fields, a Mr. Gertler, had a huge piece of land, and the people working for him had proper tools and equipment for the job. So when Mr. Gertler assigned individuals the task of standing guard over his land, we benefited since our lots were right next to his.

By trial and error, we somehow managed to reap our first harvest. Our garden provided us with fresh vegetables in the summer and potatoes, beets, cabbage, and cauliflower in the fall. Since our apartment was on the first floor and had a small crawl space, that is where we stored our winter supply of vegetables. Unfortunately, sometimes the produce would freeze when it got too cold.

By our second spring in the ghetto we were "professional farmers." We turned part of the bedroom in the apartment into a hot house allowing us to start some of our seeds early. We even began growing tomatoes. We also learned to make better use of the land we had. Rows of potatoes took a few weeks to germinate, so we planted lettuce between the seedlings. By the time the potatoes germinated, we had a crop of lettuce. For city boys, it was quite an accomplishment.

Achieving our objectives was extremely hard work—raking, watering, planting, weeding, and, especially, fretting. Since the earth we worked was not particularly fertile, our job was tougher than it should have been. To my surprise, in spite of the heavy loads I had to carry, I became very fond of working in the field. Though it was only a temporary diversion, during the time I spent there I was able forget the daily problems of ghetto life.

It was fortunate that Leon and I were assigned to work at the leather factory, the Leder and Sattler Ressort. It was also fortunate that it was under the supervision of Director Podlaski, the father of a friend and classmate of mine from the Jewish Gymnasium in Lodz. Though I had some *protexia,* sneaking out early every day to go work in the field was a dangerous proposition. But as Leon and I increasingly appreciated how vital this source of extra food was to our survival, we had no choice but to try to literally be in two places at once.

Because my family had additional sources of food, do not assume we were immune to hunger. The lack of proper nourishment was especially difficult for Tatush to endure because he suffered from stomach ulcers. Before the war, Mamma was always very careful to prepare proper meals for him, steering him away from spices and other invitations to stomach aches. Whenever he went off his diet, he had to take medication—bicarbonate of soda or another acid neutralizer—which seemed to help him greatly. But in the ghetto it was impossible for Tatush to maintain the diet required to avoid repercussions of his ailment. The bad food soon caused him to experience ever more frequent attacks.

Still, Tatush never complained, though he knew his situation was desperate. It was the expression on his face that would give him away. He would cringe and sometimes even cry or groan in pain. There was no proper medication available to either relieve the agony or treat the condition. In desperation, every now and then, when the torture became unbearable, he would risk visiting the ghetto hospital, though it had limited equipment and little medication.

November 13, 1942 was a work day like any other. It was after dark and I was home. Mamma had prepared whatever there was for dinner, which was never enough, and Tatush was having an acute, terribly painful ulcer attack. The only thing we could do was rush him to the hospital, where the doctors examined him and told us that their best efforts could not stop my father's internal hemorrhaging. Since the doctors had no appropriate medicines or surgical equipment, all they could do was watch him painfully bleed to death.

It is curious, and I have no logical explanation, but what happened to me then was the same thing that happened to me the day we had to surrender our beloved Lala to the Germans. I have tried and tried to remember the particulars of that turning point in my life, but my brain refuses to recover those memories. I cannot remember how we got him to the hospital, who came with us, or who stayed with Tatush to try to comfort him at the end. I can't remember the doctors or how we were told that my father was no longer in agony, no longer in pain, and would not suffer anymore because his body had given up and his soul was finally at rest. Knowing what I know now, I am grateful God spared him.

I don't even know if a doctor told me directly about Tatush's death, or if he told Mamma and she told us. I cannot remember his funeral or how we took his body to the cemetery for burial, or who joined us on that day. How a sixteen-year-old can't distinctly remember the day of his adored father's passing is hard for me to understand, but no matter how I try, I cannot remember anything that happened after that last meal Mamma cooked for him. I can only assume that my brain suffers from selective amnesia to prevent me from constantly re-traumatizing myself. Perhaps that is a blessing in disguise.

Later on, I went through other traumas and my brain buried them so deeply that I cannot recall certain events. Our brains work in strange ways. Perhaps mine shuts down whenever I witness unbearable sights and feel so deeply, in order to allow me to survive and rebuild my life.

Tatush's loss left an indelible mark on our entire family. It made the brutality and death in the ghetto personal; up to that point, I had only lost Lala. Now my mentor, my primary teacher in life, my anchor, was gone. I felt vulnerable, helpless to face what was bound to come. My world was never the same without my beloved, heroic, and noble father.

Seven
Working in the Ghetto

"In the face of death, we sang."

As summer faded and turned into fall, we grew concerned about the possibility of our crops being raided. We doubled our nightly guard, fearing someone would try to sneak into our plot and make away with our well-earned bounty.

The freezing winter weather presented us with yet another challenge. It was common for many in the ghetto to freeze to death—especially the very young and very old—and those who died that way could not even be buried because no one would cart their bodies to the cemetery in the killing cold. Since we received only tiny rations of coal and coal substitutes for heating our apartment and cooking, keeping warm was a constant battle, so much so that we were forced to wear our clothes day and night. But then I had an idea. During our first year in the ghetto, when we spent time in the ghetto school in Marysin, I had noticed that there were a great many old, dilapidated, and uninhabited wooden houses in the area. I thought we might be able to scavenge some wood from those abandoned structures.

Leon and I figured out a way to create wooden pallets with four handles, a sort of wooden platform, and we put a few old cans of paint on top to misdirect anyone watching us. Making the pallets for the sole purpose of stealing the wood was not easy, though we did have ready access to a hammer and some nails. Leon and I knew that if we were successful, we could carry much-needed wood to the apartment without being obvious, safely passing by both German and Jewish guards who would think we were just carrying painting materials for our work detail. But getting out at night to "capture" the wood and build our little platforms was dangerous because we were breaking rules.

Weight was also an important consideration. If we made the platforms too heavy, we would be unable to carry them without stopping to rest. There was also the question of timing. We decided that the best time to build them was after dark, since then we could carry our pallets during daylight hours when we would be less likely to attract unwanted attention. We also decided not to include any other members of our family because we worried that involving too many people might raise suspicions.

Thank God we were lucky in this endeavor. The supplemental fuel Leon and I were able to provide to our family kept us warm enough to prevent us from freezing to death in the glacial cold of the Polish winter.

Then there was the ghetto slave labor workforce, to which we all belonged. To simply exist in the ghetto, every person had to work. In order to obtain food rations, individuals had to be gainfully employed in the factories or in the ghetto administration.

Food was intrinsically linked to work. Hans Biebow, the German in charge of every factory in the ghetto, personally benefited economically from the slave labor he used—with the cooperation of the directors of the ghetto factories and private German industry. The production quotas set up for the workers were tied to food rations. The more you worked, the more food you received. What this really meant was that if you were able to exceed the already high production demands, you earned yourself an additional meager piece of bread. The Germans had thus designed a diabolically cruel system, a method that killed us slowly through starvation and overwork, while using what little energy we had to produce cheap goods for the German economy.

Supplemental food rations were provided based on the type of work you did. Policemen and high-ranking officials in the administration received additional food rations. So did those burdened with extra heavy workloads. The balance of the ghetto population, meaning most everyone else, received just enough food to cause them to slowly die from malnutrition and overwork.

In addition to providing goods to the German Army, Biebow was happy to accept orders from privately owned German companies. His customers provided us with the necessary raw materials and machinery. Because he was familiar with the directors and the technical staff of each and every workshop and knew the precise costs of production, Biebow would then calculate starvation wages for his workers. Since he controlled a workforce of about 75,000 people and made a profit of roughly 750 percent per worker, his vast enterprise made him immensely wealthy.

It is almost impossible to imagine the effects of constant, gnawing hunger and what it does to your body, mind, and soul. Your mind focuses solely on how to obtain food, operating at basic survival level, and you lose any sense of what the consequences might be of acting on that burning desire. Observant Jews were exempted by the rabbis from eating only kosher food because it was a matter of life and death (*pikuach nefesh*). Many people didn't care if they ingested harmful items, like certain leaves growing around the ghetto that we knew were poisonous. People ate them just to eat. And unfortunately, there were still many who did not realize that when they exerted themselves in the factories for that extra little food ration, they were doing much more damage to their bodies than they could repair with the few extra bits of bread they were awarded.

The quota system was extremely damaging (and like everything else the Germans did, was deliberately diabolical) because it created an air of intense competition that benefited no one but the Germans. The problems were especially severe in the clothing factories, where the workers were primarily women, most of them mothers. (Mamma worked there, too.) These caring women wanted the extra food for their children. That resulted in a large number of premature deaths from exhaustion—some women simply died at their sewing machines while stitching piece goods as quickly as they could for that tiny extra bit of ersatz bread.

The situation at the Leder and Sattler Ressort where Leon and I worked was very different. It was unique because most of the workers were youngsters sewing knapsacks, belts, and all types of leather goods and accessories for the German Army. Everything we did was done by hand and, at the beginning, though none of us knew how to sew, we learned quickly and became quite skillful.

No sooner did we get the hang of the work, however, when

our instructors immediately reported an increase in production to the director. In no time we were being pressured by him to increase the number of units we produced each day. It didn't take us long to realize that if we didn't properly organize ourselves and slow down the pace, we, like the women in the clothing factories, would die of exhaustion at our work stations. We also realized that if we reduced the number of knapsacks and other items we were making, there would be that many fewer knapsacks to provide to the enemy's troops.

In this manner, we banded together and formed the "Slaves' Union." Our leadership, responsible for coordinating solidarity among the workers, consisted entirely of teenagers like me, and included a few of my good friends: Niutek Radzyner, Sonnabend, David Sierakoviak, Nonek Flug, and Rysiek Podlaski. We realized we could not stop producing or they would deport or kill us. And so, when we planned our slow-down strike, we had to consider Rysiek's father, other factory directors, and Beibow's reaction to what we were going to do.

Biebow was strict, demanding, and ruthless. People like him, more so than the Germans in charge, fully appreciated and understood the extent of the economic benefits of using Jewish slave labor in the ghettos. Any factory visit from him never failed to result in more stringent regulations and demands for increased production. It is easy to understand why we dreaded it whenever he "popped in."

Personally, as one of the organizers, I was in a particularly precarious position. Director Podlaski already knew me well because of Rysiek, so I tried to remain as inconspicuous as possible. This was complicated by the fact that I was sneaking out early, almost daily, to go to my "mini-farm," and I couldn't afford to be under constant scrutiny. After all, that vegetable patch was the difference between life and death for my family.

Of course, our supervisors immediately noticed that the number of piece goods we produced was beginning to drop and reported the problem to the director. They were all extremely frustrated and tried various threats and incentives to force us to increase production. But we persevered and didn't budge.

I knew full well that we, as well as plant management, were

at great risk because of what we youngsters were doing. There was a possibility the director would be dismissed and stiff penalties could be imposed on us if we were caught by the Germans—specifically withholding food rations or being summarily executed as saboteurs. Deportation was the third and most frightening possibility. I figured the most immediate risk was to management. They would have to bear the brunt of the responsibility for allowing a slow-down to take place.

It therefore made perfectly good sense to me that management would "unintentionally" conspire with us to hide their deficiencies at the factory. This was a dangerous risk that carried grave consequences, but I also realized the alternative was even worse. Director Podlaski, knowing I was central to the plot, called me into his office on several occasions to deliver his personal reprimands. I was a teenager; he was in his fifties.

During our meetings in his office—a separate room off the factory floor—he would shout at me, "Don't you know I know you're part of this scheme? What are you trying to do? Kill me and everyone else? Don't you realize if the Germans find out, we will all be executed as saboteurs?"

He could not fathom how I and his son could be part of a conspiracy against him. I tried to keep a straight face and never let slip any of our plans or collateral information. I tried to convince him that working the leather was very difficult and that, in order to do the job well, it took lots of time, especially since poor workmanship was wasteful and penalized the worker. After all, we were just kids.

During our "conversations," I would think back to what my father meant when he told his friend he could never accept a high-ranking position in the ghetto because he would not be able to look people in the eye after the war.

Director Podlaski never mentioned it to me, but he knew his own son, Rysiek, was one of the chief organizers of the slow-down strikes. When he lectured me, he implied that the leaders would be the first ones penalized and it was my duty and obligation to fulfill the demanded quotas. He made it clear, in no uncertain terms, that I was to abandon my participation in these slow-downs, and that it was for my own good.

Minimizing the amount of work we had to do helped me in another way. If I worked fast, I could meet my quota in approximately three hours—early in the morning—which allowed me to sneak away from the factory floor and get to work on my "farm." This was trickier than it seems because I had to be present if Podlaski arbitrarily called me in for one of his "meetings."

Sometimes our instructors did notice I was gone, but they did not want to report me and thereby risk their own necks for not imposing enough discipline. I also assumed that because they were aware of my "special" relationship to Podlaski, they wouldn't want to report anything negative about me.

All in all, we surprised ourselves when we organized this form of resistance. It surprised us more that it worked even when we came under extreme pressure from management. Director Podlaski vacillated between offering rewards and making threats, all of them involving the food rations. Management tried to bribe us by giving us a few soccer balls to pacify us and to demonstrate how much they cared about our well-being. Nothing they tried worked. To keep our esprit de corps intact, to maintain solidarity, we wrote satirical lyrics to popular tunes. They were about the factories, our work, and, of course, the directors. We had to be very careful not to sing them too loudly. We also had to be on constant alert for unexpected visits from the German authorities—Hans Biebow in particular. At those times, we couldn't appear not to be busy—we had to work. During these unexpected visits, Biebow would tour the factory, talk to the director, and examine individual output. In case he showed up with his cronies, we always kept some unfinished pieces at our disposal. When the Germans arrived, they would see a few hundred individuals hunched over their workbenches, diligently sewing knapsacks for German troops.

Rysiek and Niutek, both sons of directors, had amazingly strong convictions and high ideals, and doing what they did against their own fathers meant putting their fathers' lives, and their own, in jeopardy. Blessedly, no one at the leather factory was ever caught, and the slow-downs were never officially noticed. I strongly believe that what we did greatly inspired strength and a will to live in many people, helping them to spiritually rise above the appalling conditions prevailing in the ghetto.

I feel privileged to have been associated with these young childhood friends, who assumed the leadership of the underground resistance in the Lodz ghetto. Most of them came from well-to-do "capitalist" families before the war, but in the ghetto became staunch socialists. They conducted clandestine meetings, discussed the theories and history of socialism, and applied those principles to fight the Germans. I attended some of those meetings, and though I was intrigued by their resistance and admired their courage I was never attracted to their philosophy, and so was never totally involved with them. In the end, however, despite their courage, most of them did not survive the war.

Almost everyone attending the meetings was a teenager though there were a few adults who helped lead the discussions. Sometimes the adults were able to provide us with tidbits of news from the "outside" about the tides of war. My primary obligation, however, was to my family, and that meant I had to tend to that vegetable patch every moment I could.

As I looked at books and documents about the Lodz ghetto while writing these memoirs, I realized that there is very little known, and even less that has been explored, about "indirect" resistance in the ghettoes. Besides slow-down strikes at the factories, there were many forms of spiritual resistance being practiced by ghetto residents in Lodz and other cities.

Sixty years later, it seems to me that among my memories the most audible (and visible) form of resistance in the ghetto was music. Through the ages, music has been central to Jewish life. Our liturgy is filled with melodies that are familiar to Jews no matter where they live or to what denomination they belong. Some of our melodies are centuries old, some are almost operatic in quality, while some of our traditional Yiddish songs are downright bawdy. We have old melodies that express joy and pain, longing and love, hope and the love of Israel, despair, grief, and even just plain fun.

Music captures the *nefesh*—the soul—of the Jews. In the ghetto, we added another dimension to our melodies: we added the music of defiance to the Jewish repertoire. During the ghetto years, musicians composed and performed at the peril of their lives, and their music accomplished more than guns ever could. Their music became the message of life, even if the lyrics and melodies sobbed with death. Mostly, the ghetto musicians played popular classical pieces, but there were those who went beyond the pale, like the brilliant composer, violinist, and conductor, David Baigelman.

Baigelman would arrange clandestine concerts in empty, unheated halls known only by word of mouth or from small announcements posted around the ghetto. Once in a while, I would go on my own and be dazzled by the sights and sounds of the symphony orchestra gathered in a *hovel*. The musicians wore special gloves that left their fingers partially exposed so they could play their particular instruments. The beautiful sounds they created reached up to heaven, inspiring hope in the audience and the thought that perhaps, at the end of it all, something better awaited us. It was not a denial of what we were going through, it was an attempt to help us forget, for a few precious moments, what those bitter days had brought.

This music was played under the most unimaginable and terrifying conditions, but it gave thousands of us enslaved Jews a needed spark, willing ourselves to live another day, another day, and yet another day.

There were times when I thought the ghetto was bursting with incredible contradictions. On the one hand, there was unceasing, torturous hunger and the relentless starvation, disease, and death, not to mention the ominous deportations. On the other hand, I was surrounded by quiet, varied forms of spiritual resistance—the rabbi who would teach children the *aleph beis* and prepare them for their bar mitzvahs; the mother who instilled humane values in her child despite the abysmal conditions in which they lived; the actors who would put on a play; the musicians who performed in those clandestine concerts. We had poets and writers, teachers and artists, all of whom continued to create, simply in defiance of those who wanted to turn them, and us, into groveling animals with no self-respect.

It is quite amazing that the human mind was able to observe, absorb, and appreciate beauty during those ghastly times in the ghetto. To me, those composers, actors, artists, rabbis, and teachers are the unknown spiritual leaders of our people, unsung heroes of the Holocaust, and the Lodz ghetto in particular.

Eight
The Beginning of the End

"Ignorance . . . is it truly bliss?"

Before I had a real chance to absorb and adjust to the loss of my father, Mamma was arrested and taken to the *Kripo (Kriminalpolizei),* the office of the criminal police. This was another one of those painful events my brain prefers to bury. I can't remember how they took her from our apartment, or whether I was even there at the time. All I remember was standing in front of the *Kripo* offices and the building that housed the Jewish police, trying to get any information regarding her whereabouts.

The internal affairs of the ghetto were run by the Jews, but absolute control resided, of course, with the German police. They victimized the inhabitants of the ghetto and held the arbitrary power of life and death in their sick minds, in their hands, and in their lethal weapons.

There were three groups of German police in the Lodz ghetto. The *Schupo,* or *Schutzpolizei,* guarded the ghetto. The *Geheime Staatspolizei* were the infamous and viciously cruel Gestapo, who held the highest ranks, and were dreaded more than any other force. All police authorities in the ghetto and Lodz proper were under Gestapo control. They controlled the food supplies and decided who would be deported. The head of the Gestapo for Jewish affairs was the infamous S.S. Obersturmführer Fuchs. All you needed to do was hear his name and you could feel cold terror crawl up your spine.

Finally, there was the *Kripo,* the criminal police who took Mamma away that day. The *Kripo* had multiple duties, but their primary function was to torture prisoners to obtain information about the location of any hidden valuables. Their headquarters were located in a pre-war church and they turned the cellars into

70

holding cells by building walls thick enough to muffle the sounds of screaming agony as they tortured the prisoners. *Kripo* agents also patrolled the streets to prevent smuggling, and were also instrumental in facilitating every deportation.

I am convinced that the *Kripo* took Mamma because she was a recent widow of a resourceful man and was now the head of our family. I also believe that because she was a woman, they felt she would be easy to intimidate and terrorize. These were the usual *Kripo* tactics. They enjoyed arresting people at their most vulnerable moments because it made it easier for them to extract the information they sought, using whatever means they had at their disposal. Their cruel and barbaric interrogations most often resulted in slow death for their victims.

For several days, Leon, my sisters, and I anxiously awaited word about Mamma. Every free moment we had, we stood vigil in front of the *Kripo's* headquarters, waiting and watching. When she finally emerged from that gate to hell, her body was trembling; she was dazed and completely disoriented. Her eyes were filled with terror, and she was mumbling incoherently. We took her back to the apartment where we tried to provide her with some needed nourishment and words of support and love, but she was in shock and non-responsive, almost catatonic.

She had no idea where she was and uttered some words to us in unintelligible Yiddish. That was strange, because she had never spoken Yiddish with us. We spoke very softly and tried to soothe her, but her bewilderment seemed permanent, and her eyes were wild with fear.

We wanted her to rest so that perhaps she might sleep. Finally she laid down on the bed, but she refused to remove her clothing. It took us days to convince her to change her clothes and get ready for bed. Obviously, she was petrified that she might be called in for additional interrogation. It was a number of weeks before Mamma lost that confused expression on her face and in her eyes, and to realize that she was back with her own family, no longer a prisoner of the *Kripo*.

Mamma never fully recovered from that ordeal. She never told us what transpired in that place of living nightmares or what they had done to her, except to say that one of the German interrogators spoke Yiddish quite well. Perhaps that was why she was mumbling in Yiddish when we brought her home. We understood how lucky we were. Mamma was one of only a few who survived a visit to the *Kripo*.

I have never been able to figure out if the Germans took Mamma in for questioning on their own initiative because they knew we were once a wealthy family, or because an informant had given them our name. I knew there were Jewish informants who cooperated with the German and Jewish police forces, but considering the atrocious conditions in the ghetto, and the promises of reward for betraying fellow prisoners, there were relatively few stool pigeons in the ghetto. This, I believe, is a credit to all of us.

For two years after the *Kripo* incident, Leon and I continued to work at the Leder and Sattler Ressort and tended to our vegetable garden. Mamma worked part-time in the general kitchen and in the clothing factory. The older of my two sisters, Dasza, and the younger one, Renia, occasionally worked in the bakery, and Renia also worked in the shoe factory run by Director Sonnabend.

Ghetto life remained essentially unchanged for those two years. Starvation, deportations, no medical supplies, excessive workloads, and the occasional beating were what filled our days. As I walked the narrow and dark streets on the way to and from work, I saw the withered bodies of men, women, and children sprawled in the mud. Most of them had been stripped of their clothing by the living. As the hours passed, the corpses were collected, counted for The Chronicle, and placed on wagons pulled by human beasts of burden working for that extra piece of bread. The same extra ration was paid to those who agreed to carry the human excrement in the ghetto to specially designated dumping areas.

Life continued along its sorrowful path despite proclamations to the contrary by high-ranking officials, particularly Rumkowski, King of the Jews, as he rode around the ghetto in his horse and buggy. He exhorted us about the importance of working even harder in order to keep the ghetto going, and reminded us how lucky we were to be there and to be alive. He had songs written proclaiming his greatness, and every now and then we would have to sing them in the workplace as well as at home. Rumkowski's word was the law.

Because the slave laborers were constantly dying of starvation or disease, there was constant turnover in the ghetto. As people were deported or died, other Jews arrived to replace them. They came from other cities in Poland, and from other countries, too. It was only because of these replacements that the ghetto workforce remained intact.

The constant deportations were abject reminders that Rumkowski's power was not as absolute as he thought it was. In fact, he was extremely vulnerable to the whims of the Germans. As tens of thousands of Jews were assembled in Lodz, the Germans intensified their actions and began massive deportations of children, the infirm, dissenters, and generally unsavory characters.

I read later that during the first few months of 1942, more than 50,000 Jews and about 5,000 gypsies were deported. More than 2,000 hospital patients and several hundred children were also deported and sent to the infamous extermination camp Chelmno. Rumkowski acknowledged such large-scale deportations as follows: "I received an uncompromising order and carried it out myself to prevent others from doing it."

Rumkowski's emotional reply to the tragic decree made by the Germans in September, 1942 that demanded the surrender of all children and elderly people was: "The decree cannot be revoked. It can only be slightly lessened by carrying it out calmly." Rumkowski, tearfully and with trembling voice, pleaded, "A grievous blow has struck the ghetto. They are asking us to give up the best we possess—the children and the elderly. I was unworthy of having a child of my own, so I gave the best years of my life to children. I've lived and breathed with children. I never imagined I would be forced to deliver this sacrifice to the altar with my own hands. In my old age I must stretch out my hands and beg: brothers and sisters, hand them over to me! Fathers and mothers, give me your children!"

Rumkowski continued his plea: "I must take the children because if not, others will be taken as well." And so 20,000 children, the infirm, and the elderly were deported to certain death. Giving up the children to the Germans may surely have been the greatest personal tragedy endured by Rumkowski. For the rest of us remaining in the ghetto, it was a black day indeed.

For our small family, the deportation of the children was particularly onerous. Though we had work permits and jobs, we understood that we were defenseless. As teenagers, we realized that this deportation, more than the others, was a harbinger of things to come, and it was likely that soon we too would have to ride the cattle cars into an unknown abyss.

The debates about Rumkowski rage to this day. He was deported to Auschwitz in August 1944, where he was murdered, and there are three conflicting stories about how he died. We can only speculate which one, if any, is the truth. One story says he was instantly recognized upon his arrival in Auschwitz by deportees from Lodz and that they beat him to death. The second account says that when he arrived he presented a letter of introduction from Hans Biebow, was accorded the privilege of inspecting Auschwitz, and that when he visited the crematoria he was burned alive. The third, and perhaps the most plausible story, is that he was treated like everyone else and was sent to the gas chambers because he was too old to work.

Locked in the ghetto for what seemed like an eternity, we hardly knew what was actually happening in the outside world. We were not even aware that the Warsaw ghetto uprising had begun on the first night of Passover in 1943 and that it had been completely destroyed.

At the end of the summer of 1944, the Lodz ghetto was in a state of constant flux and turmoil, bordering on chaos. In practical terms, nothing had really changed. The ghetto was still totally isolated from the main city of Lodz, separated by barbed wire and open spaces. There were no smugglers to bring us newspapers or information. Yet, even without tangible proof, we sensed something foul was in the air.

Though Tatush and others had thought the war would be a short one, we now knew they were wrong. Sometimes I would catch a rumor that implied things were going badly for the Germans on the battlefront, but who knew if it was true? Perhaps, as the old saying goes, ignorance, especially in this case, may well have proven to be bliss. The last thing I could afford now was false hope.

Every day we noticed the changes in the behavior of the German and Jewish authorities. Discipline was slacking off, workload demands were chaotic, supplies were scarce, and production plummeted. For the first time since I had come to the ghetto, people were just milling around in the streets, doing nothing but speculating on their fate.

Then the Jewish police started helping the Germans round up increasing numbers of Jews for deportation. People were grabbed off street corners and dragged out of their beds. Masses of hungry people rampaged in their hunt for food. They assaulted the warehouses and bakeries, battering down the doors, and grabbing anything they could get their hands on.

As I watched them riot I realized that we needed to create a security plan to protect our own food supply—our little garden—from the mobs, especially since the vegetables were just about ready for harvest. My fellow landowners had similar thoughts. We had a hasty meeting and decided that we would stand guard together and surround as much of the gardens as we could. We armed ourselves with sticks and brooms, bent on protecting what was still in the ground. We survived the first onslaught but word of our farms began to spread, the mob began to grow, and the attacks along our perimeter were constant. Then the rioters broke through and trampled the fields, ripping whatever they could get out of the soil.

In just two hours, the fruits of our hard labor disappeared as if they had never been. There wasn't a shred of evidence to prove that just that morning there were crops ready to harvest. Nothing green was visible in the fields. Every leaf and stem was gone.

I stood in the middle of the field with my head bowed, unable to stop sobbing. All the hard work, tender care, and countless hours spent cultivating that once barren land was erased in moments. When my anger and despair subsided, I became practical and reminded myself that our current food supply had been wiped out and we needed to get provisions for the coming winter.

I also realized that during the rampage, people pulled out what they could see. There were still potatoes growing deep in the soil and that thought brought me a bit of comfort. Still, I stayed in my field for a long, long time, full of grief and sorrow, until darkness began to fall. Slowly, I turned and left for home.

The next day Leon and I went back to dig up what was still left in the ground. We had no idea that soon even those potatoes would no longer matter to us.

The massive deportations continued unabated and seemed to take place more often. We were terrified that we would be next. No one was volunteering and people stopped loitering on street corners so they wouldn't be rounded up.

In order to empty the ghetto, the Germans used the Jewish police, as they did in the Warsaw ghetto, to surround certain blocks and evacuate them one at a time, transporting the occupants by truck to the railroad station where they were crammed into cattle cars and sent to unknown destinations. We knew our family's deportation was inevitable, but we wanted to stay in the ghetto as long as we could. We somehow knew that what was going on outside the ghetto was infinitely worse than what we had already been through.

We prepared a hiding place in a wardrobe with a double partition at the back. If we squeezed together, there was enough room to accommodate the five of us. There were several occasions when we heard unexpected footsteps outside our door and silently rushed to the wardrobe. We climbed out only if there was total silence in the hall.

Our cat-and-mouse game lasted only a few weeks. I don't remember how we were caught and I don't remember what came next. I only remember that my brain began to function again when I heard the loud slam of the cattle car doors as they locked us in. When I came to, I was lying in the inky and evil blackness of a tiny little corner in the cattle car. Mamma, Dasza, Renia, and Leon were all with me.

Not so long ago, my sister, Renia told me what had happened on the night we were deported. The Germans found us hiding behind the wardrobe and led us to the trucks. Even as she told me in detail what happened, my brain continued to protect me from those devastating memories, as it still does. And while I do not remember how we got to the railroad station, the sound of the cattle car door slamming shut haunts me to this day.

Nine
Auschwitz . . . Children of the Holocaust

"Abandoned by God . . . betrayed by men."

When I talk about the Holocaust, one word summarizes everything—Auschwitz. I specifically mean the three-part complex comprised of Auschwitz, Birkenau, and Buna-Monowitz. Auschwitz was the concentration camp, Birkenau was the killing center, and Buna-Monowitz was the slave labor facility.

Composed of an area of approximately fifty square kilometers, Auschwitz was centrally located in the countryside, with rail lines readily accessible. Isolated from any large cities, it was guarded by some 6,000 SS men from the Death's Head Unit, divided into twelve companies. At the camp's entrance was a huge wrought iron sign that sardonically read, ARBEIT MACHT FREI ("Work Will Set You Free"), but the only freedom truly offered was the freedom of death.

I deliberately make distinctions between Auschwitz and Birkenau for a number of reasons. Birkenau was the larger part of Auschwitz, the place where the vast majority of the slaves lived and where the large-scale crematoria were—where most of the Jews were systematically exterminated. I was incarcerated in Birkenau, a few miles from Auschwitz, the original camp.

Auschwitz-Birkenau was hell on Earth. Though hell is normally defined as a place of punishment for the wicked after they die, we weren't sent to that hell after we died or punished for any crimes or sins, other than the German-manufactured criminal act of being born Jewish. Auschwitz-Birkenau was the quintessential living nightmare created to destroy the innocent in a master plan that sought the elimination of all Jews.

Auschwitz and Birkenau must be linked for eternity as one,

for it would desecrate the memory of the innocent if future generations argue that it would have been impossible to kill so many Jews per day in the original, small Auschwitz camp. We must always think of Auschwitz-Birkenau as a single entity designed to destroy lives.

Some called Auschwitz-Birkenau "The Inferno," "The Valley of Death" or "The Abyss." However you try to grapple with it, Auschwitz-Birkenau was its own definition and defies comparison, metaphor, or analogy. It stands apart at the apogee of evil. In that place the unthinkable and unimaginable were real. It was an industrialized assembly line for human slaughter and enslavement. Using the techniques inspired by Henry Ford and his Model-T factory in Detroit, Michigan, the entire German process of slaughtering and recycling Jews was conceived, planned, built, executed, and managed by people, not devils, demons, and ghouls—by thousands and thousands of human beings—not all of them Nazis.

The process began when the Germans sorted deportees like vegetables headed for market then stripped them of their belongings, including their hair. The killing factories were entirely self-sufficient and included gas chambers, morgues, and furnaces linked by a mechanical conveyor system. Smoke saturated with the souls and stench of the departed constantly belched from the enormous chimneys. In some cases, skin and hair were recycled into blankets and lampshades, gold teeth were smelted and shipped to Switzerland, people were turned into guinea pigs for "medical science," ashes were turned into fertilizer, and there were false rumors that the little cakes of soap marked RJF were made of Jewish fat. In Auschwitz-Birkenau, a Jew didn't go to waste.

In addition to the actual perpetrators of these monstrous acts were the private German industries involved in the conception, construction, and operation of the crematoria: AEG, Falk, Industrie-Bau-A.G., Kluge, Koehler, Kontinentale Wasserwerks-Gesellschaft, Rieder, Segnitz, Topf, Triton, and Vedag. Added to this cross-section of German "Big Business," Allianz Insurance Company, the international mega-insurance company, was the major insurer for Auschwitz-Birkenau, bizarrely insuring the machinery of doom.

The initial expansion of Auschwitz-Birkenau was meant to accommodate Russian prisoners of war and house I.G. Farben's ever-growing slave labor force. But that was abandoned in order to make it the largest holding and killing camp—and, incidentally, the largest Jewish cemetery—in the world. Run by Germany's industrial giants like any other business investment and meticulously managed for cost effectiveness, the Germans demanded the annihilation of "useless" Jews (the very young, the old, the sick) immediately upon arrival, so that funds wouldn't be wasted on rations and rags. They investigated various ways of dealing with the "industrial waste" (corpses). Blueprints were drawn up and discarded, processes were tested and revised, until those in charge were satisfied that the assembly line of carnage and the salvaging of the victims' possessions and body parts was as efficient as possible.

The Germans had sealed the fate of European Jews on January 20, 1942 at the infamous Wannsee Conference. That is where the Nazi "experts," the second tier leaders, organized the precise logistics of how to create and implement the most efficient death machine to fulfill Hitler's plan leading to the murder of millions of Jews called the "Final Solution." By itself, Final Solution is a meaningless phrase. The innocuous-sounding words really meant that the Germans were going to kill every Jewish person they could find by putting them through the devilish "production" process. While most Jews would go up the chimneys immediately and have their remains recycled, others would be worked to death as slave laborers. This strategy was named with a play on words over the Auschwitz gate: "Arbeit Macht Frei" (Work Will Make You Free), when in actuality it meant "Tod Durch Arbeit" (Death Through Work).

The estimated length of time it took to work an inmate to death was ninety days. The construction of Crematoria IV and V, the use of "fast-killing" cyanide gas, Zyklon B, and the introduction of all the latest technologies for mass murder were designed to bring death to the inmates as quickly and as cheaply as possible. Unfortunately, these hi-tech innovations did not deliver as promised, and the victims suffered gruesomely while they were being gassed.

The camp administration received between three to six marks per diem for each slave laborer's output, while the cost incurred for maintaining a slave was approximately 1.35 marks. Jews replaced Russian prisoners of war as the primary commodity in the camp and supply was constantly replenished, so the Germans were conducting quite a profitable business—one that did not include the additional profits from the plunder taken from prisoners when they first arrived.

In his memoirs written between his arrest and execution, Auschwitz Kommandant Rudolf Hoess spoke of two million men, women, and children killed at Auschwitz. After careful analysis, it seems that Hoess' figures may be an exaggeration. In the post-communist era, Auschwitz historian Franticek Piper has calculated the dead by taking the number of people who arrived at Auschwitz, transport by transport, subtracting the number of people who left Auschwitz for other camps, and the amount of prisoners found upon liberation. Therefore, he came to the conclusion that between 1.1–1.3 million men, women, and children were murdered at Auschwitz-Birkenau, 90 percent of them Jews. Even if we were to accept the lower figure as indicated by Mr. Piper, this calculation is still so huge, so overwhelming, and so demoralizing, it boggles the mind.

While some individuals and companies personally profited from the construction and operations of Auschwitz-Birkenau and Buna-Monowitz, the camp was not created solely for their benefit. The project was designed to benefit a nation, and it was the entire nation of Germany and the local populations of "occupied countries" who worked diligently to invent and improve means of torture and mass murder.

It must never be forgotten that the Nazis did not work alone, nor did the guards in the concentration camps or those managing ghettos and labor camps function in isolation. Their support system included architects, engineers, scientists, and doctors—from Germany's top schools and leading universities—and the willing assistance of the indigenous populations. There were military men, politicians, lawyers, and writers, all of them actively engaged in conceiving, inventing, and building the best and most efficient machinery for mass destruction.

My first memory of my deportation from the ghetto emerges from the moment I opened my eyes in the bitter blackness of the cattle car, a blackness fractured only by tiny shafts of light that broke through chinks in its walls. My ears were waking up, too. I could hear the sounds cracking the dense atmosphere, creating a din. Voices, male and female, young and old, cried and wailed, screamed in terror, moaned and keened. When I came to, people were still being jammed into whatever space remained in the heavily packed car.

Once the doors were slammed shut, the tidal wave of noise subsided and questions filled the air:

"Moishe, are you there?"

"Hannah, where are you?"

"Yossel, are you okay?"

"Mammeleh, what did they do to you?"

Sometimes we heard the answers. Most often the pleading questions were met with silence. The questions soon turned into mourning. The sounds of heartbreak and tears soon spread throughout the car, sounds of sorrow augmented by fear.

The weeping slowly faded as our fellow passengers realized we were facing immediate concerns of a more physical nature. There were more than 150 people crammed together in the boxcar, most of them forced to remain upright because there was no way to sit or lie down. If you tried to sit down between the forest of legs, you could be trampled. As the unbearable became excruciating, the steel wheels screeched into motion as the train began its inexorable journey. That's also when the yelling, pushing, shoving, and fighting started, as people jockeyed for an extra centimeter of space.

I firmly believe my family was the beneficiary of yet another small miracle because we were fortunate enough to be thrown into the same corner. I couldn't even imagine what it might have been like to be separated from Mamma and the others. Because we were together, we were able to carve out a small area for ourselves that protected us from the shoving matches around us. Together, we held our ground during the terrifying trip. I was so preoccupied with my immediate concerns, it didn't occur to me to indulge in one of my "comparison pastimes," and compare this trip to the one we had taken from Podębie to Lodz on that long-ago summer night when we were overrun by the Germans. That happy childhood, so suddenly interrupted, seemed to have happened on an altogether different planet, in an altogether different life, to a completely different person.

The worst part of the physical deprivation hit us when we realized that there was no place to relieve oneself and no place to vomit, except on yourself. There was no water, though some people wisely packed provisions to last for a day or so. The stench was overpowering, the thirst unbearable. Such were the luxurious accommodations of the Kniker family on their last voyage by train from Lodz in the fall of 1944.

The torture train continued rolling down the tracks, stopping now and then to let a military or cargo train pass. Those able to position themselves near the cracks that let in what little light and fresh air there was, peered through them and tried to deduce where we were. Sometimes we heard noises from the outside, yelling, and men shouting orders, but we were never able to determine where we were or where we were headed.

By the time the first night fell, the violence in our ranks was no longer contained. In the filth and stench it erupted like a volcano and you couldn't tell who was hurting whom, which added yet another dimension to the horror. Being with my family was all the spiritual comfort and physical protection I had, and I began to relax just enough for slow exhaustion to overtake me and to fall into an uneasy sleep. My last thought before drifting off was, "Where are they taking us and for what?"

Every once in a while we were jostled awake by the train's sudden stops. We could hear the coupling and uncoupling of railroad cars, but we were still in the dark, both literally and figuratively, as to what was going to happen to us.

I became accustomed to the stench and, though it seems unbelievable, it became tolerable in light of other things I witnessed. Everything became increasingly worse, but I barely seemed to notice. People began calling out for water, and soon the cry for water was unceasing. We couldn't help ourselves, and we certainly couldn't help those who were so sick. People fainted. Soon we discovered that some of our fellow passengers were beyond anyone's help and had passed on to a more peaceful place.

The stronger men picked up the corpses and stacked them in a corner like cordwood, one atop the other. A day or two later, the bodies began to reek. The pile grew very quickly. On the third day, during one of the irregular stops, the door was opened. Half-blinded by sunlight, we could barely make out the Germans who threw a few loaves of bread and a few buckets of water into the car. In our desperation for food and drink, we could almost feel the tantalizing taste of bread on our tongues and the cool wetness of something, anything, to drink, on our lips. But before we could even figure out where these supplies had landed, the doors slammed shut again and we sank back into the fetid darkness.

This diabolical German way to distribute food and water was based on the same sadistic methods they used in the ghetto, just to see what we would do. First they wanted to dehumanize us, make us grovel and kill each other, destroying any shred of dignity and decency we possessed, as they watched our physical and spiritual deterioration with amusement.

Obviously everyone wanted bread and water, but how could it be divided up fairly among us all? Driven only by the desire to eat and drink, a mini-riot exploded in the scramble for the spoils. We were so far from the doors, I didn't bother getting into the melee. Those standing closest to the doors hoarded what they could and the stronger men walked over the dead and living to grab their share and more. What chance did the rest of us have?

I didn't think about it at the time, but, considering the conditions that prevailed in the concentration camps, except for a handful of really evil people, I remember that the prisoners generally showed a great deal of compassion for each other. What I witnessed in the cattle car that day was the worst human behavior of Jew against Jew I ever saw during the war.

The bread was captured and held by bullies, who kept it for themselves. The water became victim of those who tried to grab the buckets, spilling the precious fluid as they tried to tip the buckets toward themselves. Fights broke out and the result was that almost all the water fell through the floorboards to the tracks below, where no one could benefit from it. People crawled around in the filth, trying to lick the water from the floor. Eventually, as the strength of those who fought for food waned, the violence stopped.

The location of our family in one corner of the cattle car may have been advantageous on that first night, but now we were prevented from getting our share of the minuscule quantities of bread and water because we were simply too far from the source. It was probably just as well. To get some crumbs and risk severe injury or worse by getting trampled in the process, we would have had to expend precious energy to no avail.

As time passed, our demoralization intensified by constantly worrying about where we were being taken and what would happen next. To take our minds off hunger, thirst and wretched refuse, we obsessed about the future, if there was one. If this ghastly journey was the dismal harbinger of things to come, what little hope we had to survive was in danger of extinction.

The fourth day of our journey started with a bang. The train stopped suddenly and before we could recover our balance, the doors of the car were jerked wide open. Bright, burning sunlight blinded us; the clamor of barking, growling German Shepherds and Dobermans distracted and confused us. There was shouting and screaming, chaos and panic. We didn't know it yet, but we had arrived at a place in the world where human beings who were members of the world's most technologically advanced nation were indulging their most perverted, vicious, cruel, and fatal fantasies upon a helpless population—while robbing them blind.

Our eyes were not given the chance to adjust to the intense and dazzling sunshine. As we tried to get our bearings, to awake from our semi-conscious states, we heard the shouted command, *"Alle raus,"* all out. Strangely, this order was a welcome one. Anyone still capable of moving on his or her own power was relieved to be away from the pervasive and intolerable stench in the boxcar and to breathe the first fresh air we'd had in days.

The scene on the platform was incomprehensible. Dogs barked, growled, and attacked; people were being beaten to the ground if they didn't move fast enough, and men in striped uniforms mingled among the prisoners, pushing and prodding us into lines.

Above the din were the distinct sounds of women and children, shrill with fear, penetrating my awareness. The high-pitched and breathless sobbing of those children were the most painful sounds I have ever heard in my life and still haunt me to this day. I often wonder if their cries ever broke through heaven's gates. The descriptions of hell I studied in Dante's *Inferno* paled in comparison to the scene unfolding before me.

I hadn't been able yet to collect my thoughts, and moments after clambering out of the car, with no time to figure out what the consequences might be for my family, men in striped suits surrounded our group, yelling at the top of their lungs, *"Alle raus. Laufen! Macht schnell!"* ("Everyone out. Run. Make it fast.") The men in striped uniforms punctuated their commands with snaps of vicious whips, and the Germans used the solid butts of guns and rifles to mercilessly clobber anyone who didn't move fast enough or who got in their way.

Moving fast after being cramped and huddled together in that filthy boxcar was almost impossible. My legs could barely move, my eyes were painfully trying to normalize themselves, and the pitiful racket assaulting my ears petrified me. We were already the victims in a calculated effort by the Germans to instantly instill us with panic and terror. They succeeded admirably.

One of our fellow travelers had been a policeman in the ghetto and, having survived the trip thus far, figured he might be able to use his position to improve his particular situation. As he emerged from the train, he announced to the men in stripes that he had been a policeman in the ghetto and would be happy to help them carry out their tasks. As soon as those men heard that, they jumped him, punched him, and slammed him in the head and all over his body. Once he was down, they kicked him in the head and neck, then stepped on his face. There was blood every-where and in moments he was dead. He didn't know it, but he was one of the lucky ones.

That was how the Kniker family was welcomed to Auschwitz-Birkenau.

Ten

Life in Auschwitz

"Where was God? Where was man? Where were you and me? And for all of us the ultimate question . . . where will we be next time when children cry out in pain?"—*Children in the Holocaust*

How can I describe the unspeakable? What can I write about the gruesome sights and sensations I experienced when I arrived at Auschwitz-Birkenau, that infamous portal to unfathomable malevolence and doom?

True, on that day, I was not physically harmed, but I was, nonetheless, deeply scarred. Those still-raw scars are invisible to the naked eye—they burn my soul and will do so until the end. Strangely, my brain did not function as it had before—by burying the anguished memories of personal traumas so deeply that I still can't remember them. The memories of that first day in that place are so vivid, it is as if they were recorded by the latest digital technology and permanently burned into my hard drive.

When I think about that as a psychological phenomenon, I arrive at a single conclusion: my brain must have gone on automatic eyewitness mode because it somehow understood that this was no longer just my personal story. This was the story of my family. It was about my community and my Jewish people. I must have somehow intuited that if any one of us ever managed to survive this man-made purgatory, we had to remember what we saw in order to be able to tell the world what had happened.

Later I learned that the Auschwitz-Birkenau "welcoming committee"—the men in striped uniforms who yelled, screamed, and beat us—were part of a Jewish commando unit that called itself "Canada."

By the time we got to Auschwitz-Birkenau in 1944, there were those working in Canada who had been deported for "criminal behavior"—some real, some not. They brutalized the police-man from Lodz because the ghetto police had arrested them in the first place. The Canada contingent was well taken care of be-cause they had access to the goods the new deportees were bring-ing in. It didn't matter that they would be killed if they were caught pilfering, they still stole valuables from new prisoners and traded them for favors like food, warm clothing, and even sex.

There were many German soldiers patrolling the railhead, some on horseback and some on foot holding their hounds, ready to order them to kill. It was apparent that the Germans were dili-gent supervisors, overseeing the process that pushed the new ar-rivals onto the conveyor belt of death leading to the gas chambers or the slave quarters.

The Germans excelled in brutalizing their new guests. The riders who towered above the huddled masses on their huge horses added pure menace to the mix. They used the horses to separate families and groups by trotting right into them and forcing them apart, as they slashed at them from above with whips that cut as sharply as finely honed swords. They coordi-nated the "Canadians," who used whips with ball bearings at the end of each cord, designed to inflict maximum damage on the un-wary. Sometimes the dogs were ordered to rip chunks of flesh from the newly arrived simply because their masters enjoyed watching them do it.

After the relative tranquility of the ghetto, such viciousness was incomprehensible to me. In those first few minutes, I was sure of one thing and one thing only: I was no longer a human be-ing. I stopped thinking. I stopped planning. I stopped hoping. I stopped caring. I mindlessly did precisely what I was ordered to do. I, too, became part of the machinery of malevolence. I became like Sony's Aibo, the robot dog, my grandchild's toy, programmed to mindlessly do what I was programmed to do until my batteries ran out.

I was on that platform, but my soul had detached itself and flown to a safer place, where I could not find it. Today I am aston-ished at how quickly I became numb to the pitiless and cruel acts taking place in front of me. I became blind to the sight of children snatched from their mothers' arms, deaf to their heartrending screams and cries, to the roar of the guards and growls of the beasts they handled.

I don't know when I realized that there was a method to this madness: they were forming us into queues. I had no idea the Germans were preparing us for incorporation into the "production process" and had already achieved the first step, instantly dehumanizing us, by shocking our psyches. Sixty years later, I have only to close my eyes, let my mind wander back to that time and the image that first comes into focus is the scene at the gate where the Germans promised us, *"Arbeit Macht Frei."*

On that day, I, like so many others who could not conceive of what was about to happen to them, had to accept that my mother and sisters were to be torn from me as surely as those infants had been ripped from their mothers' arms. It happened as we were herded into separate lines for men and women. We had been holding hands, huddled together, when the Kapos ordered us to move.

At the moment of our separation, Mamma whispered to me and Leon to take care of each other. Those were meaningful and prophetic last words, words that helped us as we journeyed through the Stygian camps. By sticking together and watching out for each other, Leon and I were able to survive. But we didn't know that yet. I also did not realize that I would never see my beloved Mamma again.

Directing women and men to different bathhouses, no matter how cruelly, seemed a somewhat normal and reasonable thing to do. Naïvely, we assumed that despite what we witnessed on the ramps, we would be reunited after being disinfected and showered.

Rushing us, to make sure we stayed disoriented, the guards drove us like cattle into a decontamination area where we were stripped of everything, deloused, and had our heads shaved. The "Canadians" and Germans sorted through whatever remained of our previous lives, and warned us that if they found any contraband sewn into our clothing, we would die.

To emphasize what they meant and to convince us to give up everything we had with us, particularly jewelry, the German guards pointed to the white-blue smoke pouring out of the nearby chimneys and told us we, too, would go up in smoke if we didn't hand over everything. These orders were punctuated by beatings with gun butts and lashes from the cat o'nine tails. The words gas chamber and crematorium were suddenly added to my vocabulary.

Hundreds of us were shoved into a sizeable area with shower heads in the ceilings and stood there shivering as very cold water poured over us. When they herded us out of the showers, we were handed ill-fitting, threadbare uniforms and wooden shoes—and woe to anyone who complained. They were answered with the whip. Someone figured out that we needed to trade with one another. At the time we had no idea how important it was for those wooden shoes to fit. Later that could make a difference between living and dying.

Through it all, I remained on auto-pilot.

We were broken into smaller groups and led from the bathhouse to the barrack, a long wooden structure. I noticed that identical buildings stood in rows for as far as the eye could see, and each had a chimney protruding from its roof. Once inside, I could see the single stove in the center of the vast room, flanked by a row of double bunkbeds lining each sidewall. When we came in that afternoon, the barrack was empty.

Once they pushed us through the door, we were ordered to move on so the others could come in behind us. When the room was packed, and we were crammed into the bunks, we had to jostle each other to make room for additional prisoners. Three to five people were forced to share the same bunk. Conditions were deplorable, but the one consolation I had was that Leon and I had somehow managed to stay together.

The stove heated only the small area surrounding it. Our own feeble body heat, conserved by crowding ourselves together, warmed us on freezing nights. There were no toilets or latrines nearby. What was available for our use was a row of pits, where we were forced to stand in our own waste.

As devilish as the ghetto system was, this was even more diabolical, consisting of calculated measures designed by the Germans to extinguish whatever sense of self-worth any of us might still possess. It was the way they "softened us up" for our own destruction. Many of my fellow inmates succumbed to the psychological torture and became what we called *musselmen*—zombies who didn't care if they lived or died. Those of us who could, tried to care about living. If we cared enough, we might make it out.

Leon and I, jammed together in the bunk, drifted off to sleep from sheer exhaustion, but it seemed only moments before I was snapped awake by shouted orders that reverberated through the barrack: "*Alle raus! Appel!*" ("Everyone out. Roll call!")

Tired, worn out, we staggered into the semi-darkness. The sky was that strange color it becomes just before dawn. We were ordered to stand in straight lines along with thousands of others. Leon stood next to me and instinctively we realized our survival was dependent on our ability to stay together.

The Kapos and Block Elders (the *Blockalteste*) were also prisoners of the camp and included Eastern European and German criminals. They had unfettered power to torture us, to whimsically decide who lived and who died, as they made believe they were military men and we were their troops. Twice a day they demanded we stand smartly at attention while we were being counted, no matter the weather.

Imagine that after four interminable days in a cattle car with absolutely zero consideration for your humanity, you are hustled into this firestorm, separated from your mother, and dragged out of "bed" after a few minutes of sleep to be forced to stand at attention for hours in the frosty dawn. You couldn't do it unless you made a superhuman effort to pull yourself together. Those who stumbled, fell, broke ranks, or shifted the line, were literally beaten into the ground until they died.

The Block Elder warned us that the treatment we were getting was nothing compared to what would happen if we disobeyed orders. He made it perfectly clear that he would not tolerate any break in discipline. Whatever he commanded, we had no choice but to do precisely what he ordered.

Inmates too weak or battered to stand were moved off to the side, as the rest of us stood there waiting to be counted. When the count was completed we were dismissed to the barrack. That first day, some of us tried to drag our weaker "comrades" back into the barrack, but the Kapos prevented us from performing even that tiny act of kindness by using their whips on our backs and harshly ordering us not to help. "No help is to be given," the Kapos barked, and then assaulted the inmates who dared to care. "Let that be a lesson to you," they yelled.

While the Germans were actually in charge, they didn't really care what the Kapos did as long as there were no deviations in the head counts. If there was a discrepancy in the count, we had to stand through the night or for an entire day until they figured out the problem. Finally, after the "accountants" figured out they had to add the dead to the count, the numbers began to balance, and the *appels* took less time.

I don't know how long it was before I heard that the barrack we lived in was once part of the Roma (Gypsy) camp, and that the Roma had all been "dispatched" via chimney sometime earlier. Rumor had it that there were two possible outcomes for us: we might be sent directly to the gas chambers and crematoria, or, because of our age and relatively healthy condition, we could be used as slave laborers in the Auschwitz-Birkenau complex and satellite camps.

We hadn't been tattooed yet, and that scared us. Without those numbers, we surely had no clue what was in store for us. Later someone told us that we weren't tattooed because there were so many new arrivals after the liquidation of the Lodz ghetto, the processing staff was overwhelmed and had no time to number us.

As I began to adjust to my new living conditions, it began to sink in that we now served in an institution of organized bedlam. There was no rhyme or reason for a particular prisoner to be singled out and tortured by Kapos, Block Elders, or German officers. I noticed something else, too. If you were given a thorough lashing, your time on Earth was extremely limited.

One of the favorite commands given by the Kapos or Block Elders was simply *"Funf und zwanzig"* (25). This meant a chosen victim was forcibly bent over so his hands were dangling toward his feet—or sometimes he was held over a specially constructed platform that exposed his back—and was whipped, full force, twenty-five times with the cat o'nine tails. Sometimes, if the torturer felt his prisoner hadn't shown enough agony, he would order another "*funf und zwanzig*." The louder the screams of their victims, the more the Kapos relished what they were doing.

The cries that came from these victims were like constant static in the noise of the camp. From what I saw so far, I knew I needed to make myself as invisible as possible if I wanted to survive.

The Kapos, Block Elders, and their Germans superiors were constantly inventing new methods of torture. One day I watched prisoners forced to do push-ups until they dropped from sheer exhaustion. When one of them fainted, he was revived with cold water and ordered to continue.

The worst part of all of this was watching the faces of the perpetrators, who smiled and obviously enjoyed what they were doing. During the head counts, if anyone displeased the Kapos for any reason or even for no reason at all, he could be ordered to remain standing at attention indefinitely. In the summer you broiled under the relentless sun. In the winter or whenever the temperature dropped below freezing, it was particularly unbearable and life-sapping, since we had no proper clothes or shoes to protect us from the Polish winter—frostbite and the extreme fatigue induced by these endurance marathons killed inmates very quickly.

These cruel and callous events were the substance of my days. My impulse was to help the victims or intervene to prevent bloodshed, but the deterrent of instant death—or worse, a slow agonizing finish by beating—was extremely effective. We could only help each other in hidden ways. If someone could manage to stand upright but could not make it to the *appelplatz* on his own, we could prevent him from falling and held him off the ground just enough to make it look like he was walking so the Kapos wouldn't notice.

Gunshots and the thunk of the gallow's platforms dropping often punctuated the screams generated by the brutality of our caretakers. Whenever they set up the gallows, you could see them from our barrack. In retrospect, I came to understand that these direct methods of murder were humane compared to everything else going on around me.

Hanging above it all was the omnipresent smoke of Jewish souls pouring forth from the chimneys. The white-blue haze that covered the camp was a persistent, stench-filled reminder that the crematoria were waiting for us. That stink of burning human bodies permeated everything and was inescapable, twenty-four hours a day. It was beyond dreadful, and has always remained with me. Today, when I see a massive chimney stack, it takes me back to those times.

Our daily rations were strictly controlled by the *Blockalteste* and their associates, and supposedly consisted of a small piece of fake bread and a meager portion of watered-down potato peel soup. But because the Kapos and *Blockalteste* skimmed as much of our rations as they could off the top, there was hardly ever enough "bread" and "soup" to go around. In addition, if the *Blockalteste* felt like it, he would play "kick the kettle," knock over the food, and then stand back and laugh as prisoners groveled for the dregs on the ground.

Because you had to be prepared for the unexpected and for sudden sadistic "pranks," it made sense to be one of the first in line at mealtimes. On the other hand, because of the capriciousness of the *Blockalteste* and Kapos, it increased your chances of being noticed and getting singled out for some "fun and games." Leon and I were definitely on the horns of a dilemma. Do we stand in the front or the back of the line? You might risk getting a beating that will kill you slowly if you were noticed in the front and you might starve to death if you stayed at the back. After thinking it through, Leon and I decided we would rather risk starvation than getting thrashed to within an inch of our lives. We stayed at the back of the line.

Our decision did have consequences. The constant lack of food caused us to lose more and more strength each day. When I saw my condition reflected in the living skeletons of others walking around me, I realized I needed to eat soon or perish. We were sacks of skin and bones who mechanically followed orders and fell to the ground before they could even bludgeon us. Many became the walking dead, catatonically wandering around the barrack like wraiths from hell.

I sometimes found corpses in my bunk when I woke up in the

morning, and had to drag them out to the *appelplatz* to be counted. Then the bodies had to be dragged back to the barrack and piled in a corner. Every second or third ·day the *Sonderkommando* would pick them up and take them to the crematoria for disposal.

I grew desperate as my health deteriorated. I dreaded getting sick, starving, or being whipped, and I wondered how long it would be before, I, too, became a *musselman*. Either I figured out a way to get food for myself and Leon, or we would both die sooner rather than later.

It finally dawned on me: every day a procession of prisoners, surrounded by Kapos, carried loaves of bread across the compound on a large blanket. When I would see them pass, my hunger would grow more intense, as though I was being subjected to conditioning like Pavlov's dogs, only my hunger went much deeper than that. One can never understand this feeling unless one personally experiences it. One day, as I looked at this mountain of bread on the blanket, my hunger ambushed my brain. In desperation I did something foolish that almost cost me my life.

When I thought the Kapos weren't watching, I ran to the mountain of bread, grabbed a loaf and ran behind the barrack, clutching my loot to my chest. It was true I had risked death by going for that loaf of bread, and I was lucky the Kapos did not catch me in the act. But I did not foresee that there were hundreds of other hungry eyes watching the bread parade, and before I could take a bite, a group of hungry inmates who had followed my desperate stunt jumped me, piling on in their attempts to get at the life-saving bread. I don't know how many men piled on top of me or how long it took before I could stand on my own two feet, but when the Kapos noticed the disturbance, they came to break it up, slashing with their whips. When the mountain of men on top of me was finally dispersed, I tried to get up.

I stood there trembling. I could barely open my hand, the one that had clutched so tightly at the bread, and needed to pry my fist open with my other hand. When I managed to do that, there was a tiny mound of crumbs, all that was left of the bread, sitting in the middle of my bloody palm.

I needed to understand the lunacy that had possessed me. Was this parade of bread among the starving a deliberate attempt to demoralize us more than we already were? Was I completely self-destructive because I couldn't cope with not knowing where Mamma and my sisters were? It was as if they had disappeared into a black hole, and there wasn't even a way to ask for information.

I was not the only prisoner to lose my mind. Many others became irrational as well. I could never understand prisoners who would barter their entire daily ration for a single cigarette. Others simply slipped into a netherworld in their own heads, not caring if they lived or died. I did not want that to happen to me—at least not yet. I couldn't understand what had sent me over the edge, unless it was because I couldn't deal with the differences between our old lifestyle and our new deathstyle.

Leon and I had led a fairly sheltered life, even in the ghetto. But there, at least, we had the support of other family members, a little bit of privacy, and the comfort of a clean place to relieve yourself and wash. You could read a book; you could always find something to distract yourself from the constant misery around you. And until the very end, there was something we had in the ghetto that we never had in Auschwitz—the music of a young child's laughter. In Auschwitz, the only laughter we heard was brittle, cruel, and cold as ice.

During the four years in the Lodz ghetto, we witnessed horrible and brutal daily events that were similar to the ones we were now seeing in the camp. But life in the ghetto was nothing compared to the brutality we were experiencing in the "smoke factory."

I am convinced also that the Germans intended to add boredom to their arsenal of weapons. There was no *"Arbeit Macht Frei"* ethic here. You did nothing all day long except hear, smell, and absorb the malevolent atmosphere as you sank into catatonia or contemplated your imminent demise.

I realized all of this as I stood there behind the barrack, thinking, looking at my bloody palm. And I knew that Leon and I could not stay in Auschwitz anymore. Leon and I, knowing that teenagers had little chance of survival, had tried to make ourselves older than we were so that we wouldn't be sent up the chimney, but the longer we stayed in this place, the less chance we had of surviving. My epiphany was a turning point in our lives. We had to become proactive and take our fate into our own hands or we would never come out of this nightmare alive.

I talked my ideas over with Leon and he agreed. We decided that as soon as we could, we would attach ourselves to a work commando and try to join a work transport. We wouldn't know where we were going or what would happen, which, at this point, was more normal than not, but nothing could be worse than the situation we were in. At least now we had something to do and pretended to take control of our own fate. At the very least, it made us feel a little better.

Have my words been able to accurately describe what we went through in Auschwitz-Birkenau? No. Words are words and pain is pain, so it is virtually impossible to characterize the agony, brutality, and bestiality that stalked us at every moment. What happened in those ghettos and camps is inconceivable and beyond a human's wildest imagination. Nothing about the Holocaust is abstract except to those who didn't experience it in real time. What I still cannot understand is how it could have been carried out in a supposedly civilized world.

When I am asked how long I was in Auschwitz, my answer is, "I don't know. What I do know is that one minute in Auschwitz was like an entire day, a day was a year, and a month, an eternity. How many eternities can one have in a single lifetime? I don't know the answer to that, either."

Eleven
Gross-Rosen Concentration Camp

"I have had playmates, I have had companions in my days of childhood, in my joyful schooldays; all are gone, the old familiar faces . . . the old familiar faces."—Charles Lamb

Once Leon and I decided to leave Auschwitz, we had to figure out how to attach ourselves to a *kommando* (work unit) that periodically left the compound. Sometimes the Germans would come looking for volunteers—machine operators, tailors, shoemakers—people with vocational skills that we just didn't have. So we volunteered for the woodcutters' *kommando*. One day I was in Auschwitz-Birkenau and the next I was in Gross-Rosen, a labor camp somewhere in Bavaria. I just don't remember how I got there.

Gross-Rosen was a main compound with more than sixty satellite concentration camps. Each camp was, in turn, divided into sub-camps and occasionally, the Germans moved us from one camp to another. I never could figure out the reason. What I knew for sure was that it was winter, the frost was biting, the snow was falling, we had no clothing to keep us warm, and our "diet" was slowly killing us.

Leon and I were taken into the forests to cut wood with saws and axes, or to the stone quarries to crush rock. Under the best conditions, these are physically demanding jobs requiring brute strength. Without proper shoes, clothing, and food to sustain us, the jobs assigned to us proved to be virtually impossible to manage. On top of that, the German guards who stood over us—civilian and military—demanded perfection and perpetual production in the performance of our duties.

I was assigned to two sub-camps, Dornhau and Märzbachtal. The main concentration camp in my sub-division was Wustegiersdorf. We never knew when they were going to move us around, so Leon and I tried to remain together at all times. Others fortunate enough to be with members of their family followed the same survival strategy we did, and also worked at not being separated.

By now we realized we were lucky not to have tattoos. The Germans had no idea who we were as individuals. They kept track of us by the numbers sewn onto our uniform jackets, and sometimes we switched jackets with others to make sure we could stick together. It was a risky thing to do, punishable by death—an expensive lesson for those caught. Still, I would risk anything to make sure I stayed with Leon. Through the turmoil and mayhem of those miserable months, I never forgot Mamma's last words warning us never to be separated.

I would ask myself how we would survive these ordeals and how we'd managed to do it thus far. I had no answers. In my old age, based on my life experience, I finally figured out that there was no single answer, it's always a combination of factors and dumb luck. You had to be in the right place at the right time, trust your instincts, and take some initiative. You also needed to be desperate. I can see now how all those things clicked into place during the brutal winter of 1944–45 to keep us alive.

Soon after we got to Gross-Rosen, I decided it made sense for one of us to try to find work in the camp proper and, if possible, see if we could get work in the kitchen for the obvious reasons. The lessons of "Canada" were clearly well learned. Some of the food we could "organize" (steal) we bartered for clothing. Extra underwear or shirts that we could wear underneath the regular issue clothing was the most valuable because it kept us from freezing to death.

For all the advantages, working in the kitchen was also very dangerous, especially if you were starving. You had to use logic and discipline if you were going to succeed without succumbing to suicidal acts. When I finally managed to get myself assigned to the kitchen on a semi-permanent basis, I had to be extremely careful not to fall prey to temptation. Working in that kitchen was a serious challenge for a desperate man with a starving brother.

Only a handful of us worked in the kitchen, and we were subjected to rigorous searches whenever we went in and out of the area. If I was going to try to pilfer food, I would have to be very clever. I assumed that the guards working in the kitchen had a fair idea of how much food there was in stock and would notice immediately if large quantities disappeared. I also realized that by stealing a little bit at a time, Leon and I would be better off. I managed to get a piece of string and tied my long-john cuffs around my ankles. Then I would drop a carrot or potato down the pants leg, making sure it wouldn't show from the outside and that my pants looked normal so the bulky vegetables wouldn't be noticed. The method worked like a charm. Sometimes I had a chance to smuggle a little more food, so I would tie the string at my ankle, drop in two or three carrots or potatoes, then tie another string on my leg above them, and add a few more vegetables. The second string prevented gravity from pulling the additional layer of vegetables down to the bottom of the long-johns thereby making them appear bulky.

One day, a new man assigned to the kitchen noticed what I did and copied me. But he fell into the hunger trap and stuffed his pants so full, the guards would have been blind not to notice his bulging pants. I saw him and became very nervous, thinking about the serious consequences for all of us if they caught him. I asked him to take less food with him so as not to risk all of our lives.

He replied tersely, "The vegetables are not yours and you should not be mixing in my affairs." All the while, he continued to stuff vegetables down his long-johns. He had clearly gone over the edge. As a result, I stayed clean; I didn't even take a potato peel out with me when the shift was over. And sure enough, the worst possible scenario played itself out that day. The Germans removed the vegetables from his clothing, beat him to the ground, and shot him on the spot for stealing.

Unfortunately, lack of food for an extended period of time combined with daily viciousness were more than likely cause for that poor man's impaired sense of judgment, and he paid for it with his life. The punishment for the rest of us was serious, too. From that day on, it was no longer possible to smuggle anything at all out of the kitchen and we could no longer supplement our diets.

Leon and I continued to work as slave laborers in the stone quarries and forests of Gross-Rosen. We shared everything; the harshness of the work, the meager food rations, the insufficient clothing, and above all, the memories of our home and family. It was a miracle we hadn't yet been targeted for random beatings or torture, although on several occasions I came very close. There was one day when a group of us working in the quarry accidentally derailed a fully loaded wagon and, undernourished weaklings that we were, just couldn't get the cart back on track. A German guard immediately ran over and, in a minute, managed it. The moment he finished, he took the crowbar he used for leverage on the cart and used it as a weapon against us, hitting anyone in striking distance. Some of us ended up with cracked heads and broken bones. Others, including me, were fortunate not to suffer any serious injuries.

I sustained some cuts and bruises when I dropped to the ground to avoid his blows. I had never played possum before, but a combination of luck, instinct, and some initiative spared me a harsh beating. I still remembered the first lesson of Auschwitz-Birkenau: severe punishment was the first step in a slow painful death.

It is another small miracle that Leon and I did not become seriously ill. The sick were usually put into the so-called hospital where, periodically, patients were deported to the gas chambers. It was our good fortune that we never got sick enough to need "medical services."

On one occasion, despite my best efforts to remain unnoticed by the Germans, I could not avoid becoming visible, and I paid for it dearly. I was working in the forest one morning under the command of a very demanding German, and asked him if I could relieve myself. It was not that I had to relieve myself so badly, but I was looking for a few precious moments to rest. To my regret, I had to ask the same guard for permission to relieve myself in the afternoon when I really needed to, whereupon he looked at me and shouted, *"Du verflüchte Jüde"* (You dirty Jew), you want to go to the toilet twice in the same day on my time?" He ranted and raved and started beating me. Fortunately, he had no whip, gun, or other implement of torture, and used his hands. After a few blows, I fell to the ground. He kicked me a few times and left me alone. I was lucky I wasn't beaten to a pulp.

Besides the horrible physical and psychological conditions Leon and I had to endure, I lived with a constant worry about my mother and sisters. There was obviously no way to find out what had happened to them or to send a message to let them know how my brother and I were making out. Leon and I hoped that they were still alive. While it was constantly on our minds, we were afraid to discuss it because the more we spoke about it, the more likely it would be for us to reach the logical conclusion about their fates—a conclusion we did not want to reach.

One day followed another with nothing to distinguish them. What kept us going was the thought of being back home, re-united with our family. We reminisced about the warmth of our stove in winter and all the food on the table. The thoughts made us feel warmer and made our hunger less painful. We, at least, had each other.

Then the morbid monotony of that dreary winter was inter-rupted by a startling announcement. Children in the Gross-Rosen camps were to be assembled and sent to one partic-ular camp where they would work in factories for the rest of the bitter winter instead of in the forests and quarries.

Until that moment, Leon and I had done everything we could to make ourselves seem older than the young teenagers we were. Now we were tempted to join our own age group for the op-portunity to get out of the cold. But we were suspicious, and so were our friends. Why would people who had no qualms about sending children to the gas chambers suddenly be worried about whether or not they were freezing in the forests and quarries? Overwhelmed by the severe weather and the starvation, we fig-ured we had little to lose if we were going to be considered chil-dren, and maybe the Germans would show a little compassion.

We decided to join the children, and Leon and I found our-selves in a camp filled with boys our age who had been scattered around the sixty satellite camps. Promising us better conditions brought us all out of the woodwork and allowed the Germans to concentrate us in one place. Of course, we didn't go to work in any factories, and rumors were circulating that we were headed back to Auschwitz-Birkenau. That could mean only one thing, they were sending us to the gas chambers. Any positive feelings I had about the prospects of working in a warm factory over the winter went out the window.

A few days later my uncertainty and anxiety were somewhat eased when we were called to the *appelplatz,* where we were counted, divided into groups, and sent to work in the forest. Suddenly, the cold weather and hard work didn't seem to bother me as much. I was happy to stay as a slave in Gross-Rosen instead of feeding the voracious crematoria in Birkenau.

After a few weeks the situation changed again when we were ordered to the *appelplatz* in the middle of a working day, a highly unusual circumstance. As we stood there at attention for hours, the rumors began circulating. One of them said that a trainload of adult prisoners had arrived from Auschwitz and we were going to be "exchanged" for them. Another rumor going around that day was that two children were missing and were being hunted by the Germans and their dogs. Since the Germans always needed perfect head counts, we would wait there until they were found.

It took a few hours before the Kapos and their hungry dogs dragged the two boys to the *appelplatz.* By sheer coincidence they were placed in a kneeling position very close to where I was standing. When the commander of the camp approached them, I could hear him telling his subordinates, "Inasmuch as these two had the guts to hide, let them stay here." To me, this meant one thing and one thing only: the rest of us were headed to Auschwitz and the crematoria.

I will never know how I mustered the courage to do what I did next. With the words the commander uttered to his underlings ringing in my ears, I jumped forth from the row of prisoners, looked the commander straight in the eye, and said, "Sir Kommandant, I am here with my brother. We are both young and strong and we would like to stay here and work."

The *Kommandant* had three evil choices. He could beat me to a pulp, he could take a gun and shoot me, or he could tell me to get back in line. I had seen him do these things before, and it was dangerous for me just to be caught looking at him or getting too close. I didn't stop to think of the consequences for my brazen act. I was working on instinct.

The *Kommandant* looked at me for a few seconds—seconds that seemed like hours—and asked where my brother was. I pointed to Leon, and the *Kommandant* told him to step forward. I was beyond overjoyed when he said the two of us would stay in the camp. At that point, a Jewish man, left behind with a few others to handle the transfer of the children, told the commander that he had a nephew there, and asked if he could stay in the camp as well. The German commander responded that his nephew could also remain.

Over the next few days, we learned about the eerie, strange coincidence of this exchange of children for grown-ups. Eight hundred adults had arrived from Auschwitz, but there were 805 children in our camp, a surplus of five slave laborers in the count.

In the end, it turned out that we five stayed behind because there had to be an even exchange, 800 grown-ups for 800 children, and only that exact substitution of numbers would satisfy the German accountants.

The 800 youngsters deported from Gross-Rosen were sent directly to the gas chambers in Birkenau. We learned the gruesome facts from a kindly German guard we called *Moshe Rabbenu*—Moses, our rabbi. In all my time at the camps, Moshe Rabbenu was the only humane German I ever met; hence the nickname. Much older than the rest of the guards, he was wounded during earlier fighting on the eastern front and had been sent to this camp as a guard.

Hearing about the fate of the children from such a reliable source, we understood how fortunate we were to still be alive. Five out of 805. I kept thinking to myself what an odd struggle it is to survive. My elation at still being able to breathe was tempered by the knowledge that so many of my friends were dead and I would never see them again.

Being one of only five children among the hundreds of adults in the camp brought with it certain privileges. In the first place, we no longer had to pretend that we were grown-ups. The guards, Kapos, and the Block Elder knew who we were and where we had been headed. The Germans didn't send us into the forest or the stone quarries to work, nor did they assign us to any outdoor jobs. We were given indoor work in the barracks, in the Germans' living quarters, or in the kitchen. This enabled us to regain our strength, physically and mentally.

With better nourishment and without the dreaded constant supervision and random beatings, my mind became clearer, and my thoughts turned to missing family and friends. Leon and I constantly speculated about Mamma and our sisters and wondered how soon it would be before we saw them again. We never allowed ourselves to think they were gone. It was only a matter of time, we said, that we would be together with them again.

Food and clothing were no longer a problem, because the Germans took better care of us. We were quite surprised how quickly we adjusted to the new and improved conditions, and we hoped the situation would stay that way until the end of the war. But our days in "Paradise" were numbered. The camp was closing and we were going to be transferred. I was not looking forward to another uncertain venture.

The rumor mill said we were headed to a place called Flossenburg. This time the rumors proved to be true, and the day of departure arrived. Again, I cannot remember the details of the actual transfer, leaving the Gross-Rosen camps, or how we reached Flossenburg.

Twelve
Flossenburg Concentration Camp

"For every man who lives without freedom, the rest of us must take the guilt." —*Watch on the Rhine,* by Lillian Hellman

It was easy to get used to the "good life" I briefly enjoyed as one of the five children in Gross-Rosen. Unfortunately, it made it much harder for me to face the harsh realities of Flossenburg as one among thousands of inmates there.

At first, I couldn't figure out what was going on, but soon Leon and I found ourselves in a huge barrack where hundreds of other people were already living. It took a while for me to understand that this barrack was one of four that were somewhat different from the others. Most inmates in Flossenburg left for work in the morning and came back to their barrack in the evening. The inhabitants of these particular barracks did not go anywhere.

There were pros and cons to not going anywhere. One obvious advantage was that I did not have to exert any energy by doing any work. On the other hand, it meant I was under the constant surveillance of the Germans, Kapos, and Block Elders.

In Flossenburg I soon discovered many non-Jews among our ranks. Some of the Block Elders and Kapos were Germans sentenced to the camp for their criminal deeds, and the Kapos were mostly from Eastern Europe.

The Kapos from Ukraine were the most vicious. They were sadists who derived the utmost pleasure from hurting and torturing their victims. The inmates in my section of the camp were confined to crowded barracks and small outdoor exercise areas, where the Kapos would leisurely stroll among us, brutalizing anyone who got in their way and couldn't escape fast enough.

Conditions in my barrack at Flossenburg paralleled those in

Auschwitz, but in Flossenburg we were also forced to contend with some dreadful events when the Block Elders and Kapos living in our barrack periodically hosted wild parties and orgies in their quarters. First they would get hold of some alcohol, and in no time they would be drunk. Illegally manufactured primarily by non-Jewish inmates, liquor was a commodity in great demand by Kapos and Block Elders, but it was always in short supply. As a rule, the prisoners making the liquor were not under the scrutiny of the higher-ups, and they received better treatment and additional food for providing what might have been considered an essential service.

Also on hand for the pleasure of the elite corps of camp officials were women prisoners, some of them Jewish, used as prostitutes. Some of the best foods and pastries accessible in the entire region were made available to these thugs so they could please the ladies. For their added enjoyment, the Germans and Kapos brought in some prisoner-musicians and ordered them to play.

It was incredible to watch the coarse Kapos telling the poor accomplished musicians what to do and how to play. These musicians were skilled artists in their former lives and capable of playing various instruments to perfection. In Flossenburg they existed only to satisfy the whims of their captors, who provided violins, trumpets, saxophones, and other "portable" instruments.

In return, the musicians were offered extra rations, but if one of the oafs in charge didn't like the way a musician played a certain song, he could earn a thorough beating. Through it all, we watched and listened as the former musical luminaries of Lodz pasted smiles on their faces and played as instructed, knowing that they were literally playing for their lives.

Some of these musicians were people much older than I, people I had admired in Lodz. Henry Baigelman, Henry Eisenman, and Itzhak Levine, the cream of the Lodz orchestras, were ordered to perform in my barrack. Seeing them there, with the fear in their eyes and the "smiles" on their faces, I felt as if I had been tossed into the twilight zone.

The monsters sang loudly along and the band played

on—German ditties and marches, *volksdeutsche* ballads, and
Nazi beer hall songs were among the selections. The sounds of
their wretched cursing and obscene merriment often lasted into
the wee hours of the morning. Yes, it was hard to fall or stay
asleep, but it was also worse than that. What they were doing
was dangerous.

When the Block Elders became drunk, they ran amuck and
started to hit every person in the barrack. They would break ceramic platters they used at the parties by throwing them full
force against the wooden bunks. The platters would shatter, and
the sharp, flying shards would cut us as we lay on our bunks, often causing serious wounds. There was one party, not in our
block, I will never forget, where the liquor made by the inmates
caused those who consumed it to become disoriented, blind, or vi-
olently ill. A few even died. The Kapos concluded that the inmates deliberately poisoned them and were brutal in their
revenge. They rounded up the moonshiners and brought them to
one spot where they beat them in full view of all of us. I stood
there and saw the victims turn black and blue, and watched their
heads swell to balloon-like proportions.

"Who poisoned us?" the Kapos screamed again and again as
they throttled the prisoners. When someone would faint, they
would throw cold water at him and the beating continued. It did-
n't take long before it was obvious to all of us that none of these
pitiful people had even considered poisoning the Kapos. They
had nothing to confess, despite the severe thrashings they were
getting. Not one of them did anything deliberate and everyone,
including their tormentors, knew it. But that didn't stop them
from battering their victims until every last moonshiner was
dead. It was a true bonding moment for the Kapos and Block Elders. Transcending nationality, they managed to exhibit a collective instinct for brutal murder.

One of the prisoners was a German incarcerated for political
crimes. We called him "Zweibelmax" (Onion Max) because he
was in charge of the kitchen and had access to large quantities of
onions and other food. Because the Kapos needed his services,
they gave him preferential treatment, but unlike his compatri-
ots, Onion Max was quite gentle and soft-spoken. His position in

the barrack was therefore unique. He was able to secure sizeable living quarters for himself, and somehow was not at all constrained by the Germans in charge. Since I spoke a little German, Onion Max took a liking to me and asked me to make his bed every day in exchange for a bit of food.

The Germans, Kapos, and Block Elders were always looking for contraband that would be suitable as gifts for women—most often, hosiery, underwear, and cosmetics. There was a whorehouse near the camp and every now and then some big shots were given permission to partake in pleasures of the flesh, often taken from Jewish women forced into white slavery. As prisoners, we didn't even think about fraternizing with females. This privilege was reserved exclusively for the evil perpetrators to satisfy their carnal desires, and my heart and soul went out to those poor, tormented women.

One day followed the next. As usual, Leon and I assiduously avoided unexpected beatings. Always together, literally day and night, we watched each other's backs so that it was easier for us to spot something suspicious and get out of the way, fast.

In the spring of 1945, I noticed a certain uneasiness among the Germans, and here and there, rumors wafted through the barracks, saying that the Germans were taking some serious hits in the war. I heard the German army was retreating, and when planes roared overhead, the looks on their faces turned anxious. There was something more than planes in the air, but without hard evidence, all I could do was speculate and trust my gut.

As the war ground on and rumors continued to circulate, I thought more and more of Mamma and my sisters. For the first time in a long while, I felt that maybe it was realistic to dream about returning to the life I had known before the war. But I did not want to dwell on my hope for fear of being overly optimistic. I had to take solace in the fact that at least my brother was with me. The planes, the German anxiety, and the rumors gave me an added will to survive. Daily hardships seemed diminished, and I was better able to cope with the misery around me.

Then one morning in mid-April 1945, I woke up and the Germans were gone, except for a few unlucky soldiers left to man the watchtowers. The mood in the camp was very strange; tense and anticipatory.

I did not know what to do or how to behave. All I knew was that suddenly the yoke of German might had been lifted from our shoulders and the tyrants who had plagued us since September 1939 had suddenly vanished as if they had never been. The whole camp seemed to share my sense of bewilderment. Those who normally went to work stayed put; there was no one to hound them into their work details.

There was an eerie quiet; the calm before the storm, I thought. The air was filled with electricity. I don't know how it started, but when it registered that just about every German in the camp had moved out, we went on a rampage.

Block Elders and Kapos left behind were mowed down by the prisoners they used to control, who then battered down the kitchen doors and the doors to the warehouses where food was stored. We grabbed anything and everything we could carry. Our oppressors, outnumbered, were helpless and we were desperate, hungry, and out of control.

If we weren't so pitiful, it might have been laughable to see us, the human skeletons of planet Earth, carrying a profusion of food in our arms as we stuffed what we could into our mouths. They had bread, flour, cake, fruits, vegetables, and things we hadn't seen in years. There was food enough to satisfy our hunger for the day and enough left over for tomorrow and the day after that. Was this total anarchy the freedom I had envisioned? Was it only about selfishness and food?

Again, Mamma's wisdom on that first day in Auschwitz, the words she whispered to us, saved the day. Leon and I teamed up during the rampage. I grabbed what I could and then gave it to my brother for safekeeping before I went back to get more. Food was more precious to us than gold, silver, diamonds, or pearls.

Once we satisfied our hunger, we thought about the Germans. Why did they disappear and leave a handful of guards behind? Where did they go? Why in such a hurry? How had they managed to get away without us noticing? These questions remained unanswered, but the strongest speculation was that the

Germans were retreating and the Allied forces were after them in hot pursuit.

For a moment I was elated and dared not discuss out loud the life that awaited me after the war. Leon and I made plans. We thought in basic terms. First we would eat all the foods we had missed during the war, enjoying delicacies we hadn't tasted in years. We also tried to boost the failing morale of the *musselmen*, begging them not to give up hope in these last few hours—that they must live to see their oppressors punished. I begged them to remain alive in order to tell their children about this life they had endured. This was not a time to die; it was a time to live, to bear witness, to seek justice.

Four days later my optimism vanished as the Germans returned to the camp in full force—and with new orders. They called for an *appel* and I panicked. There was chaos everywhere, and I quickly turned to Leon to discuss our options. No one knew we were Jews, we had no tattoos, and no one had time to check our body parts. We decided to mingle with the non-Jews in the camp because it seemed a safer bet than joining the Jews. Our past experience as Jewish inmates led us to that inescapable conclusion. When it was time to evacuate the barrack, and the Germans ordered the Jews to step forward, Leon and I stayed behind. We could see how the Germans were dividing the Jews into smaller groups before they marched them out of the camp. Later I learned that those small groups were taken to the railway station and packed into cattle cars.

Once the Jews were gone, the Germans came back and divided "the non-Jews" into four columns. It was rumored that we were being sent to Dachau, and 12,000 of us were ordered to march, once again, into the unknown. By this time I was an emotional wreck and couldn't begin to imagine that the nightmare would ever end. Hope just kept crashing against reality, like a shipwreck on the rocks. It was pouring cold rain as thousands of us straggled along the road on our forced march from the camp. Leon and I continuously munched from the sack of food I had liberated as we marched through the deepening night.

The approaching Allied armies never even entered my mind.

At daybreak, they took us off the road and into the forest, surrounding us with the same Germans who had guarded us back in the camps (some were on foot and some were on motorbikes). They wanted us to "rest" in the mud. We collapsed where we stood. At dusk, they roused us to our feet, formed us into columns surrounded by armed guards, and took us back to the road to march. And thus it continued for three days and nights, resting in daytime and walking at night.

Normally, before we hit the ground for an uneasy sleep, Leon would tie the sack of food to my body and then lay down next to me. Of course, what little food we had was stolen on the second day, when Leon and I both fell so deeply asleep that someone was able to cut our little sack of provisions off my back without either of us feeling it. Our exhaustion had betrayed us.

Now, without food, we became weaker and weaker by the hour. We marched in darkness along a highway lit only by moonlight. Absolute silence was punctuated by the occasional crack of a soldier's gun, ending the life of one no longer able to walk. Their bodies were left to rot on the side of the road. Three nights had passed; thousands had been murdered.

As the dead bodies lined the road in ever-greater numbers, the situation worsened. On the fourth day, before we could rest, we, the tattered and broken remains of humans, were ordered to rise and pull ourselves into lines and march some more. I found it difficult to stand erect, but mechanically I kept putting one foot in front of the other. I turned to Leon, who also, zombie-like, kept pace beside me. I admitted, in despair, "This may be my last day. I cannot take anymore. How long before I am dead on the side of the road?"

We had consoled and supported each other since we felt that liberation must be close at hand. But now my steps became slower and slower, and I drifted with Leon toward the end of the column. Suddenly, there was a thunderous noise coming from behind me that broke through my stupor. I turned and in astonishment watched as the German guards around me threw away their guns and ran into the forest.

A moment later, the source of the grinding, screeching noise—a monstrous tank with a large white star painted on the front came up over a little rise in the road, appearing as if from nowhere. The mounted machine guns rattled away at the Germans, who were trying to find cover in the trees.

The miracle was taking place right before us. The hatches of the tanks popped open, and the heads and shoulders of soldiers emerged, to wave us to safety on the side of the road, away from the woods. The soldiers, who wore green uniforms, were messengers of God who brought with them the gift of life. As some of their comrades took shots at the Germans, others threw food—vegetables, cans of C-rations, and even bottles of Coca-Cola. (We had no idea what that was.) At first we thought the single star meant the tank was a Russian one; but no, we were being liberated by the Americans.

At that moment, I was too numb to understand what freedom was. I stood on the side of the highway not knowing what to do; I did not yet belong to this world. It was dreamlike, and everything around me was totally unreal. The transition from terror in a concentration camp to freedom was so sudden that my mind could not fully comprehend its significance.

Leon and I stood there, at the side of the road, stunned, being showered with food. All around me prisoners tried to catch the food and sit down to eat. The scene was totally Kafkaesque. It was our liberation day, that long-awaited day I had prayed for and dreamed of for all those years. I did know one thing: it was a glorious day, one I often thought I would never live to see!

Thirteen
Germany After Liberation

"For me, the pleasure came when I could laugh at the Nazis and watch the killers, the 'heroes,' turn into blithering cowards."

After six years in the ghetto, in Auschwitz-Birkenau, Gross-Rosen, Flossenburg, and other camps, it was truly unbelievable. We were finally liberated. I had my freedom. I could go wherever I wanted, whenever I wanted. I could do whatever I wanted, whenever I wanted. The whole world was at my feet. But somehow, I didn't want to go anywhere. I hadn't the desire, will, or strength to do anything. The transition from slavery to freedom happened so quickly, it was mind-numbing, and at that moment the concept of freedom was as foreign to me as Chinese. Subjected to constant abuse for so long, doing something of my own free will was inconceivable.

It is true that I was free before the war, under the loving care and supervision of my parents and teachers, but that life was demolished during the war. Now I stood at the place of my liberation, clueless.

Leon and I shuffled to a nearby village, Meissenberg. Being free and having food thrown to me by the Americans provided me with enough impetus and strength to get myself moving. Arriving in the village, we approached the first farmer's house we saw and asked for a room and some food. The farmer immediately prepared us a meal. We ate and drank as much as we could, and then went straight to the beds he offered, without changing our filthy clothes. For the first time in years, I put my head to rest on a real feather pillow and lay my body under a thick down quilt. What luxury; it was heaven on Earth.

How long I slept I do not know. I started the day with a complete breakfast, prepared again by the farmer and his wife—eggs, bacon, bread, and butter. If it was there, I ate it. It was another one of those miracles that Leon and I didn't get sick from the rich food as did some of the other survivors, who were treated by the local doctors with the utmost care and respect.

As if by magic, the very same Germans who had called us *"verflüchte Jüden"* (damned Jews), who had gleefully beaten and tortured us, and witnessed our total dehumanization, now suddenly welcomed Leon and me into their homes. It was inconceivable to be sitting at a German table being served food on porcelain dishes. Absurdly, our hosts constantly smiled at me, asking if everything was to my liking and if I wanted more.

The thought of being harmed by them as I slept under their roof never entered my mind. I was aware of, but did not understand, the sudden change of attitude on the part of the Germans. I accepted what I saw and took it for granted.

When I closed my eyes, I was sure that this was not really happening to us. After eating until we were about to burst, Leon and I wandered around to have a look. To our surprise, we found a few of our friends from Lodz also wandering around the streets. We met Henry Baigelman, Henry and Joe Eisman, Izhak Levine, and most of the musicians who played for the Kapos in Flossenburg. It turned out that they, too, had hidden themselves among the non-Jews as the camp was being evacuated. They were on the same death march we were on and ended up in the same village because they were liberated in the same area.

Those first few days we lived a veritable life of luxury. To have unlimited food and down blankets was a major deal. In fact, some survivors could not bear to be separated from food for even a moment and would take it with them, even to the outhouse. Being deprived for so many years, it wasn't any wonder. Of course, the outhouse to which I refer was a real outhouse, kept in immaculate condition, where a person went alone and could enjoy complete privacy. It was nothing like the filthy communal outhouse in Auschwitz.

My body was slow in adjusting to the improvements in my eating habits. When I first arrived, Leon and I were severely underweight, and constantly hungry, and it was an effort for me to walk. It was impossible to accurately judge my own physical condition, since I am assuming we looked like walking skeletons, but not like *musselmen,* although who could tell the difference except a former inmate.

Now, in one of those strange reversals of fortune, *we* had the upper hand. The farmers didn't spare any effort to keep us happy, making sure that we were always well fed. They knew that if they withheld anything, we might destroy their property to find what we wanted.

Once my hunger subsided, I turned my attention to three specific things: getting news about our family, regaining my strength, and finding out the exact status of the Americans and roving S.S. men in Germany. I discussed this with Leon and two friends we made who were liberated in the same village—Joe and Jack—as well as our friends the musicians from Lodz, the two Henrys and Itzhak.

The question of finding family was never one of "if," but of "when" and "how." It was why I was determined to be physically fit. The journey to find Mamma, Dasza, and Renia could be long and hard, and might even entail going back to Poland. I wanted to be ready. Until I could find the necessary information and come up with a well-conceived plan, I thought it best to stay in the village and make the most of my situation.

I never even thought about why the Germans were offering us their suddenly gracious hospitality, but it was not by coincidence or borne of some miraculous sense of goodwill. It was because the area was tightly controlled by the American Army. The village-dwellers were terrified that the Allies would exact revenge because they knew quite well what had been done to us during the war.

They had seen us as slaves as we marched back and forth from the camps, on the nearby highways, always surrounded by the guards; they saw us digging ditches, working in the factories outside the camps, and cutting down trees in the forests. Perhaps in their minds, by being hospitable, they were attempting to make amends for their horrific crimes, as if amends could ever be possible.

In actuality, the farmers only kept us around because they were worried that if we left we might be replaced by less desirable former slaves. They had heard of the cruelty of the Russians, Ukrainians, and gypsies and feared them like poison.

Their fears were well founded. Among the liberated prisoners, these groups would think nothing of rampaging their way through German homes. Raping, pillaging, burning down houses, even murdering Germans was the standard method of their operation. The farmers made it their business to try to keep them away. We, the Jews, were also terribly worried about the others on the loose. We knew how they earned their reputations as cruel prisoners, Kapos, and Block Elders. But the atrocities committed by these avenging groups against the Germans constituted only a minute fraction of what the Jewish Holocaust survivors were forced to endure in the camps day after day, year after year.

It didn't take long before we depleted the food supplies of the homes in which we were staying. Now we became a group, about a dozen of us, and moved from house to house to demand—or take—anything we wanted, primarily food. Eventually, we broke off into two or three groups. Only a few of us spoke German, but all of us learned a few words such as *eier, butter, zucker,* and *fleisch* (eggs, butter, sugar and meat). It was amazing how quickly the farmers met our demands.

Seeing their fear and willingness to comply with our orders, we survivors became more and more assertive. We'd start by asking them to give us something to eat, then we'd inspect the premises to see what else was available, what we wanted, and what we would take with us. I got myself a wardrobe of decent clothing, some shoes, and a bicycle. The difference between Auschwitz and the present was totally mind-boggling.

It was also astounding how quickly the Germans learned to say in English, "Me no Nazi." Based on what they said, there was not a single Nazi to be found in the entire village! They were all peace-loving Germans who knew nothing about concentration camps, had never heard of any torture being inflicted, and didn't even know what the word crematorium meant.

Where, I wondered, did they think we came from? How could they expect us to believe them when we knew so many of them witnessed first-hand the daily procession of half-starved, slow moving skeletons walking back and forth to work? How convenient for them to deny a past still present before their eyes.

With time, I became more relaxed and my mind moved on to other things. A comrade of mine had the brilliant idea one day that we should all go fishing. It was of no consequence that none of us knew how to fish, or that we had no rods, no reels, and no bait. The important thing to consider was that the pond had fish and we wanted to eat fish. Therefore, we would find a way to go fishing. It might not make sense, and it might be unfair to the fish, but we would figure out a way.

Since the pond had floodgates at one end, I figured we could open the gates and let the water run out. With the water level lowered, the fish would flop around in a concentrated spot at the bottom of the pond bed, enabling us to collect them with a little net. I am happy to report that my plan was a success, and a delicious fish dinner was served that evening.

I constantly thought of ways to make life more exciting. My brother and I requisitioned some bicycles, and this gave us freedom to move around the village and the hinterlands, even if we didn't indulge in our pre-war bike tricks. The bikes provided the transportation that connected us to new people and new information—I knew very little about the political situation, and everything I learned was news to me. I listened very carefully with an eye toward tracking down my mother and sisters.

However, on one of our excursions, my brother became too reckless by performing the same old bicycle acrobatics he had engaged in before the war. Unfortunately, he forgot he was out of practice. After all, it had been six years since he had been on a bike. He paid a stiff price for showing off that day; he fell off the bike and broke his arm. Under normal circumstances, a broken arm would just be a nuisance. But these were not normal circumstances.

Understandably, after being confined for so many years, it was our intention to make up for lost time as quickly as possible. We wanted everything and more, instantaneously. We did not want to waste precious time, or to be restricted by limitations. In other words, we were reckless. What could be done tomorrow, we had to do today!

When I noticed some horses in the village, my thoughts went back to my childhood days and horseback riding sessions with Tatush. It was only natural for me to want to ride again because of those pleasant memories of my youthful summers in Podębie before the war. But I didn't realize that these horses were not like those in Podębie. These were not for riding; they did not have saddles and reins. For my brother, there was also the issue of the broken arm and the cast he still wore. But my brother was a stubborn boy before the war, and now, without parental supervision to curtail his activities, there was no stopping him. He wanted to ride, broken arm and all, and that was that. So, with arm in cast, he mounted a horse that was totally unaccustomed to riders. Leon was a sight to see atop this heavy farm horse and before long, of course, he fell off. But this fall was very different from the tumble he took off the bike.

The bicycle seat was low to the ground, and the result was only a broken arm. This time, Leon fell off the top of a horse and landed on his head. He was unconscious when I ran to him, and when he woke, he was delirious. Every five minutes he would say to me, "Roman, where am I? What happened?" Every five minutes, I would have to tell him again how he went horseback riding and fell off the horse.

I was able to get a doctor to examine Leon, and he told me my brother had suffered a severe concussion. However, I was further advised that it was a good sign that all of his vital organs appeared to be functioning well and that the next twenty-four to forty-eight hours would tell the full story. In the meantime, the doctor said, there was nothing much to do. For the moment, he said, the best medicine for Leon was deep sleep. My vigil began. I sat by his bedside and repeated over and over again the story of his fall until he drifted off into a deep sleep.

When he finally woke a day and a half later, he seemed perfectly all right in every respect. He asked me again what had happened, and since I was so happy to see him in a normal state, I gladly repeated the story one more time. He was a new man, but just as stubborn as the old one. Even if he stopped horseback riding while his arm was in the cast, at least that was progress of a sort.

In the weeks that followed liberation, I noticed a constant flow of Germans wandering down the highway near town. Many were in civilian clothes, but a large number were still wearing soldiers' uniforms. Usually, they came down the road in a group. And now I had a little group of my own—the same group of survivors that had first assembled in the village.

After seeing these wandering soldiers, I devised a new pastime. I was now friendly with a few of the American troops around our village and knew they were scouting the roads trying to catch high-ranking officers of the German Army, especially soldiers of the S.S. I started to put two and two together, and a plan slowly began to take shape.

I realized that we, the survivors, could be helpful in assisting the Americans in their search for German officers and military personnel, as well as those we considered "war criminals." I came up with a strategy that worked like a charm. Perhaps it was a reckless plan, but we were young, fearless, and ready for anything. My older friends thought we were crazy and would not join us.

Joe, Jack, Leon, and I, together with a Hungarian survivor whose name I've forgotten, worked to make it all come together. First, we found a broken machine gun lying by the side of the road. Though it was completely useless—the back of the gun was missing and we had no ammunition—high in a treetop, in the camouflage of the foliage, it might appear, from the ground, to be a standard machine gun. We decided that one of us would climb the tree with the gun and, once positioned, would point the barrel toward people below.

As groups of Germans walked this stretch of road, three or four of us on the ground called out an order for them to stop, put their arms up in the air, and keep them there until we gave them further orders. Then, as quickly as possible, we would search for S.S. men. At first, we were totally unsure of ourselves. After all, we were just five kids without any real weapons stopping groups of grown men. In the beginning, we only stopped groups of ten or fifteen people, but we soon became more daring.

We knew that hard-core S.S. soldiers had the double lightning S.S. insignias tattooed under their arms. While their arms were raised in the air, we checked each of our "hostages" for markings. If we didn't find the marks we were looking for, we sent them on their way.

It was mind-boggling to see how meek and submissive these former killers and murderers had become. It was incredible that five teenagers were able to stop and search groups of Germans, even detain some and turn them over to the American MPs. More surprising than that, when we did find an S.S. officer, he would usually face us with a look of helplessness. It was astonishing. "I'm not a Nazi," he would state most humbly, "never was. I was forced to have this tattoo placed under my arm." It was obvious that on his own, without a gun and the might of the State giving him the legitimate right to murder Jews, the S.S. man was indeed weak and feeble.

When caught, these former monsters offered no resistance. When we told them to kneel, they remained in that position for hours on end. This was a time of lawlessness in Germany, and we could have easily tortured them, beaten them, or killed them and nothing would have happened to us. There were no policemen to charge us with crimes. There was no government and no rule of law. Yet, for some inexplicable reason, I did not feel compelled to kill, torture, or even severely beat these men. Despite what I went through, and my desire for revenge after what I experienced in the ghetto and in the camps, and even after witnessing the colossal cruelty of the Germans, somehow I could not force myself to inflict that much pain on another human being. Maybe my father had taught me too well and I couldn't lower myself to their level.

Some said I was a coward for not avenging the Jews when I had the opportunity to do so. I guess I revered human life a bit too much. In any case, we caught a number of Nazis and S.S. men, at least one a day. Sometimes we caught several in one day, and I thoroughly enjoyed watching them kneel, obeying our orders, and hearing them beg for mercy. With time, we became even more adventurous and had the courage (or stupidity) to stop even larger groups as they wandered down the highway. The basics of our operation rarely varied, and it was remarkable to see how these large groups submitted to the commands of a few teenage boys.

As we had done with the smaller groups, we searched everyone in the larger groups very quickly, and dismissed those without tattoos. It was our experience to find S.S. men bunched together at the back of the line, and luckily, that worked to our advantage. By the time we got to them, most of the regular soldiers were sent on their way, and there was less of a chance for a fight to break out and leave us overwhelmed.

When I think back to those days, I realize that what we were doing was tempting fate. Five skinny kids took on the German troops with a broken rifle and delivered at least one S.S. officer a day to the Allies. For me, the pleasure came when I could laugh at the Nazis and watch the killers, the "heroes," turn into blithering cowards.

I recall only one S.S. man who showed any form of resistance. He pulled a knife on the Hungarian, who was searching him. We all jumped him in unison, so he didn't put up much of a fight as we subdued him. Every day, when the American M.P. patrol passed through, we would hand our cache of Germans over to them.

It soon became routine for the Americans to ask us who we had for them that day, and we all became friends. They often supplied us with those rare and valuable commodities that simplified post-war life considerably: cigarettes, chocolate, and Coca-Cola. Of course, cigarettes were the most valuable. For me personally, chocolate was a more precious commodity. But, at the time, I couldn't figure out what all the fuss was about when it came to Coca-Cola. The Americans were crazy for it. To me, it was nothing special. It was warm and had no taste.

Before the Americans made their rounds, Henry Baigelman and Henry Eisman, the musicians from Lodz who were with me in Flossenburg, would also stop by. They were always curious about who we'd manage to catch on any particular day. Now it was their turn to joke and laugh at the German beasts who'd made their lives so miserable. Henry Baigelman, who spoke a good Yiddish and was very witty, would tease them mercilessly. It was wild and very, very funny.

These killers submissively sat on the side of the highway, the butt of our jokes. The dread of the punishment that awaited them was visible in their eyes. Except for landing a few punches, all we did was laugh at them. We rarely used ropes or chains to tie them down, and they just sat there, shamed and defeated.

As the months passed, our relationship with the American soldiers became friendlier. I figured that these particular men were among the troops who had liberated many of the concentration camps. They'd seen first-hand those atrocities that proved beyond a shadow of a doubt what the Germans had done to us. What they saw when they liberated us was burned into their brains forever. They didn't live it, but they saw the results of it. They clearly understood the impossible-to-imagine inhuman treatment we had been forced to endure for years.

Because of what they had seen, and how they came to find the camps, they understood that the Nazis alone could not have pulled this off. These Americans understood that what they found when they got to the camps scattered all over Europe was done with the willing and able complicity of the German people under the leadership of the Nazis.

By and large, the entire German population needed to be held accountable. The German people had definite knowledge and visual proof of the actions of their democratically elected totalitarian government and the big businesses that backed it. Millions of Germans directly and indirectly participated in inhumane acts taking place on Europe's soil.

The replacement American troops who were later sent as occupational forces did not witness the actual carnage for themselves, and, as a result, became a major obstacle in getting Jewish displaced persons proper assistance. The Germans, in the meantime, began to reassert themselves.

It was still difficult for me to fully comprehend and appreciate this newly acquired freedom of mine. For six years I had been subjected to strict rules and regulations. I was constantly concerned with trying to avoid punishment, trying not to be caught by the Germans in the ghetto, fearing for my life in the concentration camps. The Germans had accomplished what they had set out to do as they slowly broke our will. It was only natural for us to become submissive and for free will to vanish. Strange as it seems, I still needed time to understand what freedom actually meant and what it afforded me.

When I was liberated by the American Third Army, one might have expected me to jump for joy, but I did not. I needed time to experience the taste of freedom before I could fully appreciate this liberation. After all, the concept of freedom does not switch itself on in one's brain like a lightbulb. I needed to nourish the idea, to savor it, to celebrate it.

Freedom . . .

The joy of freedom came first through food,
when I was able to eat to my heart's content.
Freedom meant sleeping in a real bed,
with clean sheets, feather pillows and a down comforter.

Freedom was finding Germans who treated us like royalty,
as if we were kings, and they were our subjects.
Freedom meant traveling from one place to another,
without asking permission.
Freedom meant no guards.
Freedom meant privacy.
Freedom meant a hot bath.
Freedom meant talking to real friends.
Freedom meant being able to look for your family.
Freedom meant being able to do whatever I wanted,
at the moment I wanted to do it.
Freedom was all that and so much more.

As I found myself gradually adjusting to the splendor of freedom, I knew the next order of business was to look for the rest of my family. I discussed the situation in detail with my brother and our friends. We all had the same priorities, and we needed to figure out how to start the search. We brainstormed to try to find an efficient way to pursue the task.

Eventually, Leon and I ventured out to other villages and

small cities to make inquiries. Whenever we met Jewish survivors along the way, we asked if they had seen or knew anyone who might have knowledge of my mother or sisters. The answers were always negative.

By that time, survivors were moving into Displaced Persons camps or into private homes requisitioned from the Germans. Some of these camps, such as Bergen-Belsen and Landsburg, were quite large. For Leon and me, the thought of living in a camp environment again, even if it was run by the Allies, was intolerable and unacceptable. We chose to live in a private home. As we renewed our strength and refreshed our souls, we wandered further afield in search of our family.

This was no simple matter. There was no central data base capable of providing information about those who survived. There was no place to obtain information about who was sent where. There were no telephones or telephone directories to assist us. No fax machines, no telegraph facilities, and certainly no Internet or E-mail. It quickly became obvious that the only way to find our loved ones was to physically go wherever the survivors had formed small communities and prepared lists of names, entering them into a register. There was also the possibility of finding our family members in Lodz, since it seemed logical to go back to the place where we had last been together.

Fourteen
Reunion At Last

"Ah . . . to be reunited . . . but at what cost?"

We began our journey from city to city, starting first in the American Zone, to Cham and Regensburg, and slowly moving toward the British Zone. Traveling was not easy. We had to improvise, and that meant hitchhiking and using public transportation. But traveling without proper papers was a serious problem that could land you in jail.

The most intimidating method of transportation was the train. My brain still balked at the idea of boarding one. The trains were always overcrowded, and I feared for the safety of Leon the Reckless, who often would stand on the steps in between the cars. Since we were always so exhausted, particularly when traveling at night, I worried he might fall asleep, fall off the train, and end up under it.

This traveling didn't require a great deal of money, but before each trip we made sure we had some. Since cigarettes were even more important than money, we concentrated on getting cigarettes—with a pack of cigarettes we could get to almost anywhere.

Finding nothing in the American Zone, Leon and I, and our two friends, Jack and Joe—the same two in our "highway patrol"—finally embarked on a trip to the British Zone. We were headed to Bergen-Belsen, a former concentration camp, now the largest DP (Displaced Persons) camp in Europe. Not far from Hanover, near the railhead in Celle, Bergen-Belsen had the largest number of Jewish survivors of any DP camp in Germany.

We finally had some success. We found friends of our sisters who told us that both of them had survived, but that Dasza was very sick and had been assigned to a transport being sent to hospitals in Sweden. Renia accompanied her because the Swedes didn't want to separate them.

This was indeed a full-fledged miracle, but it came with a catch-22. The ship sailing for Sweden was officially departing from Bremen the very next day. We had to travel all night from Bergen-Belsen to Bremen if we wanted to catch up with them.

At the same time, Joe was lucky and located his cousin in Bergen-Belsen. It was decided that Joe and Jack would stay in Belsen, while Leon and I would go to Bremen.

Before we started our all-night trip to Bremen, we were required to obtain our papers from the British authorities. We approached the British officer in charge, explained our desperate situation, and asked for the needed travel permit. We had made a simple humanitarian request, and so did not anticipate any problems, but we were wrong. He was a heavy-set captain of the British Military Police and a stickler for procedure. He told us he would not furnish the permit because "late is too late" and we would have to wait until the next day.

We tried our best to convince him otherwise, but our pleas fell on deaf ears. Finally, exasperated, I told him we would be going to Bremen that night whether or not a permit was issued. He calmly warned us that we would be put in jail if we were caught by his military police, but we didn't care. We took off, arriving in Bremen in the wee hours of the morning and discovered, much to our dismay, that the transport leaving for Sweden was now departing from Lubeck instead of Bremen. We took off for Lubeck, which was fairly close by.

When we arrived in Lubeck at the crack of dawn we asked around and found out that our sisters were in a hospital waiting to leave for Sweden the following morning. We headed directly to the hospital to find them. When we got there, a nurse directed us to Dasza's bed, and at long last we were all together again . . . but not for long.

What was left of Dasza was lying under a thin blanket. She was just skin, bones, and eyes. I will never forget her eyes. When she heard our voices they opened as wide as they could and she whispered, "It is a miracle; Roman and Leon, you are here."

With all the strength she could muster, she held on to our

hands, constantly repeating our names, saying again and again, "I knew I would see you." I wanted to cry from happiness, but cried instead from sorrow and despair.

Our reunion seared itself into my soul, but I could not show her my mixed emotions. There was the joy of seeing her alive and the anguish and grief of knowing that after surviving the ghetto, the concentration camps, and the war, she was probably not going to be with us much longer. My darling sister was a skeleton, and from my sad experience, I knew her days were numbered.

Of course, we rejoiced with Renia, who sat steadfast at her bedside, but that joy was compromised by Dasza's condition. My beloved sister was one of the *musselmen,* condemned to death. Everything about her had atrophied, except her eyes.

After a while, Dasza was so exhausted she closed her eyes and fell into an uneasy sleep. At that point, we removed our hands from her grasp and moved away to discuss the situation with Renia. She told us that the Swedish Red Cross had decided to take some of the sick survivors to Sweden and put them in medical centers for proper treatment unavailable in Germany. Before they left, we talked to some of the doctors and other hospital personnel. They confirmed that though the children of our family were now reunited, it would not be in Dasza's best interests to remain in Germany because it would be a certain death sentence.

The general medical consensus was that either way there wasn't much hope for Dasza. Her condition was too far gone, and even with the best medical treatment in Sweden, the likelihood of her surviving was slim, very slim. However, they decided that even if there was one chance in a million, she had to go to have the opportunity to live.

We were heartbroken. There we were, reunited, knowing it was but for a brief moment, because Dasza was leaving us again as soon as we had found her, and Renia was leaving as well. Leon and I consoled ourselves with the knowledge that we had found our sisters. At least Dasza had the chance to see us before she died, and Renia was still with us. Leon and I had yet to learn about Mamma's fate, but we were coping with one shock at a time.

Before they left, we found the time to sit with Renia and listen to her brief account of what had happened to them after we were separated in Auschwitz. She told us that Mamma was not sent to the gas chamber and that the three of them stayed together there and in other camps as well. Then, at one of the camps, my mother became ill and was taken to the "hospital." She was caught in one of the periodic sweeps. She became one of those souls wafting up in the blue smoke that constantly emanated from the chimneys and swirled into the sky. We now knew what we never wanted to know or even imagine: our beloved mother was gone.

The tears of happiness by seeing my beloved sister suddenly gave way to tears of sorrow for our mother, and the immediate knowledge that we would have to part right away, to give my sister a chance for life.

The next morning, the girls left for Sweden. It wasn't long before we heard that the inevitable had happened. Despite the best medical care in Sweden, Dasza died a few months after they arrived. The malnutrition and tuberculosis had taken its toll. Though she managed to come out the other side of hell, she was as much a victim of the murdering Germans as were my mother and the 6,000,000 others.

After our travels across Germany, we now garnered the courage to abandon life in the village and move on to find Jewish communal life in one of the bigger cities. Leon and I went to Cham, also in Bavaria, located not too far from the city of Regensburg. Cham was a relatively small town that for some reason attracted many survivors after liberation, and where a large contingent of American Armed Forces were garrisoned.

The American military men were cooperative and friendly, having uniquely bonded with the survivors because they had been eyewitnesses to the result of the Germans' treatment of the Jews. The U.S. Army issued strict orders that the American soldiers were not to fraternize with the Germans. However, these orders were not always obeyed when it came to socializing between U.S. soldiers and German women. This was particularly noticeable when the second wave of American troops arrived. They had no clue about what had happened to us, and frankly, most of them didn't care. Because we were in camps, they assumed we were somehow "bad." They also established cordial relationships with German officials eager to instigate problems between the Americans and the Jews.

In the past, Germans in general, and German women in particular, had considered themselves to be a special race, more honorable than others and above reproach. They truly believed that they were from a superior ethnic group. As such, it would have been unthinkable for German women to ever fraternize with lowly Americans, particularly if they were of a different color and/or from a minority race. Suddenly, German women completely changed their attitudes. An American soldier could now sleep with almost any German woman of his choice for as little as a pack of cigarettes, a bar of chocolate, or a small amount of food. There was no longer any shame on the part of the German women who participated in such arrangements, and they eagerly provided their services in exchange for American goodies.

Though such arrangements between American soldiers and German women were quite widespread, the first wave of American soldiers kept their distance from the German population at large. The still-visible horrific sights of war were ingrained in their consciousness, and they didn't forget what they found when they first came to Germany. It was a paradox. The American Army fraternized with German women, but at the same time, held the survivors in high esteem, cooperating with us whenever possible and generously providing us food and other necessities.

With the war over, the American soldiers stationed in Europe found themselves with more time on their hands and in need of entertainment. That's where I came into the picture. Leon, Joe, Jack, and I put together a band to play at American military bases. We contacted the older boys, the musicians from Lodz, and formed the Happy Boys Band. We looked for musical instruments in Czechoslovakia, because it was the best place to find them.

By that time, I had added a few extra words of English to my limited vocabulary and I was able to find work on an American base. I somehow managed to acquire an American Army uniform that fit me, and for practical purposes I was now dressed as an American soldier and could pass as one.

In exchange for working for the Americans, I was given a substantial amount of food, including such delicacies as oranges. More importantly, they gave me lots of cigarettes and chocolates, a currency more valuable than the worthless German mark. The Happy Boys were already entertaining the troops, and I intended to book more gigs, so I secured a letter of recommendation from the American Commanding Officer instructing the powers-that-be to give me all possible assistance in acquiring musical instruments.

With me in my uniform and letter in hand, Jack and I traveled to Kraslice, Czechoslovakia, well-known for producing the instruments we needed for the band. We embarked on this journey fully loaded with chocolate and cartons of American cigarettes, ready to do some serious business.

We knew the cigarettes were contraband, so we hid them in a number of old suitcases and covered them with garments. Though it was hard to find musical instruments, no one who had them could resist trading them for American cigarettes and chocolate. After a couple of days, we had an abundant quantity of saxophones, clarinets, flutes, and other portables that we put into our suitcases.

But a Czech musician in Kraslice informed on us when he spotted us with all our instruments after he unsuccessfully tried to obtain one for himself. He marched over to a police station and reported us as black marketeers, a serious charge that could land us behind bars. The cops quickly stopped us, and when they saw how many instruments we had, refused to accept our explanations.

Once we were taken to the police station, we were interrogated by a number of officials who decided that we could not be released until a judge ruled on our case. In theory that was correct, but in practice, it was different. Since there was no judge to be found late in the evening, it meant Jack and I would be locked up for at least the night. Having tasted a few months of freedom, I now found myself in confinement again. Although I was not in a concentration camp, I was behind bars without knowing what the next day would bring.

Losing my freedom again so quickly brought back many unpleasant memories. Just the sound of steel doors closing and having to stay in such a small cell was more than enough. I spent a sleepless night in the little cage, and, as promised, the very next day we were brought before the judge. I presented him with the letter of recommendation from the American Commanding Officer stating that I was purchasing instruments on behalf of the U.S. Army. That saved our necks.

The judge himself had been imprisoned by the Germans during the war for subversive activities and was liberated by the American Army. He sympathized with us, and expressed regrets for the inconvenience we had suffered. We happily departed Czechoslovakia.

Later on, whenever I watched The Happy Boys perform, I'd think about the night I spent in the Czech jail. In time, those instruments represented the birth and growth of The Happy Boys, made up of seven pre-war musicians. Jack, Joe, Leon, and I were the agents, producers, and managers who kept the show going. In between gigs, I looked for my extended family, the cousins who left the Lodz ghetto and from whom I had heard nothing. It meant returning to Lodz to thoroughly investigate the circumstances of their disappearance.

Inasmuch as I was "gainfully employed" by the American Army, and in the enviable position of securing barter commodities, I thought it best to remain in Germany and that Leon, Jack, and Joe should return to Poland. There they could check the growing databases in Warsaw and Lodz and look for the rest of our family and friends. I was particularly worried about Leon and his between-the-cars acts of defying gravity, but I was even more concerned about the fact that he was traveling across borders without papers and could be stopped at any time. I figured if he was going to go, he had to do it before governments reestablished themselves and created bureaucracies that would only make things more difficult. At this point in time, he could say he was headed home—papers or not—because almost no one had papers, and everyone was going "home."

Once across the Polish border, Leon went to Jewish community centers in Lodz and Warsaw, where he thoroughly investigated the registry of names of Jewish survivors. These centers were places where information could be exchanged, since notices were posted and itineraries noted. Unfortunately, he wasn't able to find our relatives anywhere.

To his surprise, he did find Kazimierz, the old superintendent of our father's factory, who greeted him warmly. Before the war, Kazimierz was a Socialist Party member and now he was a high-ranking official in the Polish Communist Party. As such, he had everything at his disposal. He told Leon that after we left for the ghetto, the Germans came to the factory and removed all of the machinery and all other movable assets. He did not know who took it or where it was sent. It was too dangerous to ask such questions. He did know that it took a few days to dismantle the machinery, and then everything was placed on trucks and sent away.

Kazimierz gave Leon our family picture that Tatush had given to him long before the war. The photo was taken when Leon and I were maybe four or five years old. Leon broke into tears when he saw it. Kazimierz also gave him a silver cigarette case that belonged to Tatush and a silver wine cup that we had used for the prophet Elijah during Passover. We now had three tangible souvenirs of pre-war life in Lodz and the home where we spent our childhood years.

We will always have our memories of the brutalities we suffered for six long years, but we will also carry the memories of moments of joy among family and friends, before, during and after the war. These items are like time machines. You hold them in your hand and they take you into the past. The photo Leon brought back from Lodz is the single family photo that survived our childhood years, and is the only picture I have of my dear parents and departed sister. I treasure it greatly. And yet, every time I look at it, I feel the great loss we suffered.

For the moment, we thoroughly enjoyed the carefree life we were living in Germany, without worrying about what tomorrow would bring. We continued to requisition various items from the Germans, like clothing and furniture. With an ample supply of

cigarettes, chocolate, and other food stuffs, I had enough barter-
ing power to buy myself a stylish leather coat, boots, and even
two gold watches for myself and Leon.

We brazenly rode around on motorcycles that once belonged
to the S.S. and did so in a most irresponsible fashion. Looking
back, I realize it is another one of those constant miracles we experienced: we managed to never sustain serious injuries or get
into major accidents.

Slowly, such existence became meaningless, and I started to
think about the future. For Leon and me, Germany held no future. Being there was a constant reminder of who and what we
needlessly lost. We briefly considered going back to Poland. After
all, Poland was the land of our birth and where we spent happy
childhood years with our parents and siblings, and I did speak
the language fluently. Though I longed for my former life, I realized that it was no longer available. Once Dasza had died and
Renia decided to remain in Sweden, Leon and I realized we had
two choices. One was to go to Palestine and the other was to go to
the United States.

We heard UNRRA (the United Nations Relief and Rescue
Agency) was accepting applications for orphans willing to go to
America. We figured this was as far-fetched a proposition as we
had ever been offered and that we had nothing to lose by filing.
Leon, Joe, and I filled out the paperwork and we were shocked a
few weeks later when we were accepted. We prepared to go to
America under the collective visa for war orphans. After making
our farewells, we headed to Bremen once more, this time to embark on our unexpected journey to new lives in America.

Fifteen
Coming to America

"Give us your tired, your poor, your hungry . . ."

Those of us who became orphans during the war gathered in Bremen, Germany to begin our journey to the United States. We came from all parts of Germany, but primarily from the American sector. Although Jews, Catholics, and Protestants were all represented and mixed together in this group of children, the great majority of us were Jewish.

We all shared three common denominators: we'd all lost our parents during the war, we all wanted to get away from the blood-soaked soil of Europe, and we all wanted to come to the United States, the land of freedom and golden opportunity.

We were also all clueless about "the land of freedom and golden opportunity" and had no idea about what that really meant, or, for that matter, what fate had in store for us in our newly adopted country. Instinctively, however, we knew that it would be far better for us than Germany. We asked ourselves unanswerable questions and wondered what was next.

Most of us had no relatives or friends in America, yet we had high expectations regarding our adventure into the unknown. Our association with America came through the American soldiers we met—their wholesomeness and their friendly attitudes toward us had made a positive impression representing America and its inhabitants.

I found out that old U.S. Army ships were going to be used to transport us to our new country. The names of these vessels were the Marine Flasher and the Marine Perch. These boats were used during the war as troop carriers, but in peacetime they were transformed and used for this new purpose. (Today some of them have been rehabilitated and are used as floating restaurants!)

The Marine Flasher left for America in April 1946. My brother and I were assigned to leave on the second ship, the *Marine Perch,* scheduled to depart in May. Before we left, our days were filled with paperwork. Since we had no documents to substantiate what we were writing down in the questionnaires, it all seemed meaningless to me. We had only our memories to depend upon. In the meantime, we enjoyed getting acquainted with some of the other children assigned to our vessel.

Finally the day of our departure arrived, and a few hundred of us were assembled, taken aboard, and directed to our cabins. There were several of us in each cabin, and everyone was given a bunkbed. When I heard the sound of the boat whistle and the ship started to inch its way from the harbor, I realized that my life in Europe was over for real. There was no turning back.

Only a few people on the pier waved good-bye to us, a few friends. We could not expect more since most of our families and friends were killed during the Holocaust. Slowly, the European shoreline faded in the distance, and the endless, vast ocean surrounded us.

It is difficult to describe my state of mind at the time. Yes, I was happy to leave Europe, where I had lost my parents and a sister, and where I experienced the most unforgettable, indescribable, and torturous years imaginable. Yet I took with me sweet memories and thoughts of my carefree childhood, with remembrances of my beloved parents, family, friends, and my home. I was full of hope and excitement, but I was also full of anxiety and apprehension. I had a vision of America from the movies I'd seen and the Americans I'd met.

With these mixed feelings, I eagerly looked forward to the fresh start in America. The country that had been described to me as a nation of freedom, equality, and opportunity was now going to be the land of my future. These were the thoughts that filled my mind. On the other hand, my attention was also drawn to what was happening all around me on the ship.

None of the children aboard, including me, had ever traveled on such a large ship. According to the crew, the *Marine Perch* was relatively small and did not have the proper stabilizers for ocean travel. Since we were all unfamiliar with sailing, none of us was prepared for the constant motion and the seasickness we had to endure.

The cabins were small and cramped and it was unpleasant to remain in our rooms for very long. Our quarters stank and there was inadequate ventilation, encouraging most of us to stay on deck as much as possible. But the conditions on deck were not so pleasing, either, since so many of us were seasick and constantly throwing up the food we'd just eaten. When we were fortunate enough not to be sick, we would talk endlessly about what could be waiting for us, what we would do, and what we would find out in just a few more days.

The legend about America as the *goldene medina* (the golden land) implied that the streets flowed with gold just ready for the taking. We knew that America was the country to which Eastern European Jews ran when the pogroms of the 19th century started. We also knew about its skyscrapers from a Polish song, readings, and newsreels.

We spent the week speculating and being seasick, and then one morning our lethargy was interrupted by someone announcing from a loudspeaker that we were about to sail past the Statue of Liberty. At the time, I had no idea who she was, or that she existed, nor of the significance of the statue to immigrants. I had not yet read Emma Lazarus's famous words. What I did know was that Lady Liberty was the beacon announcing that American shores were just ahead, and a few hours later, I set foot in New York City.

As wards of the United States government, we were able to avoid the paperwork, red tape, and crowds at Ellis Island and the Immigration Office. We were taken by special bus to a Children's Center on Caldwell Avenue in The Bronx. I thought I would be elated when I walked through its doors; instead I felt like I was having a panic attack as my fears and anxieties took hold of me. Where was I? What would I do? What would my future be?

Being with Leon as I went through all these emotional upheavals was beneficial. As it had been during the war, it was a great comfort to have him at my side through the misery and suffering, but also through the joys and celebrations.

The Children's Center was nothing to speak of—not in a particularly nice neighborhood, not the attractive, bright, and sunny place that I imagined it would be. But at least I was on solid ground and everything around me was no longer in motion or vibrating under my feet as it had during our ocean passage.

Again we filled out endless applications and for the next few days were exposed to different rules and regulations and subjected to various meetings with social workers. The purpose of these interviews was to generate information about our character, our religious affiliations, and our personalities in order to determine the most suitable placement with a respectable family. The social workers wanted to know whether or not there was a possibility of finding family members living in the United States and if we had particular preferences about where we wanted to live. Because I knew nothing about the States, one city was the same as another to me, just dots on the map. They explained the Children's Center was but temporary quarters, and that permanent assignments were going to be made based on the information they were gathering.

If appropriate families were found, we would be placed according to religious affiliation and sent to cities throughout the United States. In each city, different organizations would be responsible for our welfare—organizations that would file periodic reports with the United States government. Then they would supervise our placements in the most appropriate foster homes.

In the meantime, word spread through the Bronx Jewish community that the house on Caldwell Avenue was full of orphans from Europe. Every day, people would come to "visit," to ask about our relatives, to see if we were related to them, or if we knew of friends and family members they had left behind. Some of our visitors were kind enough to offer to take us around the city to see the sights, which was always a welcome interlude. One couple, in particular, frequently came to visit with me and Leon.

They were Mr. and Mrs. Yiddel Borenstein, and Leon and I formed a lifelong friendship with them. Their concern was genuine, and we kept in touch even after we left New York. They followed our exploits for years. Later, when I returned to New York to settle there permanently, we continued our relationship.

The Borensteins died many years ago, and I still keep them in my heart. As fate would have it, while I was preparing to write this book, my wife, Hannah, my son, Jeffrey, and I attended a screening and reception for a film produced by Marion Wiesel, Nobel Laureate Elie Wiesel's wife. There was a vivacious lady looking for a place to sit, so we asked her to join us at our table. As we chatted, she revealed that her maiden name was Borenstein. Of course, a good round of Jewish geography was required under the circumstances, so I asked her if she had ever heard of Yiddel Borenstein. It turned out she knew him very, very well. He was her father! I realized that our paths hadn't crossed since she was a little girl. What a small world, when after all these years I chanced to meet the daughter of the people I had loved and respected so much! I was able to give her some *naches* (a blessing) by describing the wonderful things her parents did for us.

While in New York, we also looked for our friend Jack's relatives. Jack could not come to the States as an orphan because he was lucky enough to find his mother in Poland. He had a vague idea, however, that some of his relatives were living in the United States, probably in New York. And he was right. We did indeed find a few of them and put them in contact with each other so that they could provide affidavits for Jack and his mother.

New York was huge, impressive, and overwhelming—teeming with life. It was a city of contrasts, of skyscrapers and tenements, of wealth and poverty. The skyscrapers I expected; the tenements I did not. Somehow, we familiarized ourselves with the bus system and subway lines and would seize any opportunity to explore, especially Manhattan. Times Square and Wall Street were our favorite stomping grounds. These two sections of Manhattan impressed us the most, in two entirely different ways. The Wall Street area had narrow streets and tall buildings, where the sun never seemed to shine. This part of the city, with thousands of people crowding the sidewalks during the day, was completely deserted after five o'clock in the evening.

In stark contrast, Times Square was full of life all day and all night. It was hard to tell the difference between day and night; the neon signs that glowed so brightly completely eliminated the darkness. It was fascinating to watch the flashing advertisements and see the legendary smoke emanating from the mouth of a man puffing on a Camel cigarette. When we would leave the bright lights behind, it was back to the subdued atmosphere of Caldwell Avenue. Manhattan was magnificent; The Bronx was mediocre.

In the meantime, discussions between the orphans and the social service workers continued. Slowly but surely the plan to disperse us to various cities around America began to unfold. Leon and I had only one condition regarding our placement: that he and I remain together. Normally, agencies place only one orphan with a family so our case required extra effort from the officials, since they had to find a family willing to accept the two of us.

The procedure was to send Jewish children to various cities through Jewish Family Services (JFS). Each JFS agency would then handle individual cases and place each child involved with the appropriate Jewish family. The family taking the child had to report to JFS periodically. In turn, JFS briefed the U.S. agency, because the American government was ultimately responsible for our well-being. The same procedure applied as well to all Christian family services handling Christian children.

After careful consideration of our case, and if we had no objections, the officials at the Center proposed sending us to Atlanta, Georgia, where they assured us that proper care was available. Until that moment, I'd only heard the name in conjunction with the famous book *Gone With The Wind,* which I'd read in Polish before the war. Otherwise, we both knew nothing about the city. Since there was nothing objectionable that we were aware of, and The Bronx was depressing, we readily accepted the recommendation. For the next few days, as arrangements were completed for many of us, lots of good-byes were exchanged as we were sent off to our new homes.

Then, at last, it was our turn to depart. After bidding a fond farewell to all of our new friends, and promising to keep in touch, Leon and I took off on the next leg of our long journey. "Atlanta, here we come!" I thought.

Sixteen
Living Through Ballyhoo

"The 1950s in Atlanta was the rudest awakening of all, and in some ways, it was one of the most disappointing experiences of our lives."

When Leon and I arrived in Atlanta, representatives of the local Hebrew Orphan's Home came to greet us. Compared to Caldwell Avenue in The Bronx, their offices in a beautiful building with attractive furnishings were absolutely luxurious. They sat us down and talked about their plans for us.

First, a social worker was going to take us shopping for clothing. Then we were going to see a doctor and dentist to get thorough checkups. They told us we were assigned to a wonderful Jewish family in town and that after the red tape and preliminary paperwork had been satisfactorily completed, we could register for school.

When we agreed to everything to which we were told to agree, the social workers escorted us to our new home with the understanding that the next few days would be devoted to personal issues. In the morning, a social worker would be picking us up to take us shopping.

They put us in a social worker's car and drove us through the city to the northeastern suburbs, which looked like no place on Earth Leon and I had ever seen. It was green and grassy, with lots of trees that formed cathedrals over the streets and large Victorian homes. We came up to the porch, the social worker introduced us to our hosts, and left. He told us to expect him in the morning, and to be ready to go shopping. The lady of the house, who had two children, showed us to our room, which was upstairs and had a view of the greenery in the backyard. She told us that at dinner that evening we would meet the rest of the family.

She also told us that before we'd leave in the morning, the maid would prepare our breakfast for us.

The next morning, bright and early, the social worker came and took us to tour the department stores. We spent lots of time in Rich's, Atlanta's foremost department store, and one of the top shops in America. We were overwhelmed by the gigantic size of the store itself, the variety of merchandise and the choices in each category, as well as the sales people who were helpful and pleasant. It was unlike anything we had ever experienced. I certainly had no problem buying handsome new garments. But after spending time in concentration camps, and then living on my own in Germany after the war, it was tough to be subjected to the supervision of a social worker. I was already an independent who made vital life decisions; now someone else was telling me what to do.

Though the social worker was trying to be helpful, he ordered us around and told us what we could and could not purchase. As we picked out our clothes and toiletries, I realized that every decision was being made by a man with no understanding of how we suffered from accelerated maturity, how we were "ripened" for adult life in the ghettos and camps, and that we were not typical teens. It boggled my mind that I had made life-saving decisions in Auschwitz-Birkenau, that I had stood up to the Nazis to save our puny lives, and that now I was not allowed to pick my own underwear. That really irked me.

We didn't get back to the house until late afternoon. The next morning, when the social worker arrived to pick us up to continue our "Back-to-School" shopping spree, the first thing he told us was that he had gone over budget by a few dollars, and that therefore we would have to return our pajamas and some other clothes in exchange for cheaper items.

Why do I remember such an obscure incident after almost sixty years? Because he made us return things that were insignificantly over budget! Even as a teenager, it struck me that the Orphan's Home and the social worker should have realized that such attitudes were insulting to us, the recipients of their beneficence. "The pajama incident" probably would not have left such an impression on me if it hadn't been followed by another distasteful occurrence in the doctor's office the very next day.

When the doctor examined us, he noticed that Leon and I were wearing our gold Jaeger LeCoultre watches. When he was finished with our checkups, he made us a proposition. Because our watches had large faces and large second hands, he told us it would be beneficial to his practice to have the LeCoultres, and he would trade his watch for ours. He thought we didn't know what he was doing. He was condescending and insulting, and Leon and I knew it.

We had gotten our graduate degrees from the ghettos and camps. We knew full well the value of our timepieces. We did not have money with us when we came to the States, and before we left Europe, we got these watches, our most valuable possessions, to use as hedge funds for the future. We had learned early, in "Canada," what such watches were really worth . . . they were worth our lives. How offensive that "respectable" physician was when he made his offer! Yes, we politely turned him down, but I was seething. The watch affair and the pajama incident, taking place as soon as they did after our arrival in Atlanta, certainly made a lasting impression on me. And they gave me fair warning of what Leon and I were going to face in this new land of ours.

Life in Atlanta was colorful, to say the least. After a few weeks in New York City we had become accustomed to the racial integration, and after the Holocaust, we knew full well what it meant to be "the other." It was awkward, strange, and incomprehensible to witness the segregation in the South. It permeated every facet of life in Atlanta. Black people had to sit in the back of the bus; there were separate schools, toilets, and water fountains for "colored"; in restaurants there was separation between whites and blacks; and participation in sports was segregated as well.

Virtually every prosperous white family had "Negro" help, including the cook, who was considered practically part of the family and was allowed to eat and drink from the same dishes and glasses as the family. To me this was an inexplicable contradiction. Yet, this inconsistency in treatment was seemingly accepted by both sides.

There seemed to be one standard for private life and a completely different one for public life. We experienced this dichotomy in our beautiful new home, where the colored maid cooked and served dinner to a white household. On the surface, everything appeared to be just fine, but something was very, very wrong.

It didn't take long for Leon and me to realize that despite our beautiful surroundings, something was "off." For some reason, we had very little personal contact with the family who took us in. There was no warmth and no conversation or interaction between us. Though we all had dinner together, our hosts hardly spoke to us, and we went straight to our room afterward. There was no place for us to go and they never offered to take us anywhere. They never asked us about our lives, they just seemed to be going through motions without meaning. We were, we concluded, in a house, not a home. We knew very well what a home should be. Yes, we were too old to take target practice in the halls or ride the bicycle around the dining room, but it would have been nice to listen to the radio, to talk at the table, to share, to learn—as we did with Mamma and Tatush. This was very strange. Since my brother and I still had each other, we tried not to let the problem overwhelm us, but in a matter of weeks, we'd had enough of the superficial luxury and our "parents' " empty souls and hearts.

The situation came to a head when we started school. The maid, who lived out, came to the house each morning and was responsible for serving us breakfast and filling our lunchboxes. When she arrived each day, she brought our daily food "rations," which she purchased on her way to work. First off, we couldn't understand why food had to be brought in daily. There was an ice box and the kitchen was equipped with all the "newest" gadgets.

This simple business of feeding us should have worked out, but the maid was late several times a week, so we had no choice except to leave for school without eating breakfast or taking lunch along. There was nothing to say to the lady of the house, who should have been aware of the situation, but remained completely indifferent to our physical needs.

If we'd had some of our own money, it wouldn't have posed a

problem and we could have bought lunch in the school cafeteria. As usual, no money, no food. We had no way of earning any, and there was no equivalent of a black market—so there we sat, in our fancy America, hungry most of the time.

We were frustrated and couldn't figure out how to resolve the problem. Why did these two people bring two children into a beautifully furnished home and then fail to take any interest in their overall physical and emotional welfare? After a few weeks, we decided that they took us in because we were some kind of "showpieces" for display in the local Jewish community.

Leon and I talked about it at length and we decided that if this was life in the *goldeneh medina,* we were better off going back to Europe. There, at least, we had a roof over our heads we called our own; no one told us what underwear to buy, and we would certainly not be going hungry because no one cared. Here, in the land of plenty, we were constantly hungry. In Europe, at least, we got food when we needed it, and we could take care of ourselves. In America, our hands were tied, and in some ways, it was even worse than Europe. There we could decide what was necessary for survival. Here, there was nothing to maneuver with and there was no place to go. Leon and I were trained to be-have well in civilized circumstances, and our circumstances in Atlanta were exceedingly civilized—but we were still hungry.

With that old familiar feeling gnawing at our innards and souls—the one we thought we put behind us forever—it was dif-ficult for us to concentrate on our studies. No one came to us to complain about our grades, but we knew that we weren't meet-ing our potential abilities. Now we wanted to do better in school, but we couldn't because of the constant hunger. After the maid didn't show up on time for the umpteenth time—because there was no one in the house to talk to, and because our benefactors were clueless and didn't care—we decided to pay a visit to the Hebrew Orphan's Home. The social workers, after all, were ulti-mately responsible for our well-being in Atlanta. We walked in and informed the director that it was our wish to go back to Eu-rope.

It was as if we'd set a off a stinkbomb in the middle of Eden. The director was shocked and asked us why we didn't appreciate what we had—the beautiful home with an important family, the nice new clothing, the fancy school . . . What did we mean by wanting to go back to Europe? How ungrateful could we be? Besides, they told us, they wanted us to stay. We were wards of the U.S. government, and if we left, that would give the agency a bad name.

We were hesitant to explain. Finally, we said that, in essence, what the social workers were saying was true—we were living in a beautiful house, we went to a good school, and we were well-clothed—but the bottom line was that we did not come to the United States to be hungry. And we were hungry almost all the time. We explained to the director that in our opinion sheltering us meant more than just putting a roof over our heads and clothes on our backs. We wanted our "hosts" or "foster parents" to have a positive and supportive attitude, to show us they cared about our well-being, and offer us assistance and guidance to help us adjust to life in a new country.

The director and staff of the Hebrew Orphan's Home did not believe us. They could not accept the fact that most of the time we were simply hungry while living with one of the "finest" Jewish families in the city. They tried to convince us that it could not be so, and emphatically stated they did not want us to go back to Europe; that they wanted to honor their responsibility to the United States government. Furthermore, they promised to investigate the matter and find a solution to the problem.

We promised not to make any rash decisions and agreed to wait for word from them about any new developments. Lo and behold, a few days later we were called to a meeting with the people at the Orphan's Home. Although they never openly admitted that we were in a situation exactly as we had described it, they promised to find us a new home.

True to the promise I made to Mamma, I insisted we remain together, so the officials asked for some additional time to locate a place that would accept both of us. We readily agreed to their proposal because we thought it was reasonable. It didn't take more than a few days before they invited us to meet Mrs. Millie Marks, a long-time widow with an only child, Asher, in medical school. She immediately put us both at ease with her warm welcome.

Mrs. Marks's house was in a middle-class neighborhood and had none of the grandeur of the house in northeast Atlanta. What it was missing in opulence was generously compensated for with the warmth and love she generated. We instantly felt that this house, with this lady in charge, could become our permanent home, and our original instincts were on point. The Kniker brothers' first official address in America was 412 Angier Place, N.E. Atlanta, Georgia.

What a difference it makes when someone genuinely cares about you! Mrs. Marks had no maid, but each and every morning she greeted us with a smile and hearty breakfast. She made it her business to provide proper nourishment before we left for school and packed ample lunches for us to take along. She was interested in who we were, how we were doing, and constantly inquired about our progress in school.

She was uncomplicated and kind, a woman who cared for us as if we were her own. She showered us with her love and it did not take long for us to adopt her as our second mother. For the rest of her life, Leon and I maintained our relationship with her, this special woman that I still hold in my heart. Leon kept in touch when he attended medical school in New Orleans, and I stayed in contact when I moved my business to New York. Mrs. Marks was our family, who shared my marriage to Hannah and the birth of my children, along with all of our family joys and sorrows until she died in Florida many years later.

Perhaps it was because Leon and I were too old to start calling Mrs. Marks "Mother"—and we couldn't call her Millie because that was too disrespectful to our thinking—that we always called her Mrs. Marks. My kids called her Grandma and were always on the phone, sending postcards and visiting with her in Atlanta and Florida. It bothered Susan and Jeffery that they never had the opportunity to meet their own grandparents, and so, in a way, Mrs. Marks became the substitute for the two grandmothers they lost in the Holocaust.

Our lives in Atlanta were pleasant and productive. When we changed neighborhoods, we'd also changed high schools, and we noticed some obvious differences between them. At our first high school, most of the students had their own cars and drove themselves to school. If they didn't have cars, their families made sure there was transportation available. Those options were not available to us, and there was no public transportation to speak of in the area. We were, in essence, prisoners of suburbia.

Now that we were in a middle-class neighborhood, and there was public transportation available, our new school was more accessible. Experiencing less trouble getting from place to place made life lots easier. Before I knew it, I was in my senior year at Henry Grady High School. It was a large school with predominantly middle-class students. Most of my classmates were born and raised in Atlanta. Consequently, many of them knew each other since early childhood, making it difficult for Leon and me, as newcomers with language and cultural barriers and no family ties, to break into peer groups formed in grade school or earlier.

Though our knowledge of English was still limited, Leon and I managed to do very well in school and graduated with honors given only to "top-ten" students. The award was called the Golden "G," and one could surely wonder how we were both able to do so well and achieve such recognition after we'd missed six years of school. I think it was because of the love of learning that Mamma and Tatush had instilled in us, and also because they had sent us to the Jewish Gymnasium in Lodz.

Social life in Atlanta bore no resemblance to anything we had experienced at home in Lodz or even in our few weeks in New York City. It was rigid, extremely structured, and class-conscious. Leon and I had very little interaction with the general society around us, and with no parents or relatives of our own, it was even more difficult for us to fit into any particular social category.

In 1946, Atlanta was a relatively close-knit community, a small southern city with very few Northerners. It had its own customs, liaisons, and social constrictions. Interestingly enough, *The Unwritten Rules* were even more clearly defined and enforced in the Jewish community, the same community that had witnessed the framing and lynching of Leo Frank, a New Yorker who had moved to Atlanta thirty or so years earlier.

The two social establishments in the Jewish community were the Progressive Club and the Mayfair Club. The membership of one consisted of Eastern European Jews; the members of the other were German Jews. One can correctly say the clubs were restricted, and money, of course, was the key determinant of where one "belonged."

In the 1990s, in New York, Alfred Uhry wrote a play that was produced on Broadway called "The Last Night of Ballyhoo." It was not a pretty play about the Atlanta Jewish community, but it was an honest one. What took place in the play was almost exactly what happened in Atlanta every December in the '50s. I took my son, Jeffrey, to see it and explained to him beforehand that he was going to witness interplay between the different social classes in the Jewish community of Atlanta during that period. Then, perhaps, he could begin to grasp how Leon and I felt in that eerie environment. In the play, Atlanta's circumspect and respectable Jews called New York Jews unrespectable names, and that is exactly how the Atlanta Jews felt about it in real life, too.

Leon and I were like round pegs being forced into square holes. Except for a few kind souls, we were dismissed as "greenhorns." Sadly, I found that the attitude of the Jews in Atlanta encompassed a general apathy and lack of curiosity about what happened to us and the Jews of Europe during the war. In fact, it was worse than that. It was studied indifference, complicated by a need to play the game of "Who Suffered More." The pain and suffering, loss and rehabilitation of others had nothing to do with them. Atlanta was full of such Jews, whose parents fled the pogroms of Russia and the Pale of Settlement in the late 19th century.

The older generation living in Atlanta, whenever they met us, would immediately complain about how hard it had been for them and their parents when they first came to the U.S. Not one asked us about how we were adjusting or what we had gone through; we were an affront to them. They enjoyed discussing how difficult life had been in the old days and insinuated that Leon and I were getting a "free ride." They insisted that we listen to their "heartbreaking" stories of the hardship they endured during the war—gas was rationed and some products were hard to come by. Leon and I had no idea of the trouble they'd seen. After all, we were just there to mooch. And worse. We were supposed to be blindly ignorant of everything civilized.

Old-timers acted as if we had never seen a banana or a light switch. Most insulting was the way they'd instruct us on flushing toilets, as if we had come from the deepest jungles in Africa and had never seen a toilet before. In the beginning, I was angry and offended. Then I slowly began to realize that before coming to the United States, many of these people or their parents lived in small villages in Europe where civilization was hundreds of years behind the times. The likelihood was that they thought such conditions still prevailed in Europe up to the very time we came to America. It was clear to me that they were the country bumpkins and they were the ones who had no idea about the high culture that existed in the cities of Europe or anything else. Even so, the ignorance of many people in Atlanta was shocking.

It was also obvious to me that either guilt or neglect inspired these Atlantans to ignore the war and the deaths of 6,000,000 of their own. The subject was taboo, not discussed at all—not privately, not publicly, and not even in the synagogues. If Leon and I hadn't lived through it as witnesses, we would think that it never happened.

In addition, they exhibited no special desire to make us part of their community. To them we were a living rebuke and threat to their social status.

The only ones who cared about us were the refugees from Hitler who arrived in Atlanta after 1933. These people and their families went out of their way to help us integrate into American society. I think they were as rejected by the Atlanta Jews as we were. They understood our loneliness and need for social contact. They were the ones who took it upon themselves to organize weekly or bi-weekly get-togethers for newcomers in their own homes and at the community center.

The Meyer Clan, who lived at 630 Darlington, was the only family that literally opened their doors to us. Their home became the exclusive and singular "Greenhorn Club," and their teenaged daughter, Erica, became part of our group. (Though we rarely see each other, she is still part of my life today.)

These little gatherings with other boys and girls who came over after the war were the first social functions to which we were exposed and gave us the opportunity to learn skills that would help us live in our new world.

Today, involved as I am with Jewish life in general and Holocaust commemoration and education in particular, I see the active participation and involvement of rabbis and their congregants in Holocaust issues, from coast to coast and from north to south. I know how the American Jewish community has, since 1980, taken the lessons of history and the Holocaust seriously. But the 1950s in Atlanta was the rudest awakening of all, and in some ways, it was the most disappointing experience of our lives. Our illusions of what America was like were shattered by those people. They almost, but not quite, destroyed our dreams—and not for lack of trying.

The established Jewish community in Atlanta avoided interacting with us when we needed their help most. It seemed they just wanted us to vanish into thin air, not even in smoke, because of their own guilt and their leadership's guilt for remaining silent for six years while 6,000,000 died. Very few American Jews protested about the Holocaust in Washington during the war, with only one major protest at Madison Square Garden.

Like anything else, if a person wanted to know and cared, he did. If not, not. It was our cherished Mrs. Marks and the Meyers who saved us from the bitterness most of the Atlanta community injected into our lives.

Of course, there were exceptions. They were rare, but they existed, and that is why I cherish them. I can point to instances where people opened their arms, hearts, and homes, receiving Leon and me totally and fully. One such person was Charlie Kessler who, when we first met him, must have been in his late thirties. He was a bachelor and lived with his elderly mother because she needed someone to care for her.

A member of a well-to-do family that owned a number of department stores, Charlie was a soft-spoken, unassuming gentleman who was knowledgeable about many subjects. Because a childhood disease left his face badly scarred, his prestigious, "classy" family turned him into an outsider because of his looks, avoiding him but assigning him full responsibility to care for his aging mother. He was a kind and good man with a heart of gold and the soul of an angel. I slowly learned over the next few years the kind of man he was. My brother and I spent many happy hours with Charlie, listening to him as he explained the history of southern traditions. During weekends, we went on picnics and made short trips to nearby places, and we soon learned that the goodness he displayed toward us was not an isolated case of kindness.

We understood that this tranquil man, in his quiet and un-obtrusive way, was a Godsend to those in need. Silently, he offered assistance to people without them ever knowing it. Whenever we went out with him, we would make a few stops on the way to our destination to assist sick people, to bring them food, or books, or medicine, or just a few moments of human contact with the outside world.

One time he brought a television set to a paralyzed man and mounted it high up on the wall, attaching a remote control to it so the man could operate the set himself. In the early 1950s, this was quite an achievement. I came back to Atlanta many years later to visit him and was mortified to learn that he had just died. I wanted to get more details and went to see his brother, whom I'd met briefly years before. His brother remembered me and knew I had been Charlie's good friend. He invited me to sit and proceeded to ask me a rhetorical question. "How could I not know who my brother Charlie was?" He went on to tell me that Charlie's funeral was one of the largest Atlanta had ever seen. Hundreds of people whose lives Charlie had touched and whom he had helped in some way showed up to pay their respects. The family was stunned.

At the services, people came up to his brother and told him moving stories describing in detail Charlie's voluminous good deeds. It truly saddened him that it was only after his death, after seeing the outpouring of esteem from the people at his funeral, and in looking over his papers that he realized who Charlie really was. I could only respond by saying that though I knew Charlie pretty well and had been privy to many of his good deeds, I, too, had not been fully aware of the extent of his compassion and generosity. In the meantime, though, Charlie was there for the two of us, and encouraged us to keep on going.

To earn some spending money while attending school, my brother and I decided to find part-time jobs, since we had no income of our own other than the small allowance provided by the Hebrew Orphan's Home. Through a friend of ours, we were able to obtain part-time positions in a department store, working Friday afternoon and all day Saturday. Our duties consisted of doing just about anything and everything: bringing in the stock from the warehouse, straightening out and displaying the merchandise, and selling the items to customers.

After working for about a month, the time came to pick up our first paychecks. I was very excited because it was my first paycheck in America, or anywhere for that matter. But the amount on our checks caught me totally by surprise—almost half of what we expected. It was 40 percent less than what other people in the same category were receiving.

Since we knew we were performing just as well, if not better, than the other workers, we asked the owner why there was such a discrepancy in the wages. I will never forget his "good natured" reply when he declared that, after all, Leon and I were just greenhorns, and when he first came to the United States, he had worked for $.50 a day. It would take time, he said, for us to earn the right to make as much as the other workers.

I did not agree with his logic and the following week Leon and I told him thank you, but no thank you—that we were leaving his employ. This experience was really painful. A Jewish store owner who was familiar with our background and knew the hardships we had endured during the war, had tried to take advantage of our situation.

We pounded the pavement some more and found part-time jobs selling shoes in the Kinney shoestore chain. We worked Friday afternoons, Saturdays, and holidays, since these were the busiest times in the store. We worked on commission and were not subjected to any forms of discrimination regarding our salary, our origins, even our strange accents. In fact, we made more money than our colleagues did.

Aside from the small indignities foisted upon us by some of our fellow Jews, for the most part, life in Atlanta was serene. I thought often of my sister, Renia, still in Sweden. Lonely after Dasza's death, she at first thought of joining us in America. It was complicated, though, because there was no one who could send an affidavit for her application. As students, Leon and I were not capable of supporting ourselves and could not show that we could support her as well. But then she met someone and married, and they decided to remain in Malmo.

In the meantime, I became a freshman at Emory University. In the late 1940s, Emory University was a relatively small college attended primarily by students from affluent families. Blacks were not admitted. The school was located in an exclusive part of the city, surrounded by beautiful trees and walkways. Almost all the students had their own cars, and since I obviously couldn't afford one, my lack of mobility had a negative effect on my social life, particularly since I was still living at home. Since I couldn't drive to social events on campus, I had a problem making friends. Besides an occasional game of volleyball, it was hard to participate in extra-curricular activities. Without a car, it was impossible to even consider dating anyone. Guys had to pick up their dates and bring them home to their front doors. There was no option. Using public transportation on a date was unacceptable; it was like suffering from the plague.

The Meyer Clan "newcomer" get-togethers were our saving grace. But Leon and I knew it was just a question of time before we would have to come up with a way to buy a car. It was definitely in our near future, we just had to figure out how to do it. We were inspired by a native Atlantan, the only teenaged Southerner who drifted toward our little group. He taught us how to drive, which enabled us to get our permits and licenses. Once we'd learned the art of driving, the incentive was there to purchase a vehicle of our own.

We knew the Hebrew Orphan's Home was subsidizing the cost of our education, and that they would not buy us a car or even allow us to purchase one. In their minds, for a greenhorn a car was a luxury—though they understood the necessity of having a car in their own lives. As time passed, Leon and I were more and more convinced that having our own automobile was the key to the freedom that we lacked. We put on our thinking caps and concentrated on how to arrange putting a car at our disposal. Our good friend, Dr. Ray Perlin, supplied the solution to our dilemma.

Dr. Perlin and his wife, Lee, were among the few who made us feel welcome in Atlanta. Dr. Perlin was a brilliant mathematician, a professor at Georgia Tech, and one of the first scientists involved with computers. We met the Perlins quite by accident, but immediately developed a strong bond with them.

The Perlins' house became our second home. Leon and I spent many pleasant evenings having dinner with them and talking and playing cards until the wee hours of the morning. We'd saved a few dollars by working at Kinney's, so Dr. Perlin proposed to purchase a car in his name for our use. Without our knowledge, he even added some of his own money to ours to make the purchase possible.

It was a perfect arrangement. We did not expect, nor did we buy a Cadillac. In fact, we bought an old green, beat-up Plymouth that had no heater, because the used car salesman convinced us that a heater was unnecessary in the South. We didn't know any better. What more could we have asked for beyond four wheels and a motor?

Now about that unnecessary heater. We sorely missed it on the road trip we took on a Christmastime vacation to Canada. A nasty snowstorm turned the window into an opaque sheet of ice. Alas, the importance of having a heater and defroster struck us too late. Being, of course, *tzeleygers* (wiseguys), this wouldn't stop us from going forward. We improvised by sticking six candles on the dashboard. The flickering flames from each candle melted the ice in six little circles. In this way, partially blind, we pushed forward. It was stupid I know, but we were crazy and invincible.

The big advantage in having a car was being able to participate in the rage of the day—the drive-in movie. For young folks, the drive-in had little or nothing to do with the double feature on the screen, though lots of families with little kids did take advantage of the single admission price per carload of kids.

For most teenagers, going to the drive-in was for necking. Leon and I didn't go for that, we went for the family rates because we would pack as many as ten young "greenhorns" into the car to go see the latest blockbuster for the price of a single ticket. Of course, having a car did allow us some romance, depending, of course, on the young lady we were with.

Though Leon and I weren't BMOCs (Big Men on Campus—people who made themselves known to the college community by their efforts on the football field, or other extra-curricular activities), our professors seemed to know who we were. First of all, for some reason, all North Americans who came down South were thought of as foreigners once they crossed the Mason-Dixon Line. Since Leon and I came all the way from Europe and had these strange accents, most people treated us like aliens from outer space. In a way, we were. We'd come from Planet Auschwitz, after all.

Our professors, unlike most of the people in Atlanta, asked about the "life experience credits" we had earned there, and perhaps they understood more than the others and respected us for it. They even called us by our first names. Being good students didn't hurt our reputations, either. I distinctly remember my English professor once teasing me when I told him I wanted to polish my English, and he cracked back, "What for? You've got the best Polish-English I ever heard."

However, the attention of our professors was not always a good thing. I once fell asleep during a lecture on organic chemistry and when I woke up, asked a question on material the professor had already explained. He patiently answered the question and then asked me if I had enjoyed my nap. Boy, were my ears red!

Those were the quiet years on American college campuses, and Emory was no different. Everything was tranquil and stable, and the time soon came for us to choose our major courses of study. Leon wanted to go into medicine, but I decided that being a doctor or dentist was not for me because I couldn't stand the sight of blood. The idea that I might have to operate on a human being was inconceivable to me, so I ended up in the liberal arts curriculum. Besides, deciding to go for medicine only made life more difficult in Atlanta, because there were quotas for Jewish students in those days, and the fancy Atlanta Jewish community had a lock on who could make use of those one or two precious spots at the medical school.

Leon was Phi Beta Kappa and had all of the necessary qualifications to be admitted into Emory Medical School with flying colors, but he was not accepted. In a small community, secrets are tough to keep, and it wasn't long after he was rejected that the "why" of it came to us via the grapevine.

It turned out that although his credentials were impeccable, the local Jewish doctors in Atlanta decided he should not be allowed to attend medical school in the area because he was a foreigner, a greenhorn, and had no right to take up space that, by self-declared birthright, belonged to the native Jews of Atlanta. Despite the local doctors' successful efforts to prevent his entry into Emory Medical School in Atlanta, Leon was accepted to a number of fine medical schools and chose to attend Tulane University Medical School in New Orleans. Truly, except for the Meyers, Mrs. Marks, Charlie Kessler, the Perlins, and a handful of others, the Jews of Atlanta in the 1950s made a very negative impression on me.

Though I decided (and luckily, too) that medicine was not my metier, I was still eager to continue my studies at Emory. I strongly believed in the importance of education and I never forgot how Tatush emphatically stressed the point: "Money you can lose, but education you always keep." Thus I continued at Emory and took humanities courses.

Seventeen
My Brother Leon

"My buddy, my brother, my cohort in crime, my inspiration, my hope, and my best friend."

My brother, Leon, meant so much more to me than a brother ever could. I have said that we were close from the time we were in the ghetto, and stuck together from the moment Mamma left us in Auschwitz. We watched each other's backs, we held each other up, we supported each other spiritually and physically, and we kept each other alive in the darkness of the Holocaust. We were partners in survival.

My first memories of Leon go way back to when we were still toddlers in Lodz, living in the apartment, doing target practice in the halls, and driving Mamma crazy with the bike in the dining room. The two of us formed an alliance against our two sets of "enemies": our parents and our sisters. Of course, occasionally we did side with our sisters against our common enemy—our parents—but we never lost sight of our priorities.

If we were at home, in the streets, anywhere but school, we were always on the same side. Leon and I were always united, even when it came to getting into mischief, either at home or at father's factory. During the summers in Podębie, it was also us against them—the two brothers against the two sisters. In school, though, we led completely separate lives—we had different schoolmates, friends, and activities.

Dasza's and Renia's friends were fair game, and Leon and I, again in unison, targeted them for all kinds of pranks and mayhem. Interestingly enough, our main ally in separating the girls from the boys was Tatush, who made distinctions between his daughters and sons and stuck to a double standard that today would be ripped to shreds by my daughter Susan—who would recognize them for the sexist attitudes they were.

The complaints of my sisters still ring in my ears when they cried out to our father, "You always allow the boys to do whatever they want and you give them everything!"

I must admit that my sisters were not altogether wrong. Our father did bend the rules. He did stress, "Boys are boys and girls are girls," and imposed two sets of rules in guiding our behavior. No wonder some of my father's philosophy rubbed off on Leon and me.

(In later years, Susan complained to me about the very same thing, but her complaints to me were more vocal than my sisters' were. Of course, as far as I am concerned, Susan's viewpoint comes from the Women's Lib movement. And I readily admit that I have as yet to adjust to the results of that. All I know is that Susan's constant grumbling about how I allowed Jeffrey to do things I stopped her from doing was almost identical to my sisters' complaints to Tatush.)

Yes, the war had turned Leon and me into partners for survival, but I believe it happened gradually, without either of us realizing how there was a constant strengthening of the bonds between us. It began when we cultivated the vegetables to sustain the family in the ghetto and took risks to smuggle in wood to keep the family warm. The deportation and our existence in the camps tightened those bonds further, and we valued and cared one for the other beyond anything on Earth.

Not caring about the dire consequences if we got caught, the two of us did whatever had to be done to stay together. Time and time again we risked our lives by changing our names or prison numbers. We shared our food, our clothing, our fears, and our hopes. The dream of being back home again with the entire family is what kept us going, and we reinforced each other. On the coldest days we held onto each other for warmth, and at night we shared our restless sleep.

In Flossenburg, we hid among the Gentiles, walked the death march to Dachau, and then were finally liberated by the United States Army. It was Leon who kept me going that last day, when the tank appeared over the rise in the road. The closeness we shared helped us to withstand the unbelievable hardships we faced each and every day. Together we lived through the agony of the Holocaust and together we lived through the ecstasy of liberation. We never allowed ourselves to think that we would not get through it. We gave each other the courage to endure. I believe that it worked because we eliminated the word "I" in our vocabulary and used the word "we" instead—in our words, thoughts, and deeds.

When it was over, together we crossed an ocean to start new lives in a new country, first in New York and then in Atlanta. Together, we went to Henry Grady High School, and then to Emory University. When we took our finals, he and I both made the same mistakes on exams. Although we were among others, our real family consisted only of us. Everyone, except Renia in Sweden, was gone.

We socialized together at the "Greenhorn Club," where Leon met his wife, Hanki—bright, brilliant, and so bubbly and extroverted, the opposite of Leon. She, too, was an "Official U.S. Government Orphan," and ended up in Atlanta.

When I stayed in Atlanta to pursue a business career and Leon took off for Tulane for medical school, it was the first time we were really separated. I thought that when I left school, we would still be living together at Mrs. Marks's and I would see him on weekends and evenings. But things didn't turn out that way. After all the years spent together facing the most mind-boggling trials and tribulations, the time had now come for us to separate and live apart. This was quite an adjustment for each of us. Mentally, I knew that it had to happen, since Leon was already in medical school and I was on the road a lot for business. Emotionally, however, I was not prepared for it.

Understandably, the first year at medical school was particularly difficult for Leon. Coping with the complexities of his studies proved strenuous for him, especially when he had to dissect cadavers. Working with corpses brought back many painful memories he wanted desperately to forget. Many times he wanted to quit and return to Atlanta, but we both knew that his first year would be the hardest. Having seen so much death and suffering in the concentration camps, it was difficult for him to be exposed to traumatic things again, though he well understood the distinction between helping and hurting people.

During this period of adjustment, our good friend, Dr. Perlin, spent hours at a time with him on the phone to convince him to stick with it and continue his studies. So did I. At one point, I flew to New Orleans to give him moral support, and Leon being Leon, he did eventually adjust and went forward. We were both in our early twenties by then.

Leon, at that time, was still living a bachelor's life, and I visited him as often as possible. He was an excellent guide and showed me all of New Orleans' sights and nightlife. I absorbed the jazz and blues that are the city's soul like a sponge, especially during Mardi Gras, when I always tried to visit.

Still, Leon wasn't really cut out for life in the fast lane and tired of being a bachelor. He soon married his sweetheart, Hanki. They were a wonderful couple, sharing a common background and similar interests. After marriage, Leon's quality of life seemed to improve. I attribute this to the positive influence of Hanki, who, with her sunny disposition and smile, was completely devoted to him.

In medical school, the newlyweds made new friends, some married and some not. And though things may have been tough financially, they always knew how to have a good time and enjoyed life to its fullest. There was no longer any talk about leaving school, and the hot topic of the moment became which medical specialty Leon ought to pursue.

Somehow the four years they spent at Tulane flew by quickly, and it was suddenly time for them to decide where Leon should do his internship.

I was living in New York City at the time and they factored that into the decision-making process. After reviewing their options, Leon and Hanki chose an internship at Kings County Hospital, in Brooklyn, New York. (Today it is called Downstate Medical Center and is part of the State University system.) I know that choosing New York was difficult. New York was, and still is, a tough place to live if you have to count pennies, but it was Leon's desire for all of us to be together that motivated him. Frankly, I was thrilled.

Leon and Hanki rented a small two-bedroom apartment close to the hospital—the extra room was for me. Leon's hours at the hospital were brutal, and sometimes he needed to work seventy-two-hour shifts, especially on weekends when he was operating in the emergency room. He and all the other interns were under a great deal of stress, and Leon was completely exhausted almost all the time.

When Leon's internship at Kings County ended, his exemption from military service did, too, so he enlisted in the Air Force. As a full-fledged doctor, he was given the rank of Captain and sent to Texarkana Air Force Base in Texas. During those two years, Hanki and Leon really lived it up and deserved to. After all those years spent studying and then interning for the princely sum of $50 a month, life in the Air Force was paradise.

I visited them in Texas on several occasions and saw the carefree lifestyle they enjoyed. Their quarters at the Air Force base were luxurious compared to the apartments in New Orleans and Brooklyn. They had their own home, a country-club atmosphere, and membership in the officer's club. They were afforded all the perks extended to officers, and at the end of the work day, had a terrific social life at the club and at home with the other officers and their wives.

While Leon's life had changed, in some ways he had not. This was evident to me after I heard a new story about Leon the Reckless. He still loved to take risks, like when he'd stand between the railroad cars in Europe, half-asleep. Now he was water skiing with friends, but he didn't know how to swim. The standard joke among his friends was that as a precaution, he was using two life preservers instead of one. Sure enough, one day he fell while water skiing and both of his life preservers failed him. He started to drown. Immediately, all of his buddies dove into the water to rescue him and, luckily, they were successful. Did this ever stop Leon from water skiing again? Of course not!

After a life in the Air Force, it was back to the real world. Leon returned to the grind—studying neurosurgery at the University of California in San Francisco. Those four years were quite difficult for him, but with dedication, perseverance, and a loving Hanki and two toddlers to inspire him, he succeeded with flying colors.

With the final phase of his education drawing to a close, the time came for making the big decision. Where would he settle and start his practice? We arrived at the conclusion that it would be nice if we could live close by each other somewhere in the New York area. I was very happy when I heard that a neurosurgeon in Long Island offered Leon a position to join his practice. But this proved too good to be true.

There were very few neurosurgeons on Long Island during the early 1960s, and it came to Leon's attention that one of them did not take kindly to the idea that another one might be moving into the vicinity. This surgeon wrote a detailed letter strongly stating that there was no need for more physicians because the number of doctors was more than adequate to handle patients, even during major Jewish and Christian holidays. He suggested that a system be set up so physicians could easily cover for each other to ensure that patients would not be left untreated. He also recommended that local hospitals withhold privileges from any new neurosurgeons.

The fact that this was completely against the law and was in restraint of trade meant absolutely nothing to this paragon of virtue. Leon decided that the prospective years-long battle for hospital privileges would not be worth it. Thus, the other neurosurgeon won and Leon and Hanki and their children left New York. Leon took a position as a neurosurgeon at the Kaiser-Permanente Hospital in Los Angeles.

I, married by then, stayed in New York. Now a continent divided us. Despite our wonderful life in America, with all its freedom and material benefits, it truly saddened me that our small family could not remain together. Leon and his family were out west and my wife Hannah's family had settled in Detroit. As time went by, I realized more and more that no matter how close one is to his family, unless you share daily trials and tribulations with each other, it is just not the same. The closeness slowly begins to dissipate with distance. That's because life is comprised of an unlimited multiplication of events, both large and small. Although you can still be good friends, the relationship is never quite the same without the daily sharing, and the children could never grow close because they hardly spent time together.

Leon and I were in constant touch, and through the years he eventually earned the position of Chief of Neurosurgery at Kaiser Permanente. He always demanded the best of himself and expected others to do nothing less. He was living life to the fullest, and took the time to enjoy sports like tennis and skiing. Small physical discomforts never prevented him from engaging in any strenuous, and even dangerous, activities, and he recklessly ignored any symptoms he suffered.

He cared for the health of others, but disregarded caring for his own. He, for example, had some pain in his abdomen, which he consistently ignored. As a result, one day, his appendix ruptured while he was performing surgery, and he needed to have emergency surgery of his own. When hospital personnel called his wife to say he was in the operating room, she was not concerned—it never dawned on her that Leon was the one being operated on—and she calmly responded to the news with the reply, "So what? He's in the operating room every day."

One winter, our families organized a skiing trip to Mammoth Mountain, California. We all looked forward to this get-together, and everything was fine except for one small problem. Remember the car with no defroster or heater? This time Leon was going to drive to our destination in a car that had no reverse gear. Although I wasn't aware of this "negligible" mechanical defect, we later found out that all of the hospital personnel knew about it. They noticed he always made it his business to find a parking space that did not require putting the car into reverse.

Typical Leon . . . he was fearless and could do anything . . . and never stopped to think of the consequences of embarking on a 300-mile trip through the snowy mountains without a reverse gear. He was adventurous to the point of recklessness, just as he had been in his youth. Yet, this stubborn quality was minor compared to the otherwise excellent qualities he possessed.

Fitting adjectives to describe Leon would be honest, forthright, outspoken, dependable, and brilliant. I always thought of him as being in complete control of any given situation, until one day, in 1971, when he was in his early 40s, he gave me some shocking news. "Roman," he said, "I have a maximum of two years to live."

I was stunned and could not believe my ears. I told him this could not possibly be true, and brought to his attention the fact that we had lived through the ghetto and concentration camps when there was virtually no chance of survival. I emphasized the point that we had made it then, he would surely make it now as well.

His reply still rings in my ears. He said, "Yes, you are right when you say that we made it when we didn't have much of a chance. But we had some chance. As minimal as it was, we still had some chance. Now, I have no chance. Whether I want to accept it or not, something is ticking inside of me, and I cannot stop it, no one can stop it, no matter what, no matter how much I try."

He had studied his own case meticulously and concluded that he had somewhere in the neighborhood of two years to live. At that time, and even now, there is no cure for some forms of cancer. He had cancer of the colon but, because he neglected the symptoms, it had already metastasized to his liver.

He said he might take 5 FU, a medication which indiscriminately killed off different cells, but after investigating the drug, he did not believe it could substantially increase his lifespan. In any event, he made the decision to try this treatment anyway, which he knew to be painful and uncomfortable and would diminish his quality of life.

He was correct. After each treatment, he was very sick for a couple of days and constantly questioned the benefits. He mentioned that there were other similar medications used in Russia and Japan, but both were unavailable in the United States, always raising the possibility that the negative side effects of either of these two other medications might not be as severe as the American medication he was taking.

I could act on that, perhaps I could make myself useful, I thought. I secured the Russian medication through my connections in the Romanian Commercial Office and the Japanese medication through my contacts there. Unfortunately, the side effects of both were similar to that of 5 FU.

To give himself every possible chance, Leon admitted himself to the City of Hope Hospital for surgery on his liver. I will never forget what he told me after studying the results of the operation. He said that statistically the surgery was a success because he survived it, but it hadn't lengthened his lifespan.

In cases like his, he told me, a surgeon cannot afford to be timid. In order to give the patient a chance to live, he must have a mind open to any type of radical operation. It is true that the patient might die on the operating table (instead of a few weeks later) and that statistics would not be too impressive, since the mortality rate would be high. But the individuals who do make it through will have the opportunity to lengthen their lives.

That was Leon—courageous and forthright, up until his untimely death at age forty-six. He left behind a wife and two young children. With his passing, I lost my family anchor in America, my buddy, my brother, my cohort in crime, my confidant, my inspiration, my hope, and my best friend. I had no choice but to accept his fate—still it was difficult.

Leon was gone and life for me without him has never been the same.

Eighteen
The Business World

"If you can make it there, you can make it anywhere!"—"New York, New York"

In 1949, Jack, one of the "members" of the gang we hung out with after the liberation and who had been with us in Flossenburg, contacted us in Atlanta and said he was headed for the States. He just wanted to visit his family for a few days, and then he wanted me and Leon to come pick him up in New York City and bring him and his new wife back with us to Atlanta.

I'd stayed in touch with Jack over the years and it appeared that our many discussions about the possibility of starting a business together was the main reason he wanted to come to Atlanta. Since I'd just decided to go into business instead of becoming a doctor or lawyer, the timing was right.

We hadn't been to New York for a few years, so Leon and I climbed into our old car and made the trip to fetch them. We spent a few days in The Big Apple happily enjoying the sights we'd seen when we first came to America. These jaunts included a visit to Caldwell Avenue in The Bronx and a visit with the Borensteins, who had followed our progress over the years and were always concerned about our well-being.

Then Jack and his wife gathered up the few belongings they'd brought with them from Europe, said good-bye to what was left of their families, and piled into the car with us to head for Atlanta.

Jack's arrival forced me to focus on how we needed to proceed if we were going to start a new business venture. I concluded that I had to give up my studies at Emory and concentrate on making a living. The third partner in this enterprise was Joe

Eisenman, another Flossenburg inmate, who would also have to drop out of college to get us off the ground.

Starting a business was not an easy matter. Except for a few dollars—and I mean literally a few dollars—we had zero capital and a dream. Our aim was to form an Import/Export company because as native Europeans we were interested in crossing borders, in being part of the entire world.

Those were our dreams. We had no background, no qualifications, no credentials. To meet our immediate needs for a fast source of revenue, we decided to become peddlers. I later learned that peddling was an American Jewish tradition that went all the way back to Colonial times in America, when the few Jews in the North and South who began trickling in from Europe after the Inquisition would pack general goods on their backs and walk from homestead to homestead selling and trading with the Native Americans and the Colonists. (The oldest extant house in America, built in 1713, was built as a trading post in Newburgh, NY. They used to call the place, "Gomez the Jew's House on Jew's Creek." It's still there!)

By the time the 19th century rolled around, Jews were criss-crossing the countryside in horse-drawn wagons, peddling their wares. Homesteaders, pioneers, farmers, and townsfolk would eagerly await the peddler who announced his arrival with jangling bells, carrying his pots and pans, fabrics and needles, notions, long johns, soaps and candles, and all the little luxuries you couldn't make yourself that could ease your life a bit.

In the 1950s, peddling was pretty much the same as it had been for centuries, except instead of a horse and wagon, you used a car—and the quality of your inventory was better. Also by the 1950s, people were less apt to be selling snake oil. One thing had not changed at all. In Colonial times and in the 1950s, you still needed money to get you on the road. What we needed was someone to extend us some credit so that we could stock up and get moving. We ended up making a deal with the owner of a department store in a poor neighborhood who agreed to advance us merchandise on consignment.

We happily accepted his offer. At first, he selected the goods and we had no input, but that wasn't much of a problem because he carried low-end items and our route went through rural areas where there wasn't much money.

Our inventory consisted essentially of women's wear—dresses and separates, and we did fairly well. As we expanded the route, and because we focused on satisfying our customers, we earned enough to buy a second car. As time went on, our clients asked us for other items. Before we knew it, we were paying our living expenses and starting to build capital.

Peddling literally opened up a whole new world. I traveled to outlying suburbs, where in the small villages and rural communities I met different kinds of people I never would have encountered by maintaining a static life or playing by conventional rules. Most of my customers were black women who had large families, and whose men, most of them laborers, were out at work in the fields, the factories, or on the roads. I slowly established fixed routes in rural Georgia, and I witnessed what life was like for the poorest, most neglected people in America.

I'd seen the hollow affluence of Atlanta and what the hard-working white middle-class life was like in that same city. I saw how the people who helped build this country as slaves were living in abject poverty. Their homes were mostly sub-standard shacks, jammed with children, with no running water or indoor plumbing. They reminded me of the "apartments" in the Lodz ghetto.

Though privation and penury prevailed, it always surprised me that I was invariably greeted with big smiles and warm welcomes. The older children would surround me when I arrived, and the younger ones held on to their mothers' skirts. I often heard them happily exclaim, "The Jewman is coming," as they spilled into the road to greet me.

I was taken aback the first couple of times I heard "Jewman," but I soon realized that the phrase wasn't meant to be insulting at all. It was rather an expression of joy at my arrival. To these wonderful women, the "Jewman" was the person who brought them the goods they had been looking for. One thing is certain, whenever I arrived and interrupted their humdrum lives it was a "special event." Everyone would crowd around and advise my "clients" about what looked good and what didn't, and everyone wanted to be part of the marketplace atmosphere that infused the village whenever I showed up.

Most of these women scraped for every penny, and so could rarely pay the full amount. They would put some money down, and I arranged weekly payment plans for most of them, so that they could buy what they needed and pay off their debts over time.

Looking back, it amazes me that I never had to run a credit check on any of those ladies. When those women gave their word, their word was their bond, and that was all the credit rating I needed. I relied on their honesty, and they were true to their word. There were times someone would have to miss a payment, and they would be terribly embarrassed when they had to tell me.

Whenever I opened my car doors to display the "merch," I never worried about things getting stolen. I was dealing with honorable people. I could leave the car to chat with neighbors, and when I returned, nothing would ever be missing. Think of the metal detectors, security guards, and shoplifting sensors we need to protect the merchandise in today's department stores. Times have certainly changed. And peddlers have been replaced by Wal-Marts.

As I learned more about the black community in the Deep South, it became clear to me that the crippling poverty was only one facet of the plague affecting their lives. They weren't getting a formal education of any sort, and nothing of much worth was available to them. There was also no incentive for achievement. Most of the mothers I dealt with never encouraged their children to do book learning. They couldn't read, and there were, therefore, no books in their homes. To me, spoiled as I was by my parents' insistence on getting an education and understanding its value, this was hard to accept.

I was convinced then—and I haven't changed my mind since—that unless parents, especially in poverty-stricken areas, begin to instill in their children a thirst for knowledge, yes, for book learning, their children, no matter their ethnicity or race, will be doomed to poverty, and that poverty, will be transmitted from generation to generation. I understood poverty, I understood hunger, but the apathy and disinterest regarding education was totally incomprehensible to me.

Before long, the peddling business generated enough income to rent a small office and start importing assorted giftware from the Far East, mostly Japan. We used the space we had from our peddling business as a warehouse.

I was thrilled to be doing this business and doing fairly well for a start up, but I missed Leon, and it felt strange to be so completely on my own without him. In the meantime, doing Import/Export business in Atlanta was not all that simple. We needed a solid relationship with a bank in order to obtain Letters of Credit so that the foreign suppliers could get paid. In Atlanta, a city that despised greenhorns, that was not an easy thing to do. The bankers were hardly eager to deal with three young aliens who had strange accents.

To our dismay, the banks in town wanted full collateral for the required Letters of Credit—when we could even find a bank that knew what a Letter of Credit was and how to write one. We had to shell out cold cash for each Letter of Credit, due and payable a few months down the road. It was a hell of a way to do business.

It didn't take long for the few banks we did do business with to see that we were living up to our obligations. Slowly, very slowly, they relaxed the rigid requirements they had first imposed. Later we found out their rigidity was based on ignorance. For example, they wanted to know how they would be compensated for the merchandise if the boat sank and the insurance company insuring the goods went broke. I told them not to worry . . . "If the insurance companies go broke, everyone goes broke!"

As the import business grew, we cut back on peddling until we discontinued it completely. We were now in business and needed to come up with a name for the enterprise. We proudly selected a cumbersome and localized name, The Southeast Import/Export Company, and tried to figure out how to sell the Japanese goods that were on the way to Atlanta.

First we selected an attractive sampling of gift items from the inventory we chose, and asked the Japanese manufacturers to send us sample kits via airmail so they would arrive before the merchandise did. Then we loaded our two old trusty, rusty cars with the samples and searched around for clientele.

At first we canvassed the gift shops and small department stores in Atlanta, then gradually spread throughout Georgia. Then, as indicated in our grandiose corporate name, we expanded throughout the Southeast and worked frantically to get it off the ground. To economize, we did everything ourselves—unpacking the incoming merchandise (some came in large wooden crates), packaging it, selling it, and shipping it.

The paperwork, unpacking, and repacking we did in the evenings and on weekends. Our weekdays were devoted exclusively to sales. In time, we went from selling to the small shops to selling to wholesalers and large department stores. To our delight, we were no longer just a local, Atlanta-based company—our company covered the whole Southeast.

There is hardly a city in the Southeast area that I did not visit, and I had customers in almost every one. Athens, Augusta, Savannah, Charleston, Birmingham, Tuscaloosa, Mobile, Chattanooga, Nashville, Charlottesville, I knew them all, and they were very different from the rural areas where I had been a peddler. We hired staff for the office and the warehouse and soon needed more space, so we moved to larger quarters.

Soon we grew more and more impatient as we realized the financial limitations imposed on us by the banks and larger companies in Atlanta. They still didn't trust us enough to give us the credit we needed. We were still "greenhorns" no matter how hard we proved ourselves, so we looked to the North, to New York City, where we felt our banking needs would be better met.

The banks paid more attention when we added Michael [Gold], another Holocaust survivor in Atlanta, to the team. He infused our business with some additional cash. In relative terms, it wasn't much, but when you have nothing, a five-figure sum is worth a million dollars. With the added capital, we increased our rate of expansion rapidly.

Slowly, I familiarized myself with the major cities throughout the southeastern part of the United States. Our customer base was expanding, and before long we were shipping merchandise to Alabama, Tennessee, North and South Carolina, Louisiana, and Florida. For all intents and purposes, I was becoming "Americanized," learning about diverse customs and how different life was in various parts of the nation. It was nothing like Europe. Here, I could travel hundreds of miles and still be in the same country.

In most instances, I found that people had a certain curiosity about me. My accent was very different from the southern drawl one expected to hear from a person coming from Atlanta, Georgia. So when people asked me where I came from, it broke the ice, and some of my business prospects became my friends. Many were eager to learn about my life in Europe and why and how I had come to the States. In turn, they enabled me to understand the real meaning of Southern hospitality—one that put Atlanta's social graces to shame.

As the business grew, we learned that to attract larger customers and sell a substantial quantity of goods, it would be necessary for us to have a New York address. Buyers from the larger companies were fond of coming to New York to visit the showrooms and see the sights at the same time—nightlife, Broadway, the big city. We concluded that we had these big boys in our sights, but we could only nail them if we had a New York City address smack in the middle of the gift center.

We made a few trips to New York to investigate, and even tried to sell some merchandise to see whether it would be feasible to relocate our office in its entirety. The ultimate aim was to sell our goods from North to South. East to West came later. We didn't do too badly and decided to make the move, but to do it piecemeal. Joe and I would go to New York, get a small office and a warehouse, and establish an address. We could save shipping costs by sending out the Northern orders from the New York warehouse. If that worked well, then we would move the entire operation up North.

We were ready to hit the big time in The Big Apple.

Nineteen
Big Business in The Big Apple

"New York banks didn't care who your parents were or where you came from; just show 'em bank balances, business history, and projected revenues!"

Real life in the big city in the mid-'50s was no picnic. I had lots of adjusting to do, and the first thing I noticed was that New Yorkers don't smile unless they have a reason to. They had an attitude that was diametrically opposed to Atlantans. Mrs. Marks, my sweet Mrs. Marks, wasn't there to greet me every morning with a hearty breakfast, an encouraging word, and lots of motherly love. I was now on my own, fending for myself in the single room I rented on the Upper West Side.

New York, however, had its share of compensations. I would never go hungry as long as I had some money in my pocket. With all the restaurants to choose from, I could eat when I wanted, where I wanted. The choices I had were limitless, from the cheapest fare to the most outrageous prices in the world. (A regular hamburger at The 21 Club was over $25.00! Or you could get two delicious hot dogs and a drink at Gray's Papaya for a dollar.) While I hadn't quite developed a Southern drawl, I had developed a taste for Southern-fried chicken, spare ribs, hush puppies, and grits.

In Atlanta, my accent marked me as a stranger in a strange land and was a handy sales tool. In New York, no one even noticed it and cared even less where I came from. Compared to the leisurely pace of life in the South, New York was a bullet train. The niceties of life that so ruled social discourse in the South were simply a waste of time to New Yorkers. There were things to do, people to see, and you had to keep on moving, while time and money flew by. I had to change my modus operandi to deal with the brusque way people handled themselves. Happily, when the business began to grow, the social skills I learned down South played a major role in my success as a salesman.

Our office was on Fifth Avenue and 19th Street (Fifth is where East meets West), and when I wasn't on the road, it was where you could find me, even on weekends. Joe and I were dedicated and determined to make it work. We succeeded. Mike and Jack shipped everything up to New York.

In no time, the space on 19th Street became too small, so we moved to Fifth and 23rd Street and began to look for mega-customers. Our inventory consisted of giftware, dinnerware, and housewares, all imported from the Far East. We were on a roll and outgrew the new office in no time. We were moving up, in more ways than one. But Michael was having problems adjusting to the fast pace of city life and wanted to go back to Atlanta. Though we were sorry to see him go and needed every cent of capital, we managed to scramble and buy him out.

We were still a small company, but somehow already belonged to the new breed of entrepreneurs. We made decisions rapidly and conducted business according to prevailing trends. We found our niche with catalogue houses, like Sears Roebuck and Montgomery Ward. Most farmers across America in those days used to own two books—*The Sears Roebuck Catalogue* and the *Farmer's Almanac.* We also did very well with stamp catalogue businesses like S&H Green Stamps and Top Value, which no longer exist. Today, the stamp craze is long gone, and Sears belongs to K-Mart.

In those days, American housewives were in love with collecting those stamps, enjoyed licking them, filling up their little books, and redeeming them for the "free" merchandise of their choice. We became a major supplier of certain items to a number of stamp houses, which was a huge boon to our business. To our good fortune, it was a quiet boon, and thus did not encourage much competition. Only a few wholesalers seemed to realize the potential of the market.

The catalogue and stamp business also gave us the stability that we could not have achieved if we'd sold solely to department stores and to other highly competitive, overcrowded markets.

The catalogue houses needed reliable sources. Once they featured an item, they needed their deliveries in a timely manner. If a supplier could get that done, additional business was almost always assured.

We loved it. Once we'd placed an item in one of the catalogues, you could count on continued business for years to come. As long as the item moved, the merchandise was featured in the catalogue and we could order large quantities in advance. This saved time on making sales and gave us more time to investigate and develop new products. As a result of this business, we learned that hi-fashion and trendy items didn't do too well because they required frequent changing and updating, and so we concentrated on developing a conservative, staid line for the mass market.

As we grew, we decided to add textiles to the inventory and looked to Europe, an excellent source for fabric items. The center of the fabric trade in Europe was in Lodz, Poland, my old hometown. Since most importers were concentrating on goods from the Far East, in the 1960s and '70s Eastern Europe was virgin territory. We were going to conquer it. This meant going back to Poland for the first time since the war, and I was shocked when I got to Lodz. I walked through the city, which in my child's mind had been a huge and glorious metropolis. After London and Paris, after seeing major cities around the world, coming back to Lodz was an almost shattering experience. It was tiny, minuscule, and I wondered at how a child's mind plays tricks on memories.

I looked for familiar places, but many street names had changed and buildings I thought were big were really small. The cherished visions of the home sweet home of my childhood dissolved. The city I had loved as a child was now dilapidated. The most depressing sight for me was my father's factory, which was reduced to a pile of rubble. Now I had only dimming memories. And ironically, I was in Poland on textile business and I knew virtually nothing about textiles because all I had done in Tatush's factory was play around!

In Poland we looked for someone who could manufacture the most basic, simple dry goods—namely sheets and pillowcases.

We sold the linens primarily to supply houses servicing hotels and hospitals, and were soon asked to supply them with hospital gowns as well. This did not pose a problem, since the fabric was the same and they would be easy to manufacture. Originally, the hospital gowns were cut in three sizes: small, medium, and large. To keep costs down and simplify the manufacturing and inventory procedures, I decided that we needed to make garments "one-size-fits-all." Everyone else in the trade adopted the idea as well. So the next time you are, God forbid, in a hospital and that "one-size-fits all" gown leaves some body parts hanging out, I am the one to blame.

It didn't take us long to figure out that there was more volume in selling bed linens and other textiles than there was in giftware and household items. The thrust of our expansion became textiles, and we discovered that sweatshirts and warm-up suits were hot items for the American market. We bought samples of American sweatshirts and took them to our Polish manufacturers to "knock off" (copy). The Americans couldn't make them fast enough and their prices were going through the roof.

There was no word for sweatshirt in Polish, and the mills and garment factories had never made single- or double-knit cotton fleeced garments. If we were going to speak a common language with the Poles about something that we were going to order in vast quantities, then we needed a word to describe the product immediately. Thus the new Polish word, sweatshirty, was coined. We had given the Poles a new product and the word to go with it.

For some reason our European sweatshirts did much better for us than the sweats made in the Far East—the quality was better and we could sell them at the same price points. In fact, they were an immediate hit, and that was probably because they were non-gender specific, meaning men and women could both wear them, and so could all the kids in the house. They were comfortable, casual, and easy to care for. And they appealed to the masses. Even today, sweats rule!

Since the garments from the Far East compromised on quality, we didn't want to work with manufacturers there. We bought high-quality goods at reasonable prices from Poland. And there was a psychological hook on these sales, too: the intrinsic value of European merchandise was more meaningful to the public than items manufactured in Taiwan, Korea, and other Far Eastern countries.

We sold our European sweats to Woolworth's, W.T. Grant, K-Mart, and some of the larger upscale department stores, like Macy's [before the megamergers], Gimbels, and Lord & Taylor. In reality, whether our sweats were in Lord & Taylor or in Woolworth's, the merchandise in all of these stores was the same. The only difference was the label, and, of course, the price.

Our business exploded. But again, we needed additional capital. We decided against investors because they would want to become partners and cut a big chunk out of our profits, so we tried the banks of New York, which were very different from the banks in Atlanta.

When one applied for a loan in a New York bank, they didn't care who your parents were, how many relatives you had in the area, or where you came from. They wanted to see your bank balances, they wanted to determine the history of your business, they wanted to see your business plan and your projected revenues over a specified period of time. Of course, personality and trustworthiness of the applicants mattered too, but in New York, they were serious about business. We had a good record, a good credit rating, and a good reputation. We got what we needed in order to expand.

In the beginning, it was necessary for us to travel to Europe frequently. I made a few trips to Poland and Romania, another country well known for its textiles, each year. When we finally opened offices there, I was able to keep my trips down to two a year.

In spite of the fact that Poland and Romania were both in the Soviet Bloc, they did business differently, and we used those differences to our advantage. It was never easy dealing with the communists in any of these countries, but some were worse than others, and unless you were flexible and willing to go with the flow, conducting business with them could be impossible. At the time, we were one of very few American companies willing and able to do so, but we had the patience and the know-how to make it work for us.

The main source of our problems was that we were not permitted to deal directly with the manufacturers. We had to go through a Central Office and talk with bureaucrats. If you didn't work with them, there were no deals to be made. These bureaucrats knew nothing at all about business, manufacturing, pricing, or marketing. They knew they had to write reports to their superiors, and they had to make money. They cared little for production specifications, therefore we had to go directly to the factory people so we could tell them what we needed. To make things work, you had to walk the tightrope between them. You had to deal with the Director of the Agency and see if you could be allowed to talk face to face with the director of the factory, so that you wouldn't end up with a product you couldn't give away. If the Director of the Agency didn't like you, you didn't do business at all.

In Poland, the quality of the fabric and the work was fine—it was the quality of the "notions" they were using that put our venture at risk. The buttons, the zippers, and the trimmings were so inferior they were unacceptable to the American market. What we needed to do was ship the notions from America to Poland, and that meant setting up an office in Eastern Europe. In time, we became the largest American exporter of zippers to Poland and Romania.

I fondly recall my meetings at those factories. I was greeted cordially, probably because everyone knew I was a major source of American cigarettes and they smoked like chimneys (some things had not changed since 1945). After a two-hour meeting with these fellows, you could cut the smoke in the room with a knife, and your lungs felt like you had spent a year in a coal mine.

I remember meeting the new director of one Romanian textile factory very vividly. Our company representative introduced me as Mr. Roman Kent from the United States, and at that point, I would have pulled out my business card. Instead, I pulled out a carton of Kent cigarettes and handed it to him. He looked at the cigarettes, then looked at me and said with a smile, "Thank you very much, Mr. Kent, but I would have preferred your name to be Mr. Ford!"

We also checked out the possibilities of doing business in Czechoslovakia and some of the other Central European and Balkan countries, but what always puzzled me was the American attitude toward the countries behind the Iron Curtain. Americans seemed to lump all these countries together as the Eastern Bloc, and wrongfully assumed that they were all essentially the same. I knew first-hand that nothing could be further from the truth.

In Poland, I was able to move about freely and made many friends. We could openly discuss politics, and many of us went out together socially. In fact, politics was usually the main topic of most conversations in Poland. They were very open, and no one hesitated to express his or her own views. The Poles, on the other hand, had this erroneous impression of America as the legendary place where the streets are paved with gold. This illusion was perpetuated by many Polish nationals who immigrated to the United States, and wrote back to the old country about how it didn't take them long to acquire homes and cars. Their letters made it sound like everyone in the States was a millionaire, and it wasn't a difficult thing to do. In the 1960s and 1970s in Poland, very few people owned cars, and owning your own home, a villa, was something only a millionaire could afford.

The fireworks would flash when discussing Polish foreign policy and an American could immediately sense the strong attachment, influence, and adherence to foreign policy dictated by Moscow. This blind Polish support of Moscow's policies was mind-boggling, since for generations the Russians and Poles had been bitter enemies.

Romania was different and scarier. Business transactions were permitted but socializing with Americans was not. I occasionally dined with my business colleagues there, but that was usually at official functions pertaining to business. The Romanians were very guarded in their private chats and you could see and sense the machinations of the police state all around you. Romania was a nation that most closely resembled George Orwell's *1984*. There was no freedom of action and no freedom of thought, yet Romanian foreign policy was often at odds with Moscow's—and Poland's.

By the time Jack, Joe, and I were doing business in the Eastern Bloc, I was married with children and we were living in New Rochelle in a home of our own. Whenever we brought over a delegation of European businessmen, I did my best to promote social discourse and East/West friendship. I would treat the delegations (they never traveled to the States alone, only in groups) to leisurely dinners at some of Manhattan's finest eateries, take them to see Broadway shows, and always made sure they spent at least one or two evenings in my home with my family.

With my wife, Hannah, serving as my gracious hostess, it didn't take long before my guests' iron reserve would crumble, and they would relax in their comfortable surroundings. When the guests were from Poland, it really didn't matter much because there were no language barriers between us, except when my children were around. The Romanians spoke a better English than the Poles did, and a few of them even spoke fluent Yiddish. The man in charge of practically all the textile factories in Romania was Yossi Steinberg, and, to my knowledge, he was the only Jew in the Politburo—and that was because he made money for the government.

During one such visit, when a Romanian director was staying with us in Connecticut, our second home, Jeffrey tried to plant a tree by himself on the lawn in front of the house. The director removed his jacket and tie, rolled up his sleeves and set to work with my son to properly prepare the soil. It was a symbol of East-West cooperation, and the striking tree still beautifies the front yard of that house.

By dealing with Eastern European countries, I learned about the practicalities of the capitalist system versus that of the communists. Our business was successful because we had the ability to understand these systems and to adapt ourselves accordingly. Our European backgrounds, the ability we had to speak several European languages and English, the wartime experience that taught us how to be flexible, were all part and parcel of our success.

We also had to learn to deal with the Planning Boards. It really did not matter too much to the Planning Boards whether there was a market for a product or whether or not the consumer wanted it. Top officials of the government, who knew nothing about supply and demand, directly dictated the whole process of manufacture. So it was not uncommon for an Eastern European country to be glutted with certain items while there was a dearth of basic products. Take toilet paper in Poland. There was once such a huge toilet paper shortage that newspapers wrote satires about the value of a single roll—present one at the door and you could gain entry to the most exclusive and elegant parties in Poland.

It also didn't help international business that in the 1950s and '60s, tourist conditions in the Eastern Bloc were abysmal. Hotels lacked the basic comforts and hadn't been upgraded in decades. Telephone systems were so antiquated, that in Bucharest it was simpler and faster for me to drive from office to office to talk to people instead of trying to reach them by phone.

This lack of service and class is why most American companies didn't want to do business in Eastern Europe. It was simply too difficult and complicated for them and they couldn't adjust. That left us an open field, and soon we had more than two-dozen companies making products for us in Poland and Romania.

Also, in the 1950s and '60s, the food available to tourists and foreign businessmen was limited. At the local restaurants, if you weren't with the bureaucrats, you ate what they put in front of you, take it or leave it—unless you paid with American dollars or were in the company of party officials. Then variety and quality would suddenly appear on the table.

There was also the question of transportation. Most people didn't have cars, but the big shots all got to use their "company" cars. The old adage in the Communist system, "everyone is equal, but some are more equal than others," kept running through my mind whenever I was there.

It was a good thing that only three of us made business decisions, and we didn't have to wait for boards of directors or committees. It meant that if we spotted a developing trend, we could grab it fast, as we did when guitars became the in-thing in the late 1960s and early '70s. It seemed as if, overnight, every kid in America wanted a guitar.

We noticed the trend when S&H Green Stamps had a tremendous surge in requests for acoustic guitars. A number of customers asked us for thousands of guitars. Since our guitar sources were limited, we desperately needed to find additional factories. An unscheduled trip to Japan was quickly arranged so I could scout the territory, but even Japanese production couldn't produce large quantities fast enough. I had to put on my thinking cap and finally came up with something. I discovered that Russia could be a good source of supply for the inexpensive guitars we needed, but traveling to Russia in the 1950s and '60s was not easy. To obtain a visa, protocol required that you receive an invitation from a central commercial enterprise in Russia. So the next time I visited Romania, I obtained a visa to travel to Moscow.

I stayed in Russia approximately five days, and left filled with mixed impressions. I was quite taken with the Russian people, and was surprised to discover how friendly they were to me, an American. As someone who spoke Polish, I could communicate directly, since Russian and Polish belong to the same group of Slavic languages, and I still remembered a little bit of the Russian my parents spoke when they didn't want us to understand what they were saying. (Then, I resented it; now, I appreciated it.)

While in Moscow, I took the opportunity to enjoy the Bolshoi Ballet and travel on the Russian subways. The subway stations were something to behold, filled as they were with beautiful murals and candelabra that could easily adorn the most magnificent palaces.

Doing business in Russia was even more daunting than doing business in Romania. The system was locked into the rigid, five-year communist master plan, *Piateletka,* that was impossible to modify. Fit into the plan or forget about doing business with the Russians.

It wasn't easy, but I got thousands of additional guitars. Consistent with Russian policy, the guitars were not packed individually or in master cartons. The Russians wrapped each guitar in straw and packed them in massive wooden crates for shipment to America because that was the only way they could do it. What this meant for us was a tremendous amount of extra work, but we did it. Each and every crate was unpacked by hand and each guitar was repackaged in its own box for shipping to consumers.

We were also one of the first to understand the value of the now ubiquitous plastic garbage bags. Way back when, when "plastic" was a word in a movie, there weren't enough plastic garbage bags to go around, so we secured two factories in Spain who extruded them by the container load. It was good while it lasted—that is, until the big boys, like Monsanto, took over production and distribution and we were squeezed out of the market.

Somehow, we also managed to get into the market for bunkbeds and shuttered louvers for windows and doors. Both these wooden products were made for us in Spain. We could diversify like this because we were dealing only with two or three large distributors in the United States who bought these items directly from us. Dealing with distributors and not directly with the customer required mutual trust, and relationships were very personal. When I look back now, I realize there was only one time when we were seriously ripped off.

We'd contacted one of the largest manufacturers and distributors of wooden products in America, a multi-billion dollar company. They were extremely interested in our louvered products and ordered a few container loads as a trial run. When the goods moved well, they ordered additional container loads, with their logos on the packaging. We were happy to oblige.

Then something curious happened. The company rep told us that since the products were so successful, they wanted to run a large-scale promotion. They asked me to bring their European rep with me to our factory to show him that we were fully capable of producing whatever they needed. I didn't even hesitate, and said, "No problem." I often took customers with me to various factories and never had any cause for concern. In fact, it was good for business, and it pleased the suppliers, too.

The American representative was impressed with the factory and its production facilities. I naturally expected the visit to be followed up with a substantial order. But we got no more orders, and I couldn't figure out why. I investigated and discovered that although they were no longer buying our merchandise, they were selling the identical product everywhere. I smelled a rat, and decided to discuss it with the factory managers on my next trip to Spain. When I was there, I watched them produce our merchandise and load it into containers. I even opened a fully loaded container ready to go and checked the last row of goods for quality, packing, and marking. Everything had our label on it, and I returned to the States completely confused.

Several months passed and we still received no orders from the company in question. However, merchandise with their label, originating from my source in Spain, still continued to be available in stores throughout the country. Checking the import bulletin, which lists all merchandise imported to the United States, we found that our old customer was indeed bringing large quantities of the merchandise into the country. They'd broken their agreement and cut us out of the loop, so for the first time since going into business, I filed a lawsuit. This was my very first experience with lawyers and courts and I quickly learned that there were "lawyers" and lawyers. My lawyer was neither, and when the judge realized how incompetent he was, he took the case into his own hands. The judge figured out that a container of goods that was supposed to be handled by us was clandestinely shipped directly to the client while I was in Spain trying to figure out what was going on.

The judge could not understand how I never ran into the company's representative during the three days I was there and why I never saw the inventory that was being shipped, especially since I had inspected a fully loaded container. The judge directly questioned my former customer, and got them to admit that their representative was definitely in Spain while I was visiting the factory, but was keeping a very low profile in a little village nearby. Because he knew I was there, he did not go to the factory. Fearing discovery, he didn't leave his hotel room for the three days I was in town and had all of his meals brought to his room. He'd made himself invisible and that's why I did not see him.

The judge got the company to admit that, indeed, a container was being prepared for shipment to my former customer while I was in the factory. I did not discover this during my visit because of a carefully planned deception. Convinced that I would want to inspect that loaded container, the last two rows of merchandise with my former customer's logo were removed and replaced with goods displaying my logo.

It was also determined that it was not the factory's intention to deceive me and sell merchandise to my former customer. The factory owed the bank a great deal of money, and when my former customer applied pressure on the bank, the bank forced the manufacturer to sell them the goods. We won the case, which was more of a moral victory than anything else, since we weren't awarded a single dime. I could not understand the judgment, but for the first time, I learned that in the courts you could be right, and lose anyway. Eventually the ex-customer lost his supplier because of mismanagement, so the crime did not pay for the guilty, but it also didn't benefit the innocent.

I remember 1976 very well, because our company received an invitation to visit China as a prelude to conducting business there. China was a sleeping giant with very limited access to foreigners. This applied to Americans in particular, since there were no visitors and/or tourists permitted except for diplomats and those who received special invitations from the government. When I looked into the whys and hows, I discovered that the Chinese government was inviting us because we had done substantial business with Poland and Romania. In their infinite wisdom, they thought it would benefit them if they met us.

Before this invitation arrived, my partners and I never seriously pursued the prospect of conducting business there. We were doing quite well and had our hands full. We knew some Chinese products were already available in America and were sold rather cheaply. With that in mind, we accepted the invitation and took the opportunity to investigate the potential.

Jack and Joe elected me to visit China and I could take Hannah because the invitation was issued as a trip for two. But the two of us were on the horns of a dilemma. Who would take care of Susan and Jeffrey for the three or four weeks we would both be gone? After all, they were just teenagers. We'd never left them alone in the past, and we were seriously concerned about it.

In the end, Susie convinced us not to pass up this chance to go to China, since we might never get another one. She assured us that she and Jeffrey would be fine, so we went and never regretted it.

Because of our experience in the difficult minefield of Eastern European business, at the outset I was sure we had the necessary expertise and experience to handle the rigidity of business operations in a country like China. I thought I was prepared, but nothing was further from the truth. Doing business in Poland and Romania was a cakewalk compared to the situation in China. An issue that would be settled immediately in other countries took two or three days to negotiate. Invariably, even after a lengthy two or three days, the negotiations would start all over again when the immovable Chinese would bring in a new team to solve the problem.

For example, we were buying large quantities of 45-piece dinnerware sets (service for eight) in Europe and Japan. Since the Chinese had many dinnerware factories, and for centuries were experts in producing porcelain, the simplest way to start a business relationship was to purchase 45-piece dinnerware sets from them.

In theory, I was correct; in practice, I was mistaken. I was told Chinese factories had three- or five-year plans in place to produce 20-piece dinner sets and five-piece serving sets. I said that this could work out perfectly for both of us, since their production schedule would easily enable them to fill my 45-piece dinnerware set orders. I explained the obvious; two of their 20-piece sets and one of their five-piece sets packed in one carton would make the perfect 45-piece dinnerware set I was looking for. The discussion to explain this concept took three days. In the end, they said that what I suggested was impossible; they could not pack two 20-piece sets and one five-piece set in a single box, because they were programmed to pack each set separately. Either the merchandise would have to be purchased the way it was packed, or not at all. It was extremely frustrating to witness such inflexibility.

To show good faith, and to save the trip, I bought a small quantity of dinnerware packed their way and repacked it when it came to the States. Since prices were low, it wasn't much of a risk. But when it came to textiles, we couldn't do business at all. As in Eastern Europe, the sewing and the fabric quality were fine. But the notions—the zippers, the buttons, and the trimmings—were inferior and the American market wouldn't accept Chinese quality on those items. Where the Eastern Europeans understood that importing quality notions to apply to the garments made good business sense, the Chinese just could not wrap their brains around the idea. They insisted that we use Chinese notions and we insisted that if we couldn't produce a quality product we couldn't do business.

While the trip was a fizzle for business, overall it was dazzling. Hannah and I had an incredible time visiting different parts of the country and meeting the people. At first, Hannah and I felt strange when we went sightseeing. Wherever we went, we were surrounded by thousands of curious Chinese—very few of them had ever seen Westerners before. We almost started a riot when we visited a local department store. We were a sensation from the moment we entered. Practically everything came to a sudden halt, and hundreds of people gathered around us. Everyone was extremely orderly and polite, and the handful who spoke English tried to be helpful. When the police noticed the crowd, to our regret, they dispersed it.

Our official guide was, generally, always with us. One day we attempted to go to a restaurant on our own for a change of pace, instead of eating where we were ordered to eat. There was a whole procedure that had to be followed. The hotel called the restaurant we chose in advance and told them what we wanted for dinner. Then they ordered a car to take us there, with the understanding that the car would wait for us to take us back to the hotel.

The most unusual and uncomfortable situation we found ourselves in took place during an excursion to the zoo to see the pandas. After all, how does one visit China and neglect its world-famous pandas? The pandas were fine. Hannah and I were the ones on display at the zoo, because the crowd was more interested in us than they were in the animals. It was curious, funny, and interesting to watch large groups of Chinese freeze in their tracks to observe two human beings who were observing the animals.

On our first trip, the Chinese didn't take us on the "tourist trip." But on the second trip to China, though I was alone, I thoroughly enjoyed climbing on the battlements of the Great Wall of China and visiting the Forbidden City in Peking. The sheer magnitude of the Great Wall was what impressed me most. It is a continuous wall about 4,000 kilometers in length, built on the top of mountains to protect the Chinese people from outsiders. To build it, hundreds of thousands of workers labored for years and thousands of them died from malnutrition. Today, of course, the Wall brings the outsiders in, along with their tourist dollars.

The Forbidden City was indeed magnificent. It was once a complete city, consisting of thousands of palaces and halls, each with the most beautiful artistic adornments. There were halls that could seat thousands, and the ornamentation was beyond imagination. It was indeed a city for the Emperors. In front of one of these palaces, there was an enormous stone carving, and for years no one could figure out how it got there, since there are no stones of this type and size in the region. The puzzle was eventually solved when research showed that the 40-meter long stone was brought to its resting place during the winter, when temperatures were well below freezing, and water was spilled in front of the carving and allowed to turn to ice. That way, workers were able to slide the stone hundreds of miles to its destination.

As for China itself, the countryside was absolutely lovely, and we admired its great beauty. Although we actually saw only a small part of China, we could still appreciate the vastness of the country and the extent of its rivers and waterways.

In the cities and in the countryside, the colorful outfits worn by children were contrasted by the navy blue unisex uniforms worn by the adults. Then, of course, there were the bicycles—millions of them. This was the main mode of transportation since cars were scarce. The sight of all of the bicycles reminded me of Henry Ford when he said, "You can paint a car any color you want as long as it's black." The Chinese must have heard Mr. Ford's comments, because every single bike was painted black.

Our hosts even took us to visit some pre-schools, where Hannah and I observed how well-behaved and well-dressed the children were in their multi-colored uniforms. The students made impressive theatrical presentations and we noticed how each and every production we saw had a political theme emphasizing the benevolence and importance of Chairman Mao. This indoctrination of the masses started at the earliest possible age, and so I came to understand why all of the Chinese arguments and points of view were based strictly on Chairman Mao's philosophy. It particularly became obvious when I attempted to discuss politics and economic issues by trying to bring out other points of view.

Undoubtedly, Chairman Mao was omnipotent. My wife got concerned when I presented opposing views to our guides, and constantly warned me to be careful. She feared that I might be arrested for expressing my opinions. I told her not to worry and assured her that they would not arrest me while I was a guest in their country.

In my discussions with the Chinese, I was surprised by the animosity that was expressed in the press and population at large against Russia and their system of communism. In some instances, I found that Chinese hatred of Russia was even more pronounced than their dislike of the United States.

All in all, the people with whom I associated, primarily government officials connected with industry, were extremely polite, pleasant, and most anxious to tend to our every need. At one point, their hospitality and graciousness was displayed to us in a very unusual way. During one long dinner, as lengthy discussions about politics and business took place, multiple toasts were made to honor Chairman Mao while an unlimited variety of delicious dishes were continuously served. The dinner seemed to last for hours. Indirectly, I myself could have been the cause for these endless toasts. To the delight of my host, I said that if Chairman Mao had not been a Chinese leader, he would still have been known as an excellent mathematician, painter, and philosopher.

Eventually, my back started to bother me and I got up to

take a short walk, thinking that standing might alleviate any potential problems. Noticing my brief absence, the host asked me why I had left the table. I explained that my back was starting to bother me and I thought it advisable to take a walk so as to relieve the discomfort I was experiencing. After I mentioned this to him, we did not refer to the subject again and I assumed that the matter was totally forgotten.

To my surprise, however, as the Chinese delegation drove me back to my hotel, I noticed that we were going a different way. Suddenly, the car stopped in front of a large building. Upon entering, I discovered that it was a hospital. I was told that inasmuch as I had mentioned that I was experiencing some pain in my back, they thought it best that I be seen by one of their doctors. I was brought into a private waiting room that was quite cold, but a gas heater arrived shortly to warm things up.

After a few minutes elapsed, we went in to see a doctor, who spoke Chinese to the translator, who, in turn, then spoke English to me. I replied to the translator in English and he followed it up with a Chinese translation. This was the method of communication throughout the examination that lasted for about twenty minutes.

The doctor gave me various herbal medications and, at the end of the visit, I thanked him for his time. As I was saying good-bye, I couldn't believe my ears when the doctor replied in perfect English. He said it was a pleasure to meet me and hoped that the medicine would be helpful. This incident proved the politeness of the Chinese people and their genuine concern toward a guest. Not knowing that the doctor spoke English, they had extended the courtesy of making sure to provide me with a translator.

I will never forget these incredible journeys to China. They left me with some striking impressions. Two of them were particularly significant—one negative and one positive. The negative impression: the entire Chinese population, starting from early childhood, was methodically indoctrinated with the teachings of Chairman Mao, which meticulously stressed the omnipotence of the state and insignificance of the individual. The positive impression: I did not see hunger in China. Knowing from history how many millions of people, particularly children, have died in China from starvation, the complete absence of hunger was astounding to me. Since I personally experienced hunger, and knew what constant hunger was like, I felt that its elimination in a country of this size was indeed a monumental achievement.

My feelings about China can be condensed into one sentence as expressed by Winston Churchill when referring to Russia. I paraphrase: "So many never knew so little about so much!"

Treasured Kent family portrait, 1930s. Left to right: Mother Sonia, Roman, sisters Renia and Dasza, brother Leon, father Emanuel.

School pictures taken in Jewish Gymnasium before the war, Lodz, Poland, early '30s. Upper: Play—sister Dasza in front row right. Lower: Class photo—Dasza in second row left.

Class pictures, Lodz ghetto, Poland, circa 1940. Upper: Roman in top row, fourth from left. Lower: sister Renia in front row, second from left, with Chaim Mordecai Rumkowski, Elder of Jews, standing in rear.

Workplace—Leder & Sattler Ressort, producers of leather goods and apparel for German soldiers, Lodz, circa 1941.

Upper: About to leave for America: Roman, right, with two friends.
Lower: Journey to America aboard *Marine Perch*: Roman, left, brother
Leon, right.

My comrade-in-arms, beloved brother Leon, U.S., circa 1950s.

Upper: Filming *Children in the Holocaust*, Auschwitz, 1979.
Right to left: director Victor Stoloff, Roman, Liv Ullmann,
Kathy Schneider. Lower: Celebrating end of filming and
Hannah's 50th birthday at Wierzynek (Five Kings) Restau-
rant, Krakow, Poland. Right to left: Hannah Kent, Roman, Liv
Ullmann.

Tennis, anyone? Upper: With Israeli Prime Minister Yitzhak Rabin, Florida, 1980s. Lower: With Polish President Aleksander Kwasniewski, Connecticut, 1996.

Tennis playmates, Club Med—Roman, center, celebrating winning of triple-header: men's singles, men's doubles, and mixed doubles.

Polish Consulate, New York, NY. Reception in honor of Polish President Lech Walesa.

Manhattan reception honoring Israeli Prime Minister Menachem Begin.

Congratulatory luncheon for 1983 magazine publication of *Holocaust: The Obligation to Remember*, executive offices, the *Washington Post*. From second left: Prof. Michael Berenbaum; Ben Bradlee, *Post* executive director; Ben Meed; Roman; *Post* publisher Donald Graham; Norbert Wollheim.

Upper: Roman presents Shofar of Freedom Award to Danish Ambassador Eigil Jorgensen, Philadelphia, 1985. Lower: With Isaac Bashevis Singer, discussing his work and philosophy. Left to right: Roman, Singer, Marian Turski.

Presentation of America-Friendship Award to Hon. Lawrence Eagleburger, Bnai Zion Dinner, New York, 2002. Left to right: Michael Lazar, Eagleburger, Roman, Alan Hevesi.

Upper: Kent family attending White House reception. Left to right: Hannah, Jeffrey, Roman, and Susan Kent Avjian. Lower: Wedding reception for daughter Susan, Westchester, NY, 1986.

208

Vice President Al Gore greets Ben Meed and Roman during visit to New York to commemorate Yom Hashoah.

Presenting President Bill Clinton with final report of Presidential Advisory Commission on Holocaust Assets in the U.S., Oval Office, 2001.

Roman and Hannah laying wreath at mass grave,
Bergen-Belsen, 55th anniversary of concentration
camp liberation, 2000.

Upper: Elie Wiesel congratulates Roman and co-honoree Romana Strochlitz Primus at Wiesel Holocaust Remembrance Award presentation, 2000. Lower: With Irena Sendler, a Polish heroine whose actions during the Holocaust saved the lives of Jewish children, Warsaw, 2007.

Acknowledging receipt of "Torch of Freedom" Award, 1992.

U.N. Secretary General Kofi Annan congratulates Roman at 2005 opening of exhibit commemorating liberation of Auschwitz. Kent family attending first Yom Hashoah Commemoration in January 2006 at the U.N. General Assembly.

Office of the President
of the
Borough of Manhattan
City of New York

Proclamation

Whereas: THIS YEAR MARKS THE FIFTIETH ANNIVERSARY OF THE ARRIVAL ON THESE SHORES OF MANY OF THE SURVIVORS OF THE EUROPEAN HOLOCAUST; AND

WHEREAS: ONE OF THOSE SURVIVORS IS ROMAN R. KENT, WHO AS A CHILD ENDURED THE PERILS OF THE LODZ GHETTO AND THE HORRORS OF THE NAZI EXTERMINATION CAMPS, AND WHO HAS BUILT SUCCESS AND FOUND HAPPINESS IN BUSINESS AND FAMILY LIFE IN THE UNITED STATES; AND

WHEREAS: HE HAS SERVED AS CHAIR OF THE AMERICAN GATHERING OF JEWISH HOLOCAUST SURVIVORS, VICE PRESIDENT OF THE BOARD FOR THE JEWISH FOUNDATION FOR CHRISTIAN RESCUERS, AND AS A BOARD MEMBER OF THE WARSAW GHETTO RESISTANCE ORGANIZATION AND OF THE CONFERENCE OF JEWISH MATERIAL CLAIMS AGAINST GERMANY; AND

WHEREAS: TONIGHT, HE WILL BE HONORED WITH THE HUMANITARIAN AWARD OF THE INTERFAITH COMMITTEE OF REMEMBRANCE;

NOW THEREFORE, I, RUTH W. MESSINGER, PRESIDENT OF THE BOROUGH OF MANHATTAN, IN RECOGNITION OF HIS ACHIEVEMENTS AND IN GRATITUDE FOR HIS UNSWERVING FIDELITY TO THE TASKS OF PURSUING JUSTICE AND PRESERVING REMEMBRANCE, DO HEREBY PROCLAIM SATURDAY, NOVEMBER 16, 1996 IN THE BOROUGH OF MANHATTAN AS:

"ROMAN R. KENT DAY"

IN WITNESS WHEREOF I HAVE HEREUNTO SET MY HAND AND CAUSED THE SEAL OF THE BOROUGH OF MANHATTAN TO BE AFFIXED.

RUTH W. MESSINGER
PRESIDENT
BOROUGH OF MANHATTAN

Proclamation of Roman R. Kent Day in New York City, 1996.

215

Three "Kent dividends," our precious grandchildren Eryn, Sean, and Dara Avjian.

Hannah and Roman Kent—survivors of the Holocaust, united by fate.

Twenty
The Birth of Namor

"How could I have known, there were traitors in my midst?"

The legendary Empire State Building beckoned. It was then, and is at this writing, the tallest, most famous building in New York City (after 9/11 changed things). It's a superstar of a building, 350 Fifth Avenue, on the southwest corner of the equally renowned 34th Street. The classic art deco building with its gleaming chrome and black granite lobby and romantic observation deck played key roles in movies I can think of: one was *King Kong,* starring the Gorilla and Fay Wray (which I had seen in a movie house in Lodz before the war) and *An Affair to Remember* with Cary Grant and Deborah Kerr. Now that same Empire State Building was going to play a major role in my life and that of my partner. It was the early 1970s, and we were moving in!

We chose a suite on the 35th floor, and while that is not the 110th floor, the views were still incredible. I could see from the Hudson River to the East River, and had a view of the magnificent downtown skyline. I was more concerned, however, with getting a showroom, sales staff, and administrative people organized in our new space. By then, Jack and I had bought out Joe, and he went his separate way.

It really was exciting, and for the first time we were able to devote some time and attention to presenting our company and our product lines in a manner that reflected our tastes and our success. I preferred classic French Empire style desks and chairs I'd purchased in the city, and hung Chinese engravings on the walls for color—and as conversation pieces. Unlike most New Yorkers, I still preferred the more relaxed, gregarious way of dealing with customers.

We were flourishing at last and did business under three

separate names. Sphinx Import Company was the parent corporation that sold general merchandise like housewares, Seaton Textiles handled our dry goods, and we used Stafford International to conduct trade in musical instruments.

As we expanded, we put various cost-saving devices into place. Some of our practices were contrary to those in the industry. For instance, once we calculated the risk of losing goods on a ship, we realized it didn't justify paying high insurance premiums on all incoming cargo. In all the years we'd been in business, we'd never lost a complete boatload. The few times we experienced partial losses, we recovered most of the loss via claims to the carrier. By changing our policies and making precise decisions on what would and would not be insured, we saved thousands of dollars a month.

Traditionally, our offices had doubled as warehouses, and we no longer wanted to do that. We had storage for items that might need to be shipped in emergencies, and then rented space near or on the docks and shipped from there. By doing that we were flexible enough to add or delete space as we needed it.

As often happens, too much of a good thing creates problems, and our expanding business was no exception. Jack and I started having serious disagreements. Since we filled our Polish and Romanian cotton import quotas, and we could still use additional merchandise, it seemed we might need to locate suppliers from other countries. Jack suggested we go to East Germany.

I told him I was strongly opposed to the idea and that I would not go there, and did not want to expand the business if it meant dealing with the Germans. My wounds from the war never having healed, I absolutely refused to go Germany or to be involved in direct meetings and negotiations with Germans under any circumstances.

Try as I might, I could not stop Jack from going to Germany to develop his own contacts. He even imported some East German goods. I was not happy. This business with Jack brought back a flood of miserable memories. I also saw major changes in his behavior—drastic changes. He became arrogant and tyrannical, and I compared that to what our German captors had been like during the war. Also, without a word of discussion, I learned

Jack was bringing his son into the business because he wanted to go to Los Angeles and pursue his Hollywood dream. That dream was the result of a book he had written about his experiences during the war and in the post-war period in Germany. We had shared many of those experiences, so I knew first-hand that what he wrote was, in many cases, grossly misrepresented.

There was one incident in particular that pertained to me personally and was most distasteful and objectionable. He retold the story of Dasza's sad death in the Swedish hospital, only in his twisted version, Dasza was the light of his life, his long-lost lover, the sweetheart who died in his arms. It was disgraceful. When I confronted him about it, he looked me straight in the eye, survivor to survivor, and sweetly told me that it wasn't my sister laying in that hospital bed in Lubeck, it was his long-lost sweetheart.

He could not have been more insulting when he insisted that the story was about his sweetheart and not about Dasza. He appropriated the story of how Leon and I had searched for our sisters, made it into his own Hollywood fantasy, and then had the audacity to accuse me of losing my memory. Did he honestly think that after the Holocaust any survivor would forget finding his own dying sister?

I was deeply hurt and insulted, and I was reaching my limit. Jack continued to insist on being less involved in the business and more involved in the arts, and kept pushing his son at me. I didn't want to take him in as a partner because I didn't like his arrogance and his attitude. He didn't have the experience to handle the business correctly and he would offend the clientele. He would be a burden, not a blessing.

We had put together a plan that called for selling the business off five years hence, but I found myself at a crossroad. Though I realized that the timing wasn't right, I wasn't willing to go forward with Jack and his son. It was time to say good-bye and go our separate ways.

The other incentive I had for selling was that I wanted the time, now that I was financially secure, to get involved in community affairs. My parents had taught me the value of charity, and so had my experiences in Europe and then in Atlanta, when Leon and I associated with Charlie Kessler.

Selling the business was a difficult emotional hurdle. The company was as near and dear to me as my own children. I had watched it grow from infancy to maturity. Other than working part-time at Kinney Shoes, I had never worked anyplace else. It was the only commercial life I had known since coming to the United States.

After a great deal of soul searching, and numerous discussions with Hannah, we decided the business had to be sold. Once the decision was made, we had to face the practical and mechanical considerations of getting it done. As a private corporation, we were told that the proper value of the business had to be established before we could disband. And, in order to ascertain the market value, one of us had to sell his stock to the other. Only after we sold the inventory would we be able to ascertain the true value of the business. Since we expected the value of the company to be much higher than its book value, we had to dispose of the inventory and then adjust the sale price.

Jack insisted on being the one to buy me out and I wasn't happy about it. He thought he was better suited to liquidate the inventory. My intuition and logic warned me that in selling my part of the business to Jack, I would end up a loser. I felt that he might not live up to our verbal agreement.

Emotionally, I somehow convinced myself that he could never betray me after all we had gone through together. He and I shared a great deal of history during and after the war. We were in the concentration camps together, were liberated together, and had spent time together in Germany after liberation. When I arrived in America, I was the one who located his family members living in the United States and after he came to this country, he chose to live with my brother and me in Atlanta instead of staying with his mother in New York. For the sake of all we lived through, and our long-time friendship, I wanted very much to overlook the negative side of his character and to trust him. So I followed my emotions—and not my gut feeling that he would never live up to the agreement.

We kept the newly decorated suite in the Empire State

Building and reluctantly shared the space, keeping separate offices. I continued to operate the dinnerware and housewares part of the business on a limited basis. The textile end of the business was to be sold, and both of us were selling the merchandise we had left.

At first, the arrangement seemed to work, but as time passed, Jack became more secretive. It was obvious his intention was to keep me in the dark so that he would not have to live up to our agreement. At the same time, it was evident that there were other things he wanted to hide. But it didn't work. It was almost impossible for me not to notice certain things, especially those concerning communal work to preserve the memory of the Holocaust.

I discovered that he had sent his own men to bookstores around America to buy up all the available copies of his book in order to manipulate the best-seller lists. These books were then sent to him, and were re-shipped, free of charge, primarily to rabbis throughout the United States. Although the books were supposedly free, they included a request for funds to be sent to a charity he established and over which he had total control.

Jack asked me to make a contribution to that charity when he paid for my shares of the business. I did not, because I realized that he had established his own foundation with the ulterior motive of benefiting himself. In my eyes, this was a gross exploitation of the memory of the Holocaust, and was totally reprehensible.

When I confronted him, he did not take my comments kindly and I intuited that he would attempt something drastic. I was right. When I returned from one of my business trips, I found the door to my office locked. He informed me that since he owned the lease, the office was no longer mine. Our agreement was completely forgotten. He had broken his word.

Legally, there was nothing much I could do. Personally, this was the price I was forced to pay for trusting a person I had no business trusting. When I ran into him a few months later, I told him what I thought about his takeover of my office. I made it clear to him that he had done exactly what the Germans had done when they confiscated our apartments and possessions and threw us out. He said he knew what he did was wrong, but his son wanted my office. His explanation was even worse than I imagined it could be. I told him he had learned his lessons from the Nazis very well.

Hannah was glad my business relationship with Jack was over and discouraged me from pursuing legal action. I knew my wife had my best interests at heart, so I decided to honor her wishes for the time being.

As time passed, I was less inclined to take legal action after Jeffrey, my son, was seriously hurt in a car accident in July 1982. Everything else in my life was of secondary importance. But I must admit that after all those years with Jack, it was hard living with myself for not doing anything about seeking a semblance of justice.

A few years later, I decided to go to court to plead my case. I thought it best to break the case into separate parts and take them one at a time. Other than the case with the manufacturer/distributor in Spain, for all intents and purposes, this was my first personal experience with the American legal system, and the proceedings proved to be a real education.

I saw first-hand how the court system could be delayed and manipulated. It became obvious to me that though the courts are available to each and every one of us, without substantial resources it is difficult, if not impossible, for justice to prevail.

Once the lawsuit began, I learned how hard it is to disprove false testimony. Getting at the truth is more costly and more difficult than producing lies. I lost the first round, but I didn't give up. I went back to my corner and tried to figure out how to beat liars and the lies they tell.

I appealed the decision and took my case to the Supreme Court of New York. By then, Jack and his son had made the cardinal mistake so many liars make—they forgot what they'd said before and presented so many conflicting and false statements that the truth finally had to come out. The judge decided in my favor by awarding me a substantial settlement, but the icing on the cake was when he followed his decision with personal remarks about the defendant, my old friend and comrade-in-arms, my business partner and ultimate betrayer, Jack.

Said the judge: "Defendant made a strategic choice not to present affidavits in opposition to the prior motion, hoping perhaps that a minimum would suffice and more could threaten the subsequent suit . . . The defendant has toyed with the court. He has not been candid and forthcoming."

After winning, I was all keyed up. I gave serious thought to going forward with the other parts of my claim. However, Hannah convinced me not to expend my time and energy pursuing my case further. She noted I'd received some form of justice, and more importantly, the judge had essentially acknowledged, in his post-trial statement, that Jack was a liar.

My wife was right. I dropped the other cases, but the whole experience left me with a lingering, unanswered question that still haunts me after all these years. How could Jack have done what he did to a friend, partner, and fellow Holocaust survivor? I still cannot understand it.

Life went on. I formed my own company, Namor International Corp. (what a creative name, 'Namor,' being my first name Roman spelled backwards), which did business on a much smaller scale. I handled only household goods and was able to keep my old customers. I was in sole control and set up the business so that it practically ran itself. I hired people I had worked with and trusted over the years. I knew they were capable, honest, and dependable. One of them was Beno Lester, a man who had worked for me since his arrival in the United States, and who stayed with me until his retirement.

Now I finally had the time to do what I had promised myself I would do. I would bear witness to the past, because I realized from my adventures in Atlanta that America needed to learn from the memory of the Holocaust. There were lessons that needed teaching so that the 6,000,000 would not have died in vain.

Even today, the images of the gold, diamond jewelry, and precious items that were taken from us in Auschwitz dance in my head. How insignificant and meaningless those material possessions proved to be when they were used to try to buy someone's life. By and large, the mountains of jewelry we were forced to relinquish, to throw on the blankets, did not protect us. I learned early on that giving up earthly belongings did not prevent people from wafting up chimneys as stinking soul-filled smoke.

I believe that those experiences prevented me from becoming greedy and fixating on amassing a huge fortune. I knew I did not want to be poor because I recognized the importance of money and the comfort and independence that it could buy for me and my family. Now, with fewer business demands on my time, I eagerly committed myself to those causes I felt in my heart needed my attention.

Twenty-one
The Dreyfus Affair
(David vs. Goliath)

"The greater the power, the more dangerous the abuse."—Edward Burke

In the 1980s, I realized that it was becoming rather commonplace for big business to conduct and execute various transactions that were borderline legal, and in some instances, outright fraud. There was no doubt in my mind that many of these transactions were pernicious at best. What concerned me most was the growing greed that was rearing its ugly head. People, supposedly the "cream of the crop" of the American business world (all of whom were millionaires many times over), and the best and most creative lawyers and accountants money can buy, were devising schemes to enrich themselves at the public's expense.

A new lexicon was being developed for lawyers and accountants. Creative accounting was a new way to say you were cooking the books, and the better you cooked the books, the more creative accounting you could do. Greenmail, poison pills, golden parachutes, night raider, insider trading, and junk bonds were all phrases that exchanged clean words for dirty business. Special words coined to cover unethical behavior of businessmen, lawyers, and accountants triggered memories from my youth when I was in the ghetto and concentration camps.

In order to stay alive during the Holocaust, it was necessary for us starving prisoners to devise ways to secure nourishment we so desperately needed, as well as other vital necessities. However, even in our life and death situation, we could not bring ourselves to acknowledge that we were stealing. So we coined the verb "organize" to make it more palatable. This rationale was necessary because the things we did in order to eat were often

226

contrary to our upbringing and our concepts of decency, morality, and consideration for others.

In fact, "organize" became a respectful word that meant although we didn't use legal means to obtain food, clothing, firewood, or medicine, in our eyes such acts were fully legal. However, to take something from another prisoner, which occurred rarely among Jews, was still called stealing and looked upon with disdain and contempt. Even under the dire circumstances in the camps, the idea of stealing was repulsive to us. Words meant something then, so did ideas. And stealing food to save your life is a lot different from disguising the fact that corporate raiding is going on.

The new catchphrases in the financial industry to cover unsavory schemes designed to camouflage the lining of corporate pockets with additional millions showed the deep contrast in morality between the '80s and the '40s. At the outset, these newly coined words were used by just a select group of people. Eventually, they became widespread and were accepted by everyone, becoming part of our vocabulary. Now legal theft is common and acceptable until the perpetrator gets caught. It was difficult for me to accept that, and when I personally encountered a specific instance of such deceit, I decided that somehow, somewhere, I had to stand up and speak out. After all, I had learned first-hand during the war that the biggest crime one can commit is to sit and do nothing when witnessing injustice.

My personal saga began quite innocuously in 1987 with an investment I made in the Dreyfus Fund, one of America's largest financial institutions. I had some cash to invest and was impressed with a pamphlet I received in the mail that extolled the advantages of doing business with Dreyfus. After studying their brochure, I was still not completely satisfied and, as they suggested, I called for an appointment with one of their representatives.

Based on the explanations, suggestions, and recommendations of the Dreyfus financial advisor, I decided to invest what for me was a substantial amount of money in what was described to me as a safe, sound, and secure business investment. Much to my regret, this investment turned out to be neither sound nor secure.

For example, instead of purchasing a tax-free Connecticut bond, which would be in my best interest as a resident of Connecticut, they bought New York tax-exempt bonds—fine for a New York resident, but offering me no benefit. It even reduced my rate of return. Within months, my investment quickly lost value. It was more than evident that the funds had been improperly invested.

My faith in Dreyfus rapidly dissipated and I believed that they had deceived me. Under the circumstances, I tried to arrange a meeting with Mr. Joseph DiMartino, president of Dreyfus, to discuss the situation before it got completely out of hand. Setting up such an appointment was easier said than done, and was probably more difficult than attempting to see the President of the United States.

DiMartino was fully insulated from anyone who dared approach him concerning matters which would be unpleasant for him to face. However, I refused to give up, and eventually a meeting was arranged. To my surprise, the Dreyfus attorney was also present at the meeting and I did not take kindly to this development.

Due in large part to Mr. DiMartino's arrogance, the meeting proceeded in an unsatisfactory manner. He was completely confident in the superiority of Dreyfus's legal power against an individual like me and felt I could be steamrolled. I suggested that maybe it was possible for us to resolve the issue in an amicable manner. His attitude was, "You had your losses so go ahead and eat them, we will not cooperate in any way, shape, or form." His unwillingness to cooperate was reiterated in a letter written to me on June 3, 1987, when he wrote: "As to the matter of the investment losses incurred by you, I must repeat as you were advised at our meeting, we do not believe that you were given any misleading or incorrect information by any Dreyfus personnel. Our personnel are fully trained to advise customers as to our investment products and procedures." Because I am stubborn, it meant I had to find a lawyer and go through the courts.

I approached a good friend of mine, attorney Paul Hodys,

and explained the situation. He did not give me an immediate response, but told me that I had a problem. He would check with his associates and discuss it with me further in a couple of days.

At our next meeting, which took place over lunch, Paul said, "Roman, I have known you for many years and we have been good friends for a long time. I really cannot take this case because what I would be doing is taking your money without the slightest chance of recovering any. Dreyfus is one of the leading financial institutions, with unlimited monetary and legal resources. Whether they are right or wrong, they will prolong the case and drag it out for many years. They will not care how much money they spend because their aim and goal is not to lose.

"To fight them, and they count on it, you would have to spend a few hundred thousand dollars, appear in court for years to come, and produce an unlimited amount of superfluous documents. Even if we win and recover the losses, the process is so costly and lengthy that I cannot in clear conscience take the case. I have to advise you that you should not proceed with me as your counsel, or with anyone else. You will be spinning your wheels and it will cost you a fortune."

I was in a dilemma. I appreciated Paul's assessment, but on the other hand it was not just the money, it was the question of justice. The two basic historical documents of the United States, the very ones that I had to memorize to become a citizen, stressed justice above everything else. The first was the Preamble to the Constitution which ensures justice and domestic tranquility; the other was the Pledge of Allegiance, which declares that we are "one nation, under God, indivisible, with liberty and justice for all."

I could not let the matter drop. I told Paul that I appreciated his thoughtfulness, honesty, and advice. I informed him I would represent myself, but in a different forum. I retrieved the pertinent papers from him and studied the case over the weekend.

As I looked at the paperwork, I thought it might make more sense to go to arbitration than it would to go to court. I noticed that in most standard investment agreements with brokerage firms, arbitration was a final and binding method of resolving disputes between parties. Furthermore, these documents emphasized that by going to arbitration, the parties were waiving their right to seek remedies in court, including the right to a jury trial. The documents also noted that, typically, arbitrators were individuals affiliated with securities industries.

I decided that instead of having arbitration conducted under the auspices of a panel of securities arbitrators, I would refer the matter to the American Arbitration Association, where I thought I would receive an unbiased hearing. After lengthy and heated discussions with Dreyfus representatives, binding arbitration was agreed upon under the auspices of the American Arbitration Association. My first battle against Dreyfus was won. Now we were at war.

Dreyfus retained the very prestigious Park Avenue law firm of Rogers & Wells, whose lead partner, William P. Rogers, was a former Attorney General of the United States. During arbitration, the firm's lead counsel was Ms. Nancy A. Brown, an aggressive and hostile advisor.

Her contempt for me was easily detected in her voice and body language. She was convinced that she would have an easy time against a non-professional representing himself against such a well-established, well-oiled company like Dreyfus and her prominent law firm. Perhaps she was abrasive in order to intimidate me, but it had the opposite effect. I remained calm and cool at all times.

Paul Hodys was correct when he warned me they would request a ton of paperwork, and I was amused when Ms. Brown asked for exactly that. I simply stated that I was not in the wood-chopping or paper-manufacturing businesses, and had no intention of furnishing her with a huge quantity of what I considered irrelevant and unnecessary documents. I emphasized that if she needed lots of paper, she should get it from Dreyfus to show their complete modus operandi.

It was finally agreed that I would provide only a minimal amount of documents, namely those pertaining to the transactions in question, and my income tax returns for the previous three years. I was guaranteed that these tax returns would be held in strict confidence and would not be released for public scrutiny.

When the first day of the official hearing finally arrived, Ms. Brown showed up with her staff, including Dreyfus personnel. In walked poor little me, with my son, Jeffrey. I had asked Jeffrey to accompany me because I felt his legal knowledge and down-to-earth common sense and keen understanding of human nature would be quite valuable to me during the proceedings.

Ms. Brown immediately began hardball tactics. Since Jeff was not an attorney, and was not a party to the suit, Ms. Brown insisted that he be barred from assisting me and that he must leave the room. I was really upset, but I didn't let it show. I was truly on my own and I genuinely missed having my son at my side.

The hearings, arranged around all our appointment calendars, took a number of weeks. Conducted in a quasi-formal atmosphere, not in official court surroundings, they were not subject to rigid legal rules. In such a setting, I was able to see more readily the stupidity and lack of common sense on the part of the opposing attorneys, even though they came from such a high-ranking, leading law firm.

For example, based on my tax returns, they said it was obvious I was a businessman with a substantial amount of varied investments in the stock market. This surely proved that I was a sophisticated and experienced individual in financial matters.

I listened carefully as they spoke about my many qualities as a businessman and emphasized my extensive knowledge as an investor. When they finished their lengthy presentation regarding my extraordinary financial abilities, they thought for sure that the arbitrator would be impressed with their flattering remarks.

I quietly thanked Ms. Brown for giving me such a complimentary introduction, particularly as it pertained to my investment expertise. I noted she would have been correct if she had confined her praise to my judgment in matters of foreign trade, political issues, and overall general knowledge. She forgot to mention the most important point: that I was wise enough to accept my own limitations; namely, my complete ignorance about Wall Street and the world connected with it. I explained to the arbitrator and lawyers that my income tax returns corroborated

the point I was making, and that they would find the evidence of
that in those same tax returns. If they bothered looking, and
used common sense, they would see that I spent a substantial
amount of money each year on financial advisors. This was definite proof that professional advisors handled my financial matters—not me!

I emphasized that that was why, when I decided to go to
Dreyfus for an investment portfolio, I had turned for advice to
their representative. The only conclusion to be reached was that
Dreyfus led me astray. Their faces turned red when I stressed
this point. I could also see the expression on the arbitrator's
face—he could barely suppress his grin. The attorneys never referred to my sophistication in financial matters again.

They continued to try to intimidate me. At one point, Ms.
Brown raised her voice while firing a series of questions at me. I
looked her right in the eyes and said, quietly, calmly, and firmly,
"Ms. Brown, don't ever raise your voice to me!"

She looked askance at the judge, who turned to me and explained that it wasn't unusual for some lawyers to use this technique when questioning witnesses. I replied, "Your Honor, I do
not know how other lawyers conduct their questioning, but I
hear Ms. Brown raising her voice to me." I pointed at her. "She
has no right to do so. My parents had that right, and so did my
teachers. But she hasn't earned that right. As far as I am concerned, I am not the criminal here, her client is. Ms. Brown can
ask me all the questions she wants to ask, but it has to be in a civilized way. I will not permit her to raise her voice to me."

I think that brought the trial to its turning point. The
Dreyfus lawyers went into shock. Their legal presentation had
been discredited by a layman and was now focused on common
sense issues. What I learned from this experience is that you can
be trapped into using legalese and legalities when what is
needed is simply some basic common sense.

Dreyfus had tried to convince me and the arbitrator that
their multi-million dollar advertising campaigns, their direct
mail literature, and the disclaimers therein were all written and
published by underlings in a vacuum, without consulting top
management or the legal department. I knew very well from do-

ing business with large catalogue houses that you couldn't write the copy for a multi-million-dollar campaign and get it published without going through legal channels and also top management. There were just too many things that could go wrong, and you had to make sure there was "truth in advertising," or be liable to your customers.

To prove my point, I asked Ms. Brown to put Mr. DiMartino, the president of Dreyfus, and other top executives on the stand. She declined, because they would have to prove they had nothing to do with the ads, and it was obvious that they did.

It didn't take long for the arbitrator to see that Dreyfus management wasn't telling the truth. I was obviously not the financial genius they made me out to be, and it was clear that someone at Dreyfus had to have been "assisting" my financial decision-making.

My contention was that they had lured me, advised me, and then acted against the benefit of their own client. Dreyfus was obviously involved in each transaction, from A to Z. Denying it made no sense. The notion that they simply placed orders at the behest of clients without offering financial advice held no water.

The point I wanted to make was that Dreyfus was indeed acting as my financial advisor. The judge smiled when I said, "Your Honor, if it looks like a duck, if it quacks like a duck, if it walks like a duck, it's a duck.

"Dreyfus buys and sells. And Dreyfus is a financial advisor. Therefore, it is a duck."

I disproved every one of Dreyfus's assertions and showed that they had done the opposite of what they claimed. I established that the advertisements I received were unsolicited, that I had had discussions with their representative, and that that representative bought commercial paper of their choosing for my account.

When the arbitration hearing ended I anxiously waited for the final decision. In my summation I asked for compensatory and punitive damages. Ms. Brown was vehemently against punitive damages, but I was stubborn. I had proven my case and wanted them, regardless of Ms. Brown's objections.

Judgment was issued on March 19, 1990 and the first person

I called was my dear friend, Paul Hodys. I gleefully announced that I had won the case, and had been awarded compensation for the total amount of $16,826.80, plus interest.

"Roman," he said, "you deserve a medal."

I told him to sit down, I wasn't finished. Then I dropped the bomb. "Paul, not only did I get compensatory damages, I have also been awarded $50,000 in punitive damages."

I wasn't there to see his jaw drop, but I am certain it did.

"Did you say punitive damages?" he asked.

"Yes, I did." And then I read him the first three paragraphs of the American Arbitration Association Award.

"I, THE UNDERSIGNED ARBITRATOR, having been designated in accordance with the Arbitration Agreement entered into between the above-named Parties and dated June 25, 1987, and having been duly sworn, and having duly heard the proofs and allegations of the Parties, do hereby, Award, as follows:

"Within thirty (30) days from the date of transmittal of this Award to the Parties, DREYFUS SERVICE CORPORATION hereinafter referred to as RESPONDENT, shall pay to ROMAN KENT, hereinafter referred to as CLAIMANT, the sum of SIXTEEN THOUSAND EIGHT HUNDRED TWENTY SIX DOLLARS AND EIGHTY CENTS ($16,826.80) plus interest thereon at the rate of 9% per annum from the date of June 25, 1987 to the date of payment.

"Within thirty (30) days from the date of transmittal of this Award to the Parties, RESPONDENT shall also pay CLAIMANT the sum of FIFTY THOUSAND DOLLARS ($50,000.00) representing punitive damages."

I was proud of my singular effort which had culminated in such a total victory. Paul enthusiastically applauded me and said that this was indeed a remarkable achievement, like a mouse going up against a lion, against Dreyfus, one of the most powerful financial institutions.

I was elated with the win, especially with the punitive damages. The press covered the story, and it earned column inches in prestigious financial magazines and newspapers. I attribute the coverage to the fact that punitive damages were rarely imposed on financial institutions, especially in arbitration, and because it was even more unusual for someone who represented himself, pro se, to win a case—let alone get punitive damages.

Ms. Brown and her fancy law firm did not take defeat lightly. They appealed the arbitrator's decision to the New York State Supreme Court, despite their written agreement that the arbitrator's decision was final. They claimed that New York State did not allow arbitrators to award punitive damages.

I thought Dreyfus was utterly cynical, deceitful, and underhanded. They presented themselves to the public as a trustworthy, honest, and highly respected financial institution. They signed an arbitration agreement, and now they were breaking it because they needed to look for something that would negate the unfavorable judgment against them and the adverse publicity.

They won on appeal, and I never got my punitive damages. Still, I feel that my David vs. Goliath effort paid off and brought me a great deal of personal satisfaction. I recovered my losses, but more important was the fact that I had protected future investors. Dreyfus had to change its advertising and eventually the law regarding binding arbitration was changed. After my case, arbitrators in New York State *were* given the right to award punitive damages. Today, when a document says that arbitration is binding, that is exactly what it means—there are no more double standards. Financial institutions must now abide by an arbitrator's decision, including punitive damages. The loopholes have been closed.

It was a long and tedious fight, but in the end I proved that one man can make a difference, and that you can, indeed, fight the equivalent of City Hall and garner a sweet victory.

Twenty-two
Starting a Family

"All the money in the world means nothing if there is no love and joy at home."

Living through the Holocaust made some survivors afraid of making long-term commitments. I fell into this category. When it came to meeting the opposite sex with an eye toward the future and settling down, I was in no hurry.

I gradually reached a point in my life, however, when I realized that one's accomplishments were really meaningless if there was no one with whom to share the experience. There was also the matter of continuity and family life. Considering how quickly years passed—I was, by then, in my early thirties—I knew it would be a mistake to wait much longer to actively search for my soulmate. As I became more conscious of these factors, fate stepped in to lend a helping hand.

During Leon's internship at Kings County Hospital in Brooklyn, Hanki told me about a tenth anniversary reunion of Holocaust orphans she was invited to attend. They'd all attended a boarding school in Aglasterhausen, Kreis Mosbach, Germany, were cared for by UNRRA, and came to the United States on the *Marine Flasher.* Hanki asked me to come along and casually mentioned that a girlfriend of hers, a fellow orphan named Hannah Starkman, would be there. The get-together was in New York.

At that time, Hannah was living in Detroit, Michigan, where "they" sent her when she arrived because she had family there. I had no clue that Hannah was my *bashert,* my intended, and that fate was bringing us together.

When I headed to the reunion, I wasn't thinking about what it means when couples have things in common, or what it would be like to meet a woman who had things in common with me. After meeting Hannah, it was obvious how important such things really are and how much I had been missing in my life by not being able to share things with the women I dated casually.

Hannah and I had lots in common. We were both raised and educated in Lodz and were in the ghetto there, though she spent more time in the ghetto in Radom than in Lodz. We'd been deported to the same places and had both ended up in the boondocks of America—far from New York City, the hub of the survivor community. We needed to shape our own lives without our parents. Her surviving brother had also attended the Jewish Gymnasium in Lodz, so I had the chance to make a new friend.

Hanki introduced us and it was as if Hannah and I formed an instant bond. Of course, the fact that she happened to be attractive, well-spoken, and intelligent did not hurt. I was hooked and could contemplate a family and future with Hannah . . . I knew that much right after we met.

The geographical challenge was huge. There were 482 miles between us, and with my schedule, this was not something to be sneezed at. Of course, being a *"tzelayger"* who could drive through a blizzard with a candle defroster, I managed. Right now there are two versions of the story in circulation. Here's mine: I was doing lots of business in Chicago—about 717 miles from New York—and had to make two trips there each month. I routed my Chicago flights through Detroit, which, of course, was purely coincidental and no big deal—giving me a chance to see Hannah. I could never admit to myself, the true son of my father, that this new-fangled route to Chicago was devised solely for the intention of seeing Hannah.

Hannah's version is probably closer to the truth. She claims that the stopovers in Detroit *were* to see her, and not to drum up business in Detroit. It was the business that was coincidental, not Hannah.

As is usually the case in life, both these versions are somewhat correct, with the truth lying somewhere in between. Looking back, I admit that though I did need to make business trips to Chicago, my business in Detroit was mostly of a personal nature.

Time spent in Detroit wasn't all pleasure—I did take advantage of the opportunity to develop a few business contacts there in order to justify the stopovers to myself. In the here and now, however, in black and white, in print for posterity, I must admit that Hannah Starkman was the motivation prompting my frequent detours to Motown.

Once we had spent some quality time together in Detroit, we planned a summer vacation together at the Nevele Resort in the famous Catskill Mountains in upstate New York. Please keep in mind that in those days when a man and woman vacationed together, they had separate rooms and proper decorum was maintained at all times. In places like the Nevele, the Concord, Kutsher's, and Grossinger's, there was always something to do—from tennis, golf, volleyball, swimming, ice and roller skating, to eating meals that made the tables collapse and made the waiters feel like they had to be octopuses. In a place like the Nevele, people could get to know each other in a relaxed atmosphere without a lot of pressure. Hannah and I spent lots of time together and soon discovered that in some ways we were completely different, despite our common backgrounds.

For example, even before the war, I always loved sports, and as an adult I still enjoyed and participated in them. It soon became obvious that my future wife did not share the same enthusiasm or the ability to actively participate in such activities. Unlike other women who would kvetch and moan about being sports widows, Hannah, even though she had no interest, did not voice any objections to my participation. She even encouraged me to have fun with the boys because she knew I enjoyed it. It was essential to me that Hannah understand that, and I never even had to talk about it. I was relieved to know I would never have to listen to incessant nagging and whining, or be subject to any sort of resentment because I loved sports. Hannah, by the way, never was and still isn't ever a nag.

By the time our little Catskills interlude was over, we both knew we were meant for each other, and I guess you can even say we fell in love. (We had no clue about how that worked; it just seemed to happen.) Then, in late 1956, I invited Hannah to come to New York, and she didn't have to make a stopover in Chicago because she was traveling on business of a purely personal nature! As I had decided to marry Hannah, I walked over to West 47th Street, New York's famous Diamond Center, and bought her a pretty rock they told me was a diamond. The attentive salesman, realizing my complete ignorance and inexperience, talked me into buying it and shrewdly advised me not to worry about the size of the ring—I could always bring it back for a proper adjustment.

Now I had a ring, but I didn't have a bride—yet. When Hannah flew in, she stayed with us in Brooklyn, and I don't think she knew what I had up my sleeve. I don't remember what I was wearing or what day of the week it was, but I remember I took her to see a Broadway show, "Most Happy Fella!" I don't remember dinner, but I do remember coming back to Brooklyn, parking in front of the apartment house where we lived, and giving her the ring.

We were married in Detroit on April 7, 1957 with a few close friends and family members in attendance. It somehow didn't seem right—with all our parents killed in the Holocaust—that we should do something elaborate. We honeymooned in Florida and in pre-Castro Cuba.

My sister, Renia, and her husband, Bolek, came in from Sweden for the wedding and decided to join us on the Florida leg of our honeymoon. They figured they had come so far, they wanted to spend some time with me and Hannah and catch some quality time in the hot Florida sun before they went back to Sweden. Somehow they didn't understand that a honeymoon is not meant for four.

To get away from the constant scrutiny of my sister and brother-in-law, Hannah and I escaped to Havana, Cuba for a romantic interlude. Havana was a gorgeous city and the Tropicana Casino/Restaurant was absolutely magnificent. We had a "mahvelous" time doing the Samba and the Tango and all the latest dances. We were young, happy, and finally, carefree.

When we returned to New York we set up housekeeping in an apartment in Forest Hills, Queens. At first, Hannah had a rough time adjusting to life in the big city. She missed her brother and friends and was at loose ends. She had earned her degree in accounting and wasn't used to being idle. She couldn't take sitting around and being a *housefrau*, so she decided to find herself a job. Soon she was working in Manhattan and enjoying it.

Like all newlyweds, we were busy transforming our little apartment into a comfortable home. Once that was done, our thoughts turned to children. We knew that raising a family would really help us to complete the picture. This was particularly true for us because, as Holocaust survivors, it was of utmost importance for both of us to create this continuity in remembrance of our families. We were already in our thirties and age was a factor to consider as well.

Susan Irene was born on December 10, 1958. I wrote the verse on her birth announcement, long before it was fashionable for daddies to do that. Although I was thrilled to become a father and see this beautiful little baby, I admit I was afraid to hold the tiny baby in my arms because I thought I might drop her and do harm to the adorable little creature. Even today I am not at ease while holding fragile infants in my arms.

The baby completely changed our lives and everything revolved around her. It was a good thing that many of our neighbors in the garden apartments had young children and Hannah was able to share the new experience of being a mother with her new friends. This was of major importance to us, since neither one of us had mothers to advise us. It was healthy for Hannah to have neighbors who acted as a support group while I was away working long hours and traveling extensively. In effect, the neighbors became the substitute for the families we had both lost during the Holocaust.

I found it fascinating to see the day-by-day changes in Susie as she developed. The differences were particularly noticeable when I returned from a trip and hadn't seen her for a few days. While I was away, I looked forward to seeing my daughter again, and was always astounded by how much she had grown and the progress she had made.

Susie also precipitated the need for larger living quarters. We did not want to raise our children in the city and so we looked to the suburbs. We preferred a house surrounded by grass, trees, and a big yard, where our children could play without fear of traffic and where it would be possible for them to have a loving dog as a companion, something Hannah did not have as a child and did not understand.

We checked out Long Island and decided that Westchester was more appealing. Long Island was flat. Westchester had green hills; there were many large trees and the houses were farther apart. One of Hannah's friends from Detroit already lived in Westchester County and loved it. There were also tennis courts available for public use, and that was important to me.

To celebrate our second wedding anniversary, we purchased a beautiful new split-level home in New Rochelle. At that point, the house was not yet built; we made the selection from blueprints and hoped that our first home would be our dream house. In a way it was, and the move was easy since we did not have much furniture to take with us.

For quite a while, our new home was decorated in what I call Chinese Style. It had carpeting, scant pieces of furniture, and lots of pillows. For our little girl, it was Paradise on Earth. There were no restrictions imposed on her, and she could crawl anywhere and everywhere she wanted. She had the living room and dining room all to herself without worrying about bumping into anything.

In our larger home, our thoughts turned toward expanding the family.

Jeffrey Edward came into the world on December 27, 1960 and joined the Kents of Westchester. As an expectant father waiting at the hospital for him to arrive, I recall a huge, imposing figure giving me a big hug and congratulating me on the birth of my son. It was like a scene from a movie. I knew this doctor, but I had no idea how he'd gotten there. He was one of Leon's medical school classmates from Tulane University and best man at his wedding!

It turned out that Dr. Neil August was an anesthesiologist at the hospital. When he was filling out paperwork listing the names of the parents, he saw Hannah Kent's name as mother of the newborn infant, which did not mean anything to him. But when he noticed the name Roman as the father, he said to himself that this had to be the brother of his old friend, Leon. Life is totally unpredictable. It is absolutely strange how my wife met Neil—who now lived and practiced medicine in Westchester. Considering the way he met Hannah, and the condition she was in, it was amazing that we renewed our acquaintance and saw each other socially during the years that followed.

Our house was in a development full of families with young children, and so Hannah had the same kind of support system she had developed among her friends in Forest Hills. The women helped each other in emergencies and counseled each other on common childhood problems. This was a great comfort to me, because I was on the road a lot.

When the children were young, my business trips were short. But when I traveled to the Far East, which was rare, it involved lots of time away from home.

On one extended trip to the Orient, I was missing the kids terribly, and felt a particular urge to communicate with them. I decided to share my experiences in Japan with them by creating a homemade picture book. I bought an assortment of postcards and constructed a collage while writing a children's story about that far-away land. Then I pasted the postcards on one page, and described the scenes, with a little imagination thrown in, on the opposite page. I wrote in rhyming verses that were age-appropriate, and it turned into a fairy-tale-type book based on actual places I had seen and visited. When I mailed it home, I hoped the kids would get as much enjoyment reading it as I had putting it together.

By the time I got home, the book about Japan was a hit all around the neighborhood. The children enjoyed it so much, they brought it to school with them and showed it to their teachers. The teachers, in turn, advised my children to tell me to publish it so that other children could benefit from it too, but I never did.

We traveled quite extensively as a family while the children were going to school, taking vacations to various islands in the Caribbean, to Europe, and to Israel. One of the most memorable trips was a trip to Poland to show the children where Hannah and I had been born and had spent our childhood years. Susan came with us, but Jeffrey decided to stay in the States.

Marian Turski, one of my old schoolmates who still lives in Poland and is the historical editor for Poland's most prestigious weekly newsmagazine, *Politika,* made the trip very meaningful. He insisted on taking a week off from work to show us the length and breadth of his Poland, and no one could have shown us the country better than he.

I was going to show Susie, now a high school student, where the apartment building we lived in was still standing, where the factory used to be, and where we spent four years in the ghetto. Three of my Polish friends in Lodz joined us for that excursion. One of them was a reporter.

We arranged to meet on the corner of Srodmiejska and Gdanska Streets, where the house was located. Susie was with my friends in one car and I was in another. When I arrived, I was amused to find one of them busily explaining to her that there had been a textile factory right across the street. He went on to say that during the war the Germans took all of the machinery out of the factory and it then became a warehouse. After the war, the Polish government continued to use it as such.

Then he informed Susie that several years before our visit, there was a big fire that took the fire department three days to bring under control. The walls of the factory collapsed during the fierce blaze and the building was reduced to rubble. At that point, the Polish government decided to construct a school on the vacant land.

My friend asked me if I remembered the factory. Instead of answering I burst out laughing. My daughter innocently asked me what was so funny. "Do I remember it?" I asked. "I will never forget it as long as I live. The factory belonged to my father! That is where my brother and I spent many happy hours in our youth playing and getting into mischief.

"In fact," I added, "the small structure you see in the back, separate from the newly built school, is the little building where my family lived after the Germans evicted us from our apartment. We lived there for several months until we were forced into the ghetto." Then I showed Susie the beautiful Poznanski family palace, right next door to the apartment house.

Later that day, I took Susie to the area that used to be the ghetto and showed her where I had dug my fields and where we lived. She was very quiet and subdued, the same mood she showed when I brought her to Auschwitz on the way to Cracow and the Carpathian Mountains.

Susie was deep in thought, trying to connect to her family history for the first time, putting imagination in sync with reality. She says she was reaching into history, wondering how Hannah and I and the others could survive it all. In Auschwitz-Birkenau, she said that no book had prepared her, no stories could prepare her for the stark reality of smokestack after smokestack after smokestack. She was thinking about how impossible it was that people could do such things to each other, and thought back to the story of Lala, our dog. She said that she was tumbling through her emotions, going from highs to lows as she walked through the places of my past.

When we returned to the States, Susie described the nice part of our trip to Poland in such glowing terms, and the "other" part in such moving terms, that Jeffrey asked me to take him during our next summer vacation.

When we got to Warsaw, my friend, Marian, again insisted on taking a week off to do the same for Jeffrey as he had for Susie. Jeffrey, like Susie before him, thoroughly appreciated the trip.

The most moving moment came as we visited my father's grave in Lodz. After briefly meditating at the gravesite, my wife and son left me, and I stood there alone reflecting on the past. When I heard somebody coming, I looked up to see Jeffrey returning to my side to say Yizkor, the Jewish prayer for the souls of the departed. This was the first time Jeffrey felt connected to his grandparents. And because my son was there to stand with me at my father's grave, that particular trip to Poland will stand out in my memory forever.

During our vacations, I made it a point to always rent a car to travel through the countryside and neighboring regions so that we could see how the local inhabitants lived their daily lives. In many parts of the world, a great majority of the people lived under terrible economic conditions. In order to appreciate how lucky we were to afford our lifestyle, I wanted to make sure that my children understood the plight of the less fortunate.

In these travels, my children were exposed to different cultures, though they were already aware of the many diverse customs prevailing in various countries. I believe that dealing with individuals from distant lands helped them better understand people at a very early age. I never figured it might help them get into college, but it did. Our teenagers were quickly approaching that age when we had to think about higher education. There was no question in any of our minds that they would continue with their studies and attend well-regarded colleges.

In America, most kids want to spread their wings by selecting colleges a good distance from their homes. Knowing this, we told our kids that they could attend any college that accepted them within a 200-mile radius of our house. Hannah and I felt strongly that there were more than enough good colleges to pick from in the New York area. We wanted the children to go to schools a reasonable distance from home yet still make it possible for us to see them periodically. This way, during long weekends and holidays, they could spend some time at home and we could visit them without too much of a hassle.

Susie chose one of the finest universities in the country, the University of Pennsylvania, and we were indeed pleased that she was accepted. Two years later it was Jeffrey's turn to select a college, and the University of Pennsylvania was his first choice, too.

What happened at one of Jeffrey's interviews was quite curious. He was asked about his parents' backgrounds during the meeting. When the question of a scholarship was broached, Jeffrey replied he was not asking for any financial assistance. This seemed to surprise the interviewer, who asked, "Why not? Your father is a refugee so why wouldn't you apply for it?" I was very proud when my son told him that I believed financial help is for people who really need it. Since we did not, the scholarship should be reserved for those in need.

For six years, we visited Philadelphia regularly because our children were there and we looked forward to seeing them—and Princess, the dog. Our Princess, a beautiful Norwegian elkhound, now lived with Susie in the City of Brotherly Love. We had had Princess since she was a puppy and we really missed having her around the house, but it was interesting to see how Susie arranged for the dog to attend the same classes she did. We felt that "three of our children" were attending U of P, while we paid tuition for two. How many people can say that their family pet had almost earned a college degree?

Unfortunately, Princess did not make it to commencement. She was put to sleep before graduation, due to advanced age and ill health. Taking Princess to the vet to end her life was extremely difficult for my children, because they loved her and because they remembered the story of Lala, my beloved dog, who was probably shot by the Germans.

Once Susie left for college, it was immediately evident to Hannah and me just how quiet the house had become, and when I first heard it, the expression "empty nesters" rang true. Imagine! We even missed the constant arguments between our children. Poor Jeffrey had no one to fight with except his parents.

Two years later, our quiet home became virtually silent when Jeffrey left for college. Our friends had warned us that when our kids were gone, there would be a period of adjustment and they guaranteed that in time we would get used to it—so used to it, in fact, that when the kids would come to visit, we would be thrilled to have them back—to a point. After a few days we would happily anticipate their departures and exclaim, "See you around! Bye!" as soon as we gracefully could.

Susie loved animals and wanted to pursue a career working with them. Jeffrey went to Wharton and concentrated on finance and architecture. After graduation, Susie set out to find herself. She moved to Colorado, was happy working in a factory that manufactured costumes for square dancers, and was pleased that the move offered her the opportunity to pursue her love of skiing. But the factory job taught her that she needed more schooling to accomplish her goals.

She thought the best way to figure out what she really wanted to do was to come home and volunteer in a hospital. She did such a good job as a volunteer, the hospital offered her a paying position, but the experience also taught her that medicine was not her métier. She then wanted to become a pediatric physical therapist. Accepted at Duke University in Durham, NC, she graduated with a master's degree in physical therapy.

One Passover, Hannah prepared an entire seder at our home in Connecticut, and we "shlepped" it down to Duke so Susie and her friends could enjoy a proper Passover. Some of her friends had never been to a seder and this was a first!

Jeff was also making major career decisions. He thought about international law, and so planned a trip to Vienna, Austria, the center of East/West trade. Coincidentally, a classmate of mine from Lodz, another Holocaust survivor, was now living in Vienna and would keep an eye on him. It eased my mind to know that while he was so far from home, Jeff would have somebody to call upon for assistance.

Destiny, however, had other plans and brought Jeffrey's promising career to an unexpected halt. It began innocently enough when Jeffrey and his friend, after graduating from college, were traveling through the Canadian Rockies. They were accompanied by Jeff's cousin from Sweden, Renia's daughter, Suzanne.

The three of them flew from New York to Los Angeles to visit Hanki, now living in California. Then they rented a car and began the journey North. They eventually arrived in Kelowna in the interior of British Columbia, a beautiful spot in the Rockies, where they were to spend a couple of days.

Returning to home base after purchasing provisions for a barbecue, Suzanne insisted on driving the car. Throughout the trip she had not driven, and the boys had been reluctant to let her drive because of her lack of experience. However, since this was a small town with very little traffic, the guys finally relented and said it was okay for her to take the wheel.

While driving, Suzanne did not notice a stop sign and crossed an intersection at the same time as a large garbage truck. It slammed into their car exactly where Jeffrey was sitting. The car was no match for the garbage truck, and the impact was devastating. Jeffrey was unconscious when they pulled him out of the wreck and was rushed to the nearest hospital with internal bleeding, punctured lungs, and broken bones. Jeffrey was in dreadful shape. Fortunately, after emergency surgery, the doctors were able to save his life.

Later, in New York, other doctors discovered that Jeffrey had sustained additional serious injuries unnoticed at the time. An X-ray of his skull, a routine procedure in cases like this in the United States, was not taken in BC. Therefore, the terrible damage to Jeff's jaw and sinuses was not revealed. He is still living with the life-altering repercussions of the accident. Though the accident inflicted such extensive pain and suffering on Jeffrey, curiously, the driver and other passenger were hardly hurt. They walked away from the scene with only a few minor scrapes and bruises.

At the time of the accident, Hannah and I were just completing a fact-finding mission to Africa for the Anti-Defamation League (ADL). The next day we were due to embark on our long-awaited picture-taking safari in Botswana, but just before we left, Susie called us, hysterical, and told us that Jeff had been involved in a serious automobile accident.

Frantically, we tried to find the fastest modes of transportation to get to western North America to be there with Jeffrey in his hour of need. For the next thirty-six hours we flew more than halfway around the world. Susie joined us when we stopped in New York on the way to Kelowna. When we arrived at the hospital, the doctors told us that Jeff was still in the Intensive Care Unit and that we would have to control our emotions and remain quiet.

Regardless of the warning, we could hardly refrain from screaming aloud. Our hearts stopped beating for a brief moment when we saw our Jeffrey lying almost lifeless in the hospital bed. It was impossible not to react. The last time we saw him he was so happy and excited about his impending trip to the Rockies, and now this.

To see him there, in ICU, breathing heavily with tubes, bandages, and all other kinds of paraphernalia hanging off of him, was more than we thought we could handle. For the next few days, we remained at his side as his fight for life continued. He was in a comatose state most of the time but slowly he made enough progress to be taken off the critical list.

After a while, he improved sufficiently for the hospital to discharge him. Since he was still unable to fly back home, we rented an apartment in the vicinity. Even while he was in the hospital and not completely sedated, he constantly complained of severe pain in the jaw, particularly when he attempted to swallow. We discussed the situation with the doctors and were told that the pain he had while swallowing was totally normal and to be expected after undergoing such tremendous trauma during the accident. Little did we know that in addition to his other problems he had broken his jaw in three places. No wonder he complained of pain and had difficulty in swallowing.

The accident permanently damaged nerves in Jeff's face and his sinuses. Twenty years later, this condition is still a source of pain, suffering, and constant infection—and no doctor, so far, has been able to determine its exact cause or cure.

Unquestionably, the magnitude of the technological advances we have witnessed over the last twenty-plus years has been truly astonishing. That we can travel to the outer limits of the universe, to the moon and stars, that we transmit billions of pieces of information per second through thin air via satellites and computers is mind-boggling. Shouldn't it be child's play for the medical profession to come up with a cure for my son's condition? That fateful day completely changed Jeffrey's life by destroying his dreams for the future, and touched every aspect of our lives. The focal point of our existence was Jeffrey's health, and we are still focused on that. Jeff is still battling for good health and no matter what I had gone through before, there is nothing quite as difficult as watching your own son suffer.

Jeffrey eventually did go to Vienna for more than a year, and tried to continue with his plans. While he was there, he sought out medical experts. We will never lose hope, and we believe that among the new technologies being developed all over the world there is one that will ease Jeff's pain.

As for Susie, in order to get her master's at Duke, she had to intern in a hospital, so she volunteered to work at a children's hospital in Denver, Colorado. Lots of her friends from U of P were living there, and she could go skiing whenever she wanted. I believe it was *bashert,* predestined, because while there, her friend

Andrea casually introduced her to a fellow named Bob Avjian, who not long after they met, became her husband. They married in 1986 and settled in Denver to start their life together. Today, they are the proud parents of three wonderful, bright and adorable children, two girls and a boy: Dara, 17, Eryn, 15, and Sean, 9. At this writing, they live in Maryland, where Bob works as an engineer and Susie is an outstanding physical therapist, if I do say so myself.

Susie has devoted a great deal of time pioneering a technique that uses horseback riding to assist in the recovery of paraplegics. While horseback riding, quadriplegic patients slowly begin to regain limited use of their arms and legs—something impossible under normal circumstances. Susie is perfectly suited to this program, because in addition to her specialty in pediatric physical therapy, she happens to be an accomplished, ardent horseback rider.

Once it was determined that our nest in New Rochelle was too big for the two of us, we decided to buy a smaller house, with the caveat that it have a tennis court—or if not the court itself, then enough room to build one. There was no way I was going to live without playing tennis regularly . . . and even though I am now in my eighties, I am still an avid player!

Being on a tennis court and hitting the ball somehow enables me to forget many of my problems and worries. I have the capacity to become completely engrossed in the game, which helps me to relax. Hannah has never fully understood how and why I want to play tennis even when I am sick with a cold. For some unexplained reason, playing tennis with a cold makes me feel better—it seems to me that the cold just vanishes!

Of course, instead of buying a smaller home, we purchased a bigger one. In order to justify this, we told ourselves that we needed larger quarters because our children would come home to visit and bring their friends and/or children with them. The new house in Connecticut did not have a tennis court, but it had enough land to build one, so I did.

My love of tennis caused me to drag tennis paraphernalia with me on all my trips, particularly when I went on extended visits abroad. I somehow managed to play tennis in unlikely places. For example, I was able to play in Poland, even during the winter months, when the gym in a gigantic building built by the Russians—the Palace of Culture—was converted into a tennis court and you had to pass through military checkpoints to get to it. Imagine playing tennis on a hardwood floor!

In Bucharest, Romania I got permission to participate in a game at the Diplomatic Club, which had beautiful clay courts. I was privileged to play with a young Romanian boy named Ilie Nastase, who later became one of the top-seeded tennis players in the world. Even as a young boy he was fun, and he seemed to be able to maintain his real personality throughout his career. I remember seeing him when he was playing on the senior circuit; he was still full of life and laughter, and could never stay serious for very long. Sometimes I think it may have cost him a few championships.

One of my favorite tennis games was the game of doubles I played with Yitzhak Rabin, then the Defense Minister of the State of Israel. Knowing that he always wanted to win whenever he played, I approached him and said, "Yitzhak, if you want to win, be my partner. If you want to lose, play against me." He looked at me and said, "Let's play together." Of course, we won, and he smiled and told me, "Roman, you were right."

I met his daughter, Dalia, on a recent trip to Israel. When we reminisced about her father, I told her my tennis story and she smiled and simply stated, "He hated to lose."

I promise this is my final tennis story: Hannah and I once entertained Aleksander Kwasniewski, the President of Poland, along with his staff, at our home in Connecticut. After playing tennis with him and winning the first set, the Polish Secretary of State took me aside and told me it was not nice of me to beat the President. I turned to both of them, and replied with a smile, "Remember, he's your president, not mine."

President Kwasniewski was a gracious loser and an extremely polite and pleasant guest. We spent almost an entire Sunday together in my home, and our conversations on different topics were very cordial. The powerful position he held was not in evidence, and so we discussed various matters as friend-to-friend.

Oh, wait, there is just one more! Perhaps my proudest tennis moment took place at a Club Med somewhere in the Caribbean—when I was still "young." I entered all the tennis tournaments and to my great surprise won first place in every category: singles, doubles, and mixed doubles. Reluctantly, I must admit that the week we were vacationing, the other players were not that good. But it was exhilarating to be awarded three medals by two beautiful young ladies, right in front of my family.

Once we moved to Connecticut, I realized that the daily commute to Manhattan was becoming more and more difficult—it took an exorbitant amount of my time and energy, and I wasn't getting any younger. So Hannah and I found ourselves a little pied-à-terre in Manhattan, in Murray Hill, which was just a few blocks from my office. It came in handy after I became very involved with communal work and went to meetings that took us into the wee hours of the morning. At least once a month, Hannah says the apartment added ten years to my life. Of course, she didn't guarantee those years, but I like to think she's right about that.

The older I get, the more I understand that nothing can take the place of a fulfilling family life, but I also know that there is something to be said for having an economic advantage and financial stability. All the money in the world means nothing if there is no love and joy at home.

With the arrival of the grandchildren, my dream of continuity has been partially fulfilled. Of course, I regret that my extended family, like many others in the United States, is far away from us because they have to live where they can find work. It diminishes our closeness, just as it did when I was separated from Leon. As I mentioned previously, the inability of family members to share daily trials and tribulations prevents the added intimacy that brings families together.

Though we don't see our beloved grandchildren on a daily basis, Hannah and I are in constant touch with our daughter and her family. We are updated regularly on the goings-on at the Avjian house, and greatly enjoy hearing about their progress via telephone and periodic visits.

When I look at my children and grandchildren, I wish for

them the peace, contentment, and happiness I have experienced in my lifetime, without the pain and the agony. There were days, weeks, months, and years when I thought I wouldn't live even a moment longer. Seeing my children and grandchildren is a miracle; it is the best revenge on Hitler and proof he did not succeed.

Twenty-three
Communal Involvement

"If I am not for myself, who will be for me? . . . If I am only for myself, who am I?"—Rabbi Hillel

In the mid-1980s I devoted more of my time to various humanitarian organizations. I realized that doing something for soci-
ety-at-large meant more to me than it did before, and I was
drawn to different organizations, particularly those that pre-
served the memory of the Holocaust, worthwhile charities, and
educational foundations. The older I got, the more convinced I
became that only education can prevent a Holocaust or genocide
from ever happening again—to us or to any other people.

As I checked out my options and became more intimately involved with some of the organizations, I soon realized that while
monetary contributions were always welcome, money was not
the most precious commodity I could offer the community. My
time, knowledge, experience, and devotion counted even more.

The organizations nearest and dearest to me, and in which I
am still deeply involved in varying degrees, are The American
Gathering of Jewish Holocaust Survivors, the Jewish Founda-
tion for the Righteous, the Conference of Jewish Material Claims
Against Germany (the Claims Conference), the Presidential Ad-
visory Commission on Holocaust Assets in the U.S., the Interna-
tional Commission on Holocaust Era Insurance Claims
(ICHEIC), the Anti-Defamation League (ADL), the Holocaust &
Jewish Resistance Teachers' Training Program, the Warsaw
Ghetto Resistance Organization (WAGRO), and the German
Foundation Initiative.

WAGRO

The Warsaw Ghetto Resistance Organization is probably the oldest group that commemorates the Warsaw Ghetto uprising in April 1943 and perpetuates its significance. They, and the Bergen-Belsen Survivors Association, were the first groups I was aware of that sanctified Yom Ha-Shoah, Holocaust Commemoration Day. (In Israel it is called Yom Ha-Shoah Vegvurah—the day of the Holocaust and the day of heroism, in order not to forget the resistance.)

Forty years ago there wasn't much to talk about and people hardly cared to straggle in. Today, the commemoration that WAGRO sponsors in New York City fills Temple Emanuel in New York, and there were times the organization even filled Madison Square Garden. Presidents and vice presidents of the United States and other countries, Prime Ministers and Ambassadors, Secretaries of State, and other plenipotentiaries have all attended. The commemoration was transformed into a national event in America, called Days of Remembrance, observed even in the Rotunda on Capitol Hill with most of Congress in attendance.

WAGRO was instrumental in bringing Yom Ha-Shoah commemorations to local synagogues and Jewish community centers all over the world. It also made it an official observance in Washington, in almost every State Capitol, in the United States Armed Forces, and in places one can hardly imagine.

The credit for this work must go to the outstanding individuals who devoted themselves to making sure that they were true to the promises we all made in the camps and the ghettos, in hiding and in resistance: to bear witness. Among them are Elie Wiesel, noted author and Nobel Peace Prize Laureate and founding Chairman of the United States Holocaust Memorial Museum, the late Ben Meed, president of the American Gathering of Jewish Holocaust Survivors, the late Sigmund Strochlitz, one of the organizers of the World Gathering of Holocaust Survivors in Israel in 1981, Miles Lerman, an active leader of the United States Holocaust Memorial Museum, and Sam Bloch, head of the

Bergen-Belsen Survivors Association. Humbly, but proudly, I would also add my name to this distinguished list.

The overall support and dedication of survivors from every state in the union must be acknowledged. The creation of the United States Holocaust Museum, which grew out of the United States Holocaust Memorial Council established by President Jimmy Carter, definitely added to the impact.

In 2002, because the WAGRO commemoration had grown so large and the survivors weren't getting any younger—many of them had already passed on—Ben Meed and the members of the organization, with heavy hearts, decided to ask the Museum of Jewish Heritage—a living memorial to the Holocaust in downtown Manhattan—to take over the ceremony, in the spirit of passing the torch.

The ADL (Anti-Defamation League)

My involvement with the ADL was of a completely different nature. The ADL is concerned with fighting prejudice and hatred of all kinds, and of course, anti-Semitism is the issue that is always on its front burner.

I took two interesting leadership trips with them: one to Africa in 1982 and the other to South America in 1983. I believe that our trip to Africa, where we met with key officials and Jewish leaders in different countries, greatly improved the understanding between the United States, Israel, and the African nations. Lobbying for such understanding was the main purpose of our trip, in the shadow of the damage done by NGOs in Africa, the non-governmental organizations who were calling Israel apartheid and racist, after the UN voted in a resolution that said Zionism equals racism.

In Africa, we met with Kenyan Minister Moi who described how he, during the Israeli rescue raid on Entebbe, helped make the arrangements for Israeli planes to refuel in mid-air. We also met with President Mobutu, of Zaire, on his presidential yacht. He arrived by helicopter and hosted what he called a "simple dinner," an unforgettable banquet with a variety of foods one hardly encounters anywhere in the world. He was a dictator who raped his country and murdered his countrymen, but I must admit that night, at least, President Mobutu and his wife were the most charming hosts.

Of course, there is no free lunch, or in this case, "simple dinner."

After our sumptuous meal, we had a serious discussion about his expectations pertaining to financial aid from the United States—then blocked in Congress for non-payment of interest on existing loans. It was ludicrous to listen to Mobutu pleading poverty and the inability to repay the interest on the loans when his own net worth was in the billions of dollars. We politely suggested that if he invested a bit of his personal fortune to pay the interest, then Congress would likely release the foreign aid he was seeking. This was a particularly sensitive issue. I knew very well that the money Mobutu accumulated in his personal European bank accounts really belonged to Zaire, but he considered all of it his private property.

We finished our mission in Zimbabwe, where we met with government officials and Jewish community leaders. Once that was done, Hannah and I and a few other people from our delegation were going to go on a highly anticipated and eagerly awaited photo-taking safari in Botswana—and that was when Jeffrey was hurt in the car accident in the Canadian Rockies, aborting our safari.

On our trip to South America in 1983, we went to Argentina to see if we could get any information about the *disparacitos,* the disappeared ones—particularly the 5,000 or so Jewish students among them who vanished during the days of terror under Allende. Most of them were children of Holocaust survivors who settled in Argentina after the war. A thriving Jewish community had existed in that country since the middle of the 19th century, and this was devastating to the Jewish community there, as well as to others who had lost their children.

A new liberal president, Raoul Alfonsin, was in power when we arrived and we had our meetings with him and with various ministers and Jewish community leaders.

When we were in Buenos Aires, we saw the desperate moth-

ers and grandmothers of the *desparacitos* who gathered daily in
the Plaza de Mayo, where they prominently displayed pictures of
their missing children. We were intensely interested in the fate
of all the thousands of children who had disappeared without a
trace. When we investigated, however, it became obvious that
Jewish prisoners received worse treatment than the thousands
of non-Jewish students who were also jailed and killed. Most of
the Jewish students were killed because they were Jewish, by
members of Battalion 601, an Army Intelligence Unit with a
fearsome reputation for ruthlessness. According to civil rights
groups, individuals taken by this battalion for interrogation
were first tortured, then dragged behind a vehicle, loaded into
airplanes, and then thrown into the sea from above.

We were hopeful that personal intervention on the part of
American Jewry would help to uncover the whereabouts of, at
the very least, the corpses of these children. So, while we did receive proper "recognition" from the authorities, the bottom line
was that our meetings were not productive. We assumed that all
of the Jewish students who disappeared were dead and their
bodies would not be recovered.

Our meetings with the Jewish communal leaders in Argentina brought back painful memories. The existing climate in that
country reminded me of the mood in Europe all through history.
Argentinean Jews had to endure all kinds of persecution and
were afraid to raise their voices to exert their rights. Each member of the ADL contingent was presented with a thick folder
filled with documents, and we were given additional verbal explanations as to what the Jewish community did or did not do to
prevent the illegal seizure of their sons and daughters.

After soul-searching, I felt I had to tell them that they were
behaving as timidly as our forefathers had in Europe. They, too,
were afraid to raise their voices, and so they lost what they had.
It was time to speak up and exert their rights, I said. I tried to
impress upon them that Jews were no longer in the same powerless position they had been in before the war, and that we did not
have to act like our ancestors. The State of Israel was there to
protect us, and the Diaspora Jewish community-at-large was

united and had learned the lessons of the Holocaust. Thus, we would stand behind any actions to fight injustice.

I asked them why in heaven's name they hadn't approached the worldwide Jewish community to ask for help, and how come none of the organizations or newspapers had been informed about what was happening to the Jewish students, since they were obviously singled out as Jews? At this point we were asking rhetorical questions, and the leaders understood my frustration regarding their behavior. Even with the best intentions, it was too late to bring back lives that were lost. We left Argentina mourning the loss of many innocent Jewish lives, the future of the Argentine Jewish community—now gone just for being Jewish.

We also had some very interesting meetings in Rio de Janeiro, Brazil. The beachfront of the city was truly breathtaking. At night, however, the beauty was somewhat diminished and the area seemed to take on a sinister dimension. I was a passenger in a car driven by a local Jewish community leader and noticed he did not stop for red lights after dark. When he went through the third red light, I couldn't hold back and politely asked if it was accepted practice to ignore traffic signals in Rio.

Looks are deceiving, he told me. During the day everyone stopped at red lights. At night, carjackings were so common, no one in their right mind would dare to stop. He did assure me that he looked both ways before he entered the intersections—and all things considered, he said, it made more sense to go through the lights than to get robbed and hurt.

Our discussions with the Brazilian Jewish community leaders were mostly about the rising tide of anti-Semitism in that country. The person leading the mission was Nathan Perlmutter, National Director of the ADL, who offered educational materials, know-how, and staff to assist them in fighting the scourge. He also said the Brazilian community would have to pay for the expenses they incurred—office space, staffers, public relations, printing, administrative costs, and so forth. I was shocked when the Brazilians said that that was unfair and that they expected the Americans to absorb all their costs.

The logic behind their reasoning was as follows: since monies donated to ADL by U.S. citizens is tax-deductible, the Brazilians felt that Americans should bear all costs even if the offices are located in Brazil. I noticed Nathan's jaw drop as this convoluted logic left him literally speechless, so I opened my mouth (as a layperson, I could get away with it).

"Gentlemen, you are right. Money donated by individuals to ADL in America is tax-deductible. However, except for saving a percentage of that money on taxes, it is cash money out of each donor's pocket. Talking openly among ourselves, and based on information I have, it seems to me that the tax structure in Brazil is so full of loopholes that hardly anyone who should pay taxes, pays them in full or even partially."

I insisted that they had no valid reason to avoid paying the costs of combating anti-Semitism in their own country. I added that they should appreciate what the National Director of ADL wanted to do for them, and that they should thank the international ADL for the help they were extending to the Jewish community in Brazil. After that, there was no further talk from them about having North Americans pay for the Brazilian ADL.

I did notice something else that was interesting in South America. Most of the wealthy Jews didn't live in villas or mansions. They lived in hi-rise apartment buildings and it struck me as curious until someone told me that it was all about security. The rule of law was so far gone in Brazil, that all people cared about was protecting themselves from criminals, day and night. There were armed guards everywhere, and it was cheaper to guard many apartment homes with two armed guards 24/7, instead of paying for two of them to watch a single, luxurious home that was bound to become a target. Of course, all the Jewish community centers had their own security forces in place, which was really sad to see, but it's much more common today. It's ironic that when I left South America, I felt lucky to live in America, where we didn't need armed guards to protect our Jewish institutions. But then, that was before 9/11.

Argentina and Brazil, I thought, were both South American countries that served as safe haven for many Nazis who escaped from Europe after the war. How unpleasant to think that a good number of those who had murdered us were now leading tranquil, comfortable lives as respected citizens with the sizeable fortunes they brought with them. Today we know they influenced internal policy and were responsible for many deaths in the region, not just in Argentina, but in Peru and Chile as well. The irony was striking.

JFR (The Jewish Foundation for the Righteous)

The Talmud is often quoted in relation to the Holocaust: "He who saves one life, it is as if he saves the entire world."

When I look back at the Kingdom of Night, there is little glory and even less holiness to recall. However, there were three holy gestures which redeemed my faith in humanity and mankind. The first holy gesture was made by individuals, the second was made by a village, and the third was made by an entire nation. Each share a common idea and deed, and all three illuminated a darkened world. The individuals are represented as the righteous gentiles, the village is Le Chambon, and the nation is Denmark . . . three sacred sparks in the Kingdom of Night.

Righteous gentiles stand above all. Their deeds have earned my utmost respect and admiration, because they risked their lives as non-Jewish individuals to hide Jews. They made these decisions and carried out their obligations to those they helped without the support of neighbors and/or their villages. If caught, especially in Poland and central Europe, the consequence was usually death for the individual and his or her entire family.

If you hid a Jew it meant caring for him or them day in and day out, sometimes for months on end, under the most difficult circumstances. When hunger ravaged the entire population, secretly providing extra food was, in itself, a risky and difficult deed. Then there were the neighbors to worry about, knowing full well that any one of them could betray you.

Heroes are usually associated with short-term action. Most acts of heroism don't last more than an hour, or tops, a few days. Heroism, when related to the act of saving a Jew during the Holocaust, is an inadequate word. It can't come close to describing the dangers of choiceless choices and collective responsibility the individual samaritans had to face. Yet most righteous gentiles interviewed about saving Jews during the war offer a common reply: "We did our duty as we saw fit . . . we did nothing extraordinary. We did the right thing because it was the right thing to do."

We know that in the world of the Holocaust, the ordinary was extraordinary. We should—no, we must—honor righteous gentiles for their unselfish and heroic deeds. The survivors should remember and so should the rest of the world.

An old man was planting a tree and his grandson asked, "Why are you planting a tree, Grandfather? You will not live to eat its fruit or enjoy its shade." The old man turned to his grandson and said, "When I was your age, my grandfather planted the tree you are sitting under, the tree with the apples you eat. My task is to plant a tree so that future generations will enjoy its fruit."

Righteous gentiles planted trees of goodness, nourished them with kindness, and made them grow even during the darkest hours of mankind's history. We who rest in the shade of those trees should take our example from them and plant trees of hope and light . . . of guidance, education, and compassion for others.

It is the obligation of those who survived to turn those nightmare years into a moral vision. By sharing their memories with the world, we must use the goodness of these special people as a preventative—to protect future generations from hatred. The righteous gentiles are shining proof that the world doesn't have to be too dangerous to live in because of evil. They remind us that it is important to remember yesterday in order to shape tomorrow, and the splendid, selfless conduct of these rare individuals is an inspirational and uplifting part of our remembrance.

The Jewish Foundation for the Righteous, inspired by Rabbi Harold Schulweis, was established to honor these heroes of the Holocaust. I am dedicated to this particular organization because of its meaningful mission, and because it gives assistance to samaritan families in need. All of them are quite old now; many are in poor health and many are in poverty. The Foundation provides financial and medical support to them so they can live out their final years in some of the comfort they so richly deserve. At the time of this writing, approximately 1,700 righteous gentiles throughout the world receive stipends from us.

Because of the Foundation's dedication to Holocaust education, in 1993 we organized the first International Conference on Rescuers of Jews during the Holocaust, which I chaired. It was called "Can Indifference Kill?" and was held in Warsaw, because Poland was the country in which most of the Jews were killed. My old friend, Marian Turski, helped us organize and publicize this event.

The three-day Conference was attended by over 250 participants from the United States, Europe, and Israel, and included Lech Walesa, the President of Poland; Stanislaw Wyganowski, Mayor of Warsaw; Henryk Muszynski, the Archbishop of Poland; Per Ahlmark, Former Deputy Prime Minister of Sweden; Professor Jan Karski from the United States; Dr. Zbigniew Brzezinski; Abraham Foxman, National Director/ADL; and Professors Yehuda Bauer and Israel Gutman from Israel—among many other distinguished guests and scholars.

We had two goals: one was to honor the victims who perished in Poland during the Holocaust, the other was to pay homage to the brave men and women who saved Jewish lives. The Conference covered all the issues that were germane to the righteous gentiles in rescuing Jews—economics, politics, morality, and religion.

One of the most memorable accounts was movingly narrated by Archbishop Muszynski during the plenary session:

"When I was a young man during the war, just entering the priesthood, a peasant woman came to the confessional and asked me for absolution for her sin, but wouldn't tell me what her sin was. 'My child,' I said, 'you have to confess the sin before I can render absolution.' The frightened woman refused to confess, and we talked back and forth for a long time. She finally told me she would surely burn in hell for eternity for the sin she had committed, and that was why she was afraid to divulge the information.

"When she realized I could not offer her the absolution she was seeking without hearing the confession, she quietly muttered, 'Father, I have to confess that I am hiding a Jewish child, and for this I was told I will burn in hell for eternity.' I was startled by this confession, and after a long pause, I replied, 'Child, for your deeds you will not burn in hell, you will be rewarded and go to heaven.' "

At the time, the incident weighed heavily on his mind. Two weeks later he was brought back to reality when another peasant woman came to the confessional, and chose to ask him a question rather than make a confession. "Father, will I go to heaven if I save a Jewish child?" she asked.

For the next few months, every now and then, someone would come to the confessional to ask him the very same question, "Will I go to heaven if I save a Jewish child?"

This story confirmed my own thoughts: how many Jews, particularly Jewish children, would have been spared if the church, with all its many priests in Eastern Europe, had acted in unison to save Jewish lives?

Our hidden agenda was to also find some of those Jewish children hidden by gentiles during the Holocaust. It was obvious to us that when the natural parents didn't come to claim their hidden children after the war, the youngsters in question lost their Jewish identity and lived as Christians.

The extraordinary coverage of the Conference by the Polish media did just that. I assume we got it because of the high profile Polish clergy, politicians, literary and historical personalities, and prominent international luminaries who attended. Many men and women came forward to tell us that they had become orphans during the war, without ever knowing their birth parents, that they had been adopted and raised as Christians by their gentile saviors, and their Jewish identity was lost.

Irena Sendler and Jan Karski are perhaps the two most special examples of righteous gentiles—their poignant stories are very different, but very moving. During the Holocaust, Irena worked for Zegota, a unit in the Polish underground devoted to helping Jews in hiding. As a teacher and healthcare worker, she had access to the Warsaw Ghetto, and between 1942 and 1943, smuggled hundreds of children to relative safety in hiding. Sometimes the children had to be sedated so that they could be quietly hidden in potato sacks and coffins. There was a church in the Ghetto that had two doors. Irena arranged for Jewish children to enter from the Ghetto side and exit as Christians on the Aryan side.

On October 20, 1943, the Gestapo arrested, imprisoned, and tortured her in the notorious Pawiak prison. Even under those terrible circumstances, she refused to betray either her associates or any of the Jewish children in hiding. She was sentenced to death but was saved at the last moment when Zegota members bribed one of the Germans involved and helped her escape. The Gestapo chased her until the war was over.

After the war ended, the communist government in Poland continued to make life difficult for her because she saved Jewish children. She was unable to travel freely, was denied a number of positions, and her children were unfairly harassed and persecuted.

Now in her nineties, Irena still lives in Poland; she does not think of herself as a hero. Over the years, we have become close, and my son, Jeffrey, who met her on one of his trips to Warsaw, shares the great respect and admiration I feel for her. I visit with her as often as I can. My story does not do justice to Irena's warmth, dedication, and the sparkle in her eyes when she talks about the innocence of the children who were condemned to death.

As I pieced together her story over the years, I was amazed that one young girl had such an abundance of courage for the sake of complete strangers, especially when the slightest mistake would end her own young life. But Irena never speaks about her suffering, only about the suffering of others. When I recently visited her in Warsaw, she was confined to her bed, yet spoke only about getting help for other people in distress. When the Foundation for the Righteous gave her a wheelchair, she exclaimed, "For the first time in months, I will be able to see the sun!"

Although age is a contributing factor, the beatings she got from her German interrogators crippled her, but her mind is as sharp and clear as ever. Her main message: "I want the Jewish community to know that there was resistance and a spirit among the Jews in the Ghetto."

In 1942, twenty-eight-year-old Jan Karski was a liaison officer in the Polish underground, particularly suitable as a clandestine diplomat since he was endowed with a phenomenal photographic memory. That was an invaluable asset for a courier running between the Polish underground and the Polish government in exile in London and Washington.

In the summer of 1942, Jewish underground leaders asked Karski to undertake a mission of mercy. They asked him to agree to be smuggled into the Warsaw Ghetto so that he could witness first-hand the horrific sights and conditions there. He agreed and was stunned by the appalling conditions. The naked bodies he saw lying unattended in the streets, as well as the living skeletons still walking around, barely alive, convinced him he could not remain silent, even as a gentile. Then they asked him if he would go to the camps where the Jews, by the tens of thousands, were being sent by the trainload to be killed or worked to death.

He was smuggled into Izbica, a camp not far from Warsaw. He was a soldier himself and supposedly hardened to most atrocities, but what he saw was beyond his wildest imaginings of hell. The pitiful cries of the men, women, and children, and the smell of burning flesh, remained with him for the rest of his life.

When they got Karski to London, he met with Anthony Eden, the British Foreign Secretary; in Washington, he met with President Roosevelt, so there was no way for the Roosevelt Administration to deny that they did not know what was happening to the Jews.

Karski's greatest regret was that he failed to move these leaders to provide help and rescue. In London, Karski met with Samuel Zygelboim, leader of the Jewish Socialist Bund of the Polish government in exile, who went on a hunger strike to bring the matter to the public's attention. After the Warsaw Ghetto Uprising, Zygelboym committed suicide in an act of final desperation.

Karski was betrayed by one of his countrymen and so had to remain in the West. Instead of resting on his laurels in freedom, he persisted in his attempts to convince the Allied politicians to rescue European Jews. Karski told me he met with Supreme Court Justice Frankfurter, who when he heard all that Karski had to say, turned to his associate and said, "I cannot believe it." When asked if he thought Karski was lying, Justice Frankfurter said, "No, I don't think he's lying, but I still don't believe it."

Jan Karski and I became close friends and remained so until his death in 2000. Despite all the honors that were heaped upon him for his efforts on behalf of our people, he often uttered these few words to me: "I did not do enough, I failed."

To raise money for the humanitarian fund, to publicize the efforts of these special people, and to honor them publicly, every year the Foundation hosts a gala testimonial dinner, where we try to reunite rescuers with the rescued. It is extremely moving to share the moment when the person responsible for saving a life is surrounded by the individual one saved, and also by his descendants. To the righteous gentile, this is visual proof of what an unselfish deed can accomplish.

When these issues are on my mind I often wonder what I would have done under the circumstances. Would I have risked my life and my family's existence to save "the other," "the alien," "the complete stranger?"

My honest response is that I really don't know what I would have done, and I hope that I will never be put to the test. Unfortunately, there are others in our world who face that dilemma daily. I would hope our righteous gentiles are their role models.

The American Gathering of Jewish Holocaust Survivors

My survivor friends and I were very busy with our daily lives. With growing families and increased economic stability, it seemed that the need to get together with one another to share our thoughts about past, present, and future experiences would somehow diminish with the passage of time. The passage of time, however, proved to be a mixed blessing.

Although it did heal some of our wounds, as time flew by many of us developed a burning desire to be together and collectively affirm that the Holocaust would never be forgotten—that we didn't give Hitler a posthumous victory. We wanted to take his evil acts and turn them on their heads, so that mankind would be leery of repeating such hate-filled crimes against themselves. (Today I console myself with the thought that if we hadn't tried to make the world a slightly better place than we found it, it would be even worse than it is.)

In June 1981, just four days after Israel bombed the nuclear reactor in Iraq, thousands and thousands of Holocaust survivors and their children gathered in Jerusalem to address the issues of learning from the past and passing "The Legacy" on to the next generation. The World Gathering, as it was known, was the result of two years of hard work generated by spontaneous combustion in the survivor community. More than 10,000 people from around the world participated. Ernest Michel, an Auschwitz survivor, was one of the driving forces behind it.

This "movement" was triggered by three key events: the release of Gerald Green's Holocaust TV series on NBC in 1978 which brought deniers out of the woodwork, the publication of Helen Epstein's book, *Children of the Holocaust,* and the Zachor conferences on the psychological impact on the children of survivors that were convened around the country under the direction of Dr. Irving Greenberg (Rabbi Yitz). The results of these three very public events galvanized "the survivors and their kids."

In the planning of that event, WAGRO, the Bergen-Belsen Survivors Association, and other survivor organizations, the *landsmanshaften,* for the first time became intimately involved on a grand scale with the mainstream American-Jewish establishment, and realized that they could empower themselves.

The meeting which took place in Jerusalem in 1981 influenced American survivor leadership to bring the survivors living primarily in North America under one umbrella. One reason for uniting in this way would be to give us enough clout to be heard when we expressed our gratitude to the United States for giving us a safe haven and the equal opportunity to start our lives anew—and still give us the chance to tell it like it was. That would also give us clout in the established American Jewish community.

I couldn't be at the milestone event in Jerusalem because I was involved in the making and distribution of a film with Liv

Ullmann called "Children in the Holocaust," about the one and a half million Jewish children murdered by the Nazis. The opening and closing scenes were shot in Auschwitz, and I had to make a presentation in Europe. This was my only venture into the film industry, and I was proud when the film received the Bronze Award from the International Film and TV Festival of New York.

Since the World Gathering in Israel was so meaningful to the survivors, we decided to organize a conference in Washington, D.C. under the auspices of the recently formed American Gathering of Jewish Holocaust Survivors. I must admit that when my colleagues and I came up with the idea, we did not realize the magnitude of the undertaking.

We figured that if we could bring together 5,000 survivors and their children, we would be more than pleased. None of us had ever been involved in an undertaking of this kind, so we contacted the national Federation of Jewish Philanthropies, an organization used to putting together massive conferences. By the time we arranged a meeting with them, the estimated number of participants had risen to 8,000. To our surprise, the Federation told us they couldn't help us because our plans were too big.

The die, however, had been cast, and since information about the gathering was spreading like wildfire in the survivor community, we had no choice but to go forward. We were left to our own devices, but forward we went. It turned out that ignorance is bliss in more ways than one. When we started, we also had no clue how the American and American-Jewish perception of survivors would change forever.

Our small staff could hardly handle the avalanche of requests to participate. There was just a handful of people who could plan and organize the event: Ben Meed, Sam Bloch, Norbert Wollheim, Sigmund Strochlitz, and me.

For eight months Ben Meed and I made weekly trips to Washington to put plans into motion. We concluded that without local volunteers, the mass of survivors we expected could never be handled properly. More than 1,100 Washingtonians volunteered their help, and all of them were needed to guide the now anticipated 20,000+ survivors through the maze of registration, meals, seminars, and programs. As the numbers continued to grow, so did our strategy.

In addition to three key meetings (plenary sessions) attended by all survivors, one on each day, we wanted a computer hookup where survivors throughout the country could register, list their names, and try to locate relatives and friends. At the time, it was ambitious for us to network computers for people searches as it hadn't really been done before, and it turned out to be an astounding success. By the time the American Gathering in D.C. was over, more than 600 survivors were reunited with loved ones they thought they had lost forever.

The other major success at the D.C. gathering was the re-creation of the "Survivors' Village" that had been conceived for the World Gathering—an element that is now pro-forma at survivors' events around the world. We set aside a room filled with tables and placed the names of different countries, cities, towns, and *shtetlach* on them. We placed a microphone in the center of the room and put up bulletin boards so that people could post notices on them. If the survivors went to the table from their city of origin, they might find people they once knew.

We were very lucky and our timing in D.C. was almost perfect. The finishing touches were being put on the brand new convention center in D.C. itself, the survivors' home base when they weren't attending events on the Mall or on the Hill.

As we prepared for our opening ceremony, we could not believe that more than 20,000 people had registered. It was inconceivable! What's more, politicians smelled a huge, strange Jewish presence in town and doors that were previously closed suddenly opened wide, as they all scrambled to "support" the survivors. Michael Berenbaum and Larry Goldberg, using local staffers, coordinated politicians' appearances and local volunteers from our headquarters in D.C. arranged meetings with constituents. They were indeed indispensable.

In addition to the program schedule, we needed to worry about logistics—accommodating 20,000 people and moving them to and from key events. We also had to feed them. It was a hugely ambitious plan.

Then, in January 1983, we received confirmation that Vice

President George H.W. Bush and many other dignitaries—senators, congressmen and Supreme Court justices—would participate. At that point, President Ronald Reagan had neither rejected nor confirmed his participation, and it was just three weeks before the event that we finally received official notification that he would take part in the opening ceremonies.

Now that we had the President, we needed a place to hold the ceremony, one that could accommodate everyone, plus the press and the dignitaries. We knew we needed to be indoors because the weather in April was unpredictable. Luckily, when we went looking, we discovered that the Capital Centre, a sports arena in Landover, Maryland, could hold us all and was available on that day.

The management at the stadium presented us with a three-inch thick contract. When we signed it without reading it, they went into shock. Maybe we were foolish, but to our way of thinking we had secured what we needed and that was all that counted—and we certainly weren't in a position to debate the small print.

Hannah and I arrived in Washington three days before the official opening and I quickly paid a visit to the Capital Centre to check the stringent security measures we needed because the President of the United States was going to be our guest. When Hannah and I walked into the stadium, the sheer enormity of the place overwhelmed her. We were dwarfed by its immensity and she felt insignificant. She turned to me and asked if this was where the opening ceremony was going to be held. Before I could answer, she posed another query, "Aren't you frightened by the scale of this undertaking?" Frankly, I was, but I would never admit it. "Of course not," I answered. Looking back, Hannah was right. We had no experience in organizing such events, and I was working on ignorance and guts. Fools rush in where wise men fear to tread. Perhaps we were fools, but we were fools with guts.

The Capital Centre event, our opening ceremony, was chaired by Benjamin Meed. The keynote speakers were President Reagan and Elie Wiesel. On the second day, the key event was held on the front lawn of the Capitol Building and chaired by

Sam Bloch. Elie Wiesel, Vice President Bush, and House Speaker Tip O'Neill were the keynoters.

Despite the headaches, each day brought with it moments of interest and greatness, like meeting the President and Vice President of the United States and all the rest of the politicians and the press. At the opening event, tight security required each person to go through extensive electronic scanning devices, and even some people with clearance, like the few individuals who were on the stage with the President, couldn't move about freely. I was one of the few with clearance from the Secret Service to go back and forth as needed.

Michel Schwartz, a famous calligrapher and artist, designed the "Scroll of Remembrance" that the American Gathering was going to present to President Reagan that night. As is often the case, there was some last minute retouching needed. It became my responsibility to retrieve the scroll, but two Secret Service agents stopped me and told me they needed to inspect the scroll before I could get back on stage.

I was ignorant and asked them what could be dangerous. "It's just paper and paint," I said. They smiled and replied, "Yes, but how do we know that the paint isn't an explosive?" In two minutes, there were three gentlemen, explosives experts, checking the scroll. Only after they gave their approval was I permitted to bring the scroll to the stage to be presented to the President.

The second night, devoted to Jewish culture, was staged in the Daughters of the American Revolution's Constitution Hall. I think it was a historic first—a Jewish presentation in that prestigious and exclusive auditorium—and we simulcast the performance to the Convention Center for the overflow crowd to see. The impressive and touching program included Metropolitan Opera artists Misha Raitzin and Roberta Peters; as well as actors Theodore Bikel, Joseph Wiseman, Liv Ullmann, and others. There was Klezmer music, and an Israeli dance group performed. During the Second Generation session, my son, Jeffrey, made an excellent speech that made many valid points, and which I quote in the introduction to this memoir.

The closing ceremony on the third evening was chaired by

me, and was held in front of the dramatically lit Washington Monument on a blustery night. The keynote speakers were Congressman Tom Lantos of California, a survivor from Budapest, and Mayor Edward Koch of New York and myself. The fiery torches that ringed the perimeter felt like the protective walls of fire that led us out of Egypt and through the wilderness to the Promised Land. From the stage you could see that every second survivor held a lit candle in his or her hand, that each one was a burning memory in the night.

The meaningful closing ceremony on the Mall ended with Yizkor and the blowing of six shofars.

During this gathering, Elie Wiesel's and Ed Koch's speeches were admirable in that, while we held the gathering to thank America for taking us in after the storm, they both took on the politicians who still had to answer for some of the things they had not done during those dark years. As an American Jew who remembered the 1940s, Koch raised the issue of anti-Semitism in the State Department and at the Bureau of Immigration and Naturalization. Elie reminded everyone about the St. Louis and about how the Roosevelt Administration refused to bomb the tracks to Auschwitz. While planes flew almost overhead, he trotted all the skeletons out of the closet, and reminded the politicians that they had an obligation to keep Israel secure.

There were some scary moments—like the anonymous phoned-in bomb threat at the Convention Center. The matter was handled with dispatch, firmness, and the utmost sensitivity. There were over 10,000 people in the building at any given time, and we had to make sure we did not create panic. After the D.C. police bomb squad and their trained dogs ran a painstaking search, no bomb was found.

Another unnerving incident was the KKK request to the D.C. Police Department for permission to demonstrate in front of the Convention Center while we were there. The police consulted us, so I offered my advice: tell the KKK they can have their little demonstration, but warn them that the 20,000 survivors in attendance aren't afraid of them, so maybe they should be very afraid for themselves. The police listened carefully and must have conveyed the message. For some strange reason, the KKK demonstration never materialized.

I run out of adjectives when I try to describe some unbelievable incidents during those few days. Some were extremely gratifying—like chairing the closing ceremony, or being in the room when we gave Abe Pollin, the owner of the Capital Centre in Landover and owner of the NBA Washington Wizards, a check for $150,000 to pay for our opening night ceremony.

Ben Meed and I made an appointment to see Abe and we brought our wives with us. It's not every day you get to meet an NBA team owner. We wanted to thank him personally for accommodating us on such short notice, to express our appreciation for the efficiency and thoughtfulness of his staff, and to settle the bill.

Abe Pollin was a gracious host. He invited us into his office and offered us refreshments while we wrote out the check and handed it to him. I will never forget how he took it, looked at it, and tore it up, right in front of the four of us. His words are engraved on my brain, so I never forgot, like I forget other things.

He said, "You don't owe me anything. I am indebted to you for bringing 20,000 survivors who endured the horrors of the Holocaust, the President of the United States, and a considerable number of renowned dignitaries under my roof." He told us it was an experience he would remember for the rest of his life.

Liv Ullmann told me something similar when I thanked her for performing in our cultural program. She said, "Roman, you don't have to thank me for my performance. It is I who should be thanking you for allowing me to participate in this historic event."

When we called the White House to thank the President for participating, his staff invited us to come to the White House for a fifteen-minute "appointment." That was how Ben and Vladka Meed, Hannah, and I found ourselves in the West Wing.

An exciting fifteen minutes became a two-hour debriefing with the White House staffers who evaluated the event. They told us that it had taken a long time to make sure that the President's appointment calendar was cleared, that security was tight, that logistics needed to be worked out. But in reality, the true reason for their delay in letting us know if the President would participate was political.

To put it simply, if the President attended our meeting he would have to say something positive about the relationship between the United States and Israel, and this might have posed a problem. His staff reasoned that such a statement might create a backlash from the Arab countries and so they had considered declining our invitation.

It was President Reagan himself who decided to join us, and he chose to make a far-reaching declaration that night about America and Israel. He said, "I promise you that the security of your safe haven, here and in Israel, will never be compromised."

What also overwhelmed and pleasantly surprised us was the media interest in our gathering and the publicity it generated. Almost every daily newspaper and weekly magazine, TV news and radio station in the United States, carried stories. Hundreds of reporters from around the world were there. We hadn't prepared any press materials and hadn't sought coverage, and so we were, once again, amazed. That was nothing compared to how utterly flabbergasted we were when *The Washington Post* produced a supplement to the daily paper about our gathering.

Holocaust: The Obligation to Remember, an anthology by the staff of *The Washington Post,* was sixty-eight pages in oversized format, printed on high quality paper, without a single line of advertising! We were truly flattered that such an esteemed and celebrated newspaper, without our knowledge, took the time and trouble to honor us in this meaningful and touching fashion. It hit me like a ton of bricks: I called the publisher of the *Post,* Donald Graham, and Ben Bradlee, the executive editor, to extend our thanks in person. I invited them to join us for lunch so that the American Gathering could formally express its gratitude. But they didn't want to be our guests, they wanted us to come to *The Washington Post* offices as their guests.

A few days later, Ben Meed, Norbert Wollheim, and I arrived at *The Washington Post* to celebrate the publication of the supplement. It gave us the chance to meet the people there and offer our sincere appreciation for their impressive tribute.

When it was all over, the American Gathering board was

asked by many of the attendees to create a document for posterity, a book that would commemorate the experience. This historic book, *From Holocaust to New Life,* was edited by Michael Berenbaum, with a Preface by Elie Wiesel. Sam Bloch was Chairman of the Publication Committee. We also minted commemorative medals to give as gifts to various dignitaries and to use as souvenirs for attendees.

A few days after the Gathering, a friend of mine told me a story that reinforced my conviction for the need for Holocaust education. He flew into D.C. and told his cab driver to take him to the Convention Center. "Oh, yes!" the cab driver said, "that's where the Holocaust is taking place; I wish they had a Holocaust like this every year. It's good for business!"

Of course, the driver wasn't being facetious and he wasn't being malicious. He was operating on pure ignorance. This ignorance, multiplied by millions, is why I firmly believe that the memory of the Holocaust should be, and must be, kept alive.

The event in Washington consisted of some of the finest hours in the lives of the American Holocaust survivors, and I am proud of the American Gathering, my colleagues, and myself. As I write this, more than twenty years later, I can honestly say that no other Jewish organization has brought so many Jewish people to Washington for such a magnificent event.

It took quite a while for me to come down to earth after the euphoria of that tremendous success. Now one thing is totally clear to me and my associates: survivors want to be together. It is a heartfelt desire for us to meet old friends and comrades from before the war, or those you were with in the ghetto or concentration camp, to share common memories. Since then, the American Gathering has organized similar, smaller gatherings in Philadelphia, Los Angeles, Miami, and New York, also attended by prominent governmental luminaries—either the President or Vice President of the United States, members of Congress, Supreme Court justices, and others.

I vividly remember two meetings in particular, one held in Philadelphia, the other in New York near the Statue of Liberty. Philadelphia is known as the City of Brotherly Love, and is also the home of the Liberty Bell, so the location was specifically chosen to symbolize the brotherly love and the warm affection we felt toward the Danish people for smuggling thousands of Jews to Sweden by ferry and saving their lives. We wanted to express our gratitude to the people of Denmark by bestowing upon them the "Shofar of Freedom" Award.

I was greatly honored to be chosen to make the presentation to the Danish Ambassador, His Excellency Eigil Jorgensen. To our surprise, this event was also being documented. Unexpectedly, and unbeknownst to us, a beautiful bound volume depicting memorable moments of the gathering was compiled by Bernard F. Stehle and entitled *Another Kind of Witness*.

When I gave the ambassador the Shofar of Freedom I said, "In the world of the Holocaust, the ordinary was extraordinary, and that is why we are here to honor the Danish people." The ambassador replied when he accepted the award on behalf of the government and the people of Denmark, "We were grateful to be able to do our simple human duty." Those words were now forever recorded for posterity on the book's dedication page.

Another ceremony I participated in, one that took place in a very dramatic setting in New York Harbor, was very moving. In the shadow of the Manhattan skyline that still held the World Trade Center, with the Statue of Liberty, Ellis Island, Staten Island, New Jersey, and Governor's Island all in sight, I was taken across the magnificent bay from Battery Park to Liberty State Park by a Coast Guard cutter. There, in front of Nathan Rappaport's monument dedicated to the survivors and liberators, I gave thanks to the American Armed Forces and laid a wreath at its feet. It felt and looked like I was in a Hollywood fantasy!

Then grim reality set in, and the American Gathering had to raise its moral voice. The newspapers were reporting that the Germans were going to sell weapons to the Saudis, stacking the military deck against tiny little Israel. We decided to make our voice heard loudly by placing an ad on the Op-ed page of the *New York Times*. In a bold headline, we asked, "How many Jews will German weapons kill this time?"

In the statement underneath the headline, we voiced our concern for the pending sale of modern weapons to Saudi Arabia,

which would ultimately find their way into the hands of terror-
ists and hostile states to be used against Israel.

A German reporter noticed the ad and the story was picked
up in Germany. *Der Spiegel* ran an editorial about it, and the ad
was reprinted in German. To my surprise, I then received a call
from the German Ambassador in Washington, who asked why
we had made inflammatory statements in the *New York Times*
without contacting him first. Why hadn't we cleared the ad with
him prior to publication? He did not think Germany intended to
sell Leopard tanks to Saudi Arabia and we should have checked
with him first.

I was taken aback and offered a sharp reply. I lived in a free,
democratic country, not in a concentration camp. Therefore, I
had no obligation to clear the ad or anything else with the German Embassy prior to having it published. I told him the German government had a responsibility to provide information to
the American public, especially to the survivors, if they knew
that a $5 billion Saudi arms deal was being consummated, with
or without Leopard tanks.

I knew that German Chancellor Helmut Kohl was coming to
the United States for a couple of days to meet with the President,
so I respectfully requested a meeting between the Chancellor
and the leaders of the Gathering to discuss matters sensitive to
the survivor community. They said yes and set up a meeting at
the infamous Watergate Hotel.

A few days later, the ambassador called to say that other
Jewish organizations had also requested meetings, and that
since time was limited, the Chancellor could have only one meeting with Jewish delegates. Would the American Gathering be
willing to include other Jewish organizational representatives at
the meeting? He said he strongly supported such an arrangement.

The American Gathering leadership discussed the matter
and decided that although we were just as effective, if not more
so, in conveying our message to the Germans, we had no choice
but to agree to have one representative from four or five additional organizations join us, and permitted them to deliver short
statements. The American Gathering had two representatives,

who would make the opening comments and the closing statement. We had forty-five minutes, and since time was of the essence, it was important for us to immediately impress upon Chancellor Kohl that it was not business as usual when it came to selling advanced weapons to the enemies of Israel. We felt that this statement would have more of an impact coming from the survivor community than from any other organization.

Ben Meed opened the meeting by presenting the German Chancellor with a formal, written document stating the American Gathering's position on the matter. Representatives from the other organizations, including the World Jewish Congress, made their remarks, and then Chancellor Kohl responded.

The thrust of his remarks was that the Germans would not sell sophisticated weapons to Saudi Arabia as noted in our ad, and that the Arabs would never use them against the State of Israel. Furthermore, he did not believe the Arabs wanted to push the Israelis into the sea, sentiments often expressed in Arab media. In light of Chancellor Kohl's comments, I ditched my prepared remarks and directed mine to his points.

I noted that I appreciated his assurances that the Arabs would only use the arms in question for defense, and did not plan to use them against the State of Israel to wage war or push the Jews into the sea. But to the best of my knowledge, most of those arms were offensive weapons. I emphasized that he must take into account what we lived through in our youth is indelibly imprinted in our memories. Could we forget the book *Mein Kampf,* written by Adolf Hitler, who described in detail his plan to annihilate the Jews? In the beginning no one believed Hitler or took him seriously. This proved to be a tragedy for all mankind, and particularly for the Jews, as he succeeded in accomplishing exactly what he said he would do—and 6,000,000 Jews were killed in six years.

I told the Chancellor that we, the Jewish Holocaust survivors and the State of Israel, take Arab threats seriously, particularly since they are explicitly repeated. The State of Israel has no choice but to react in order to prevent the slaughter of her people. Therefore, as much as we would like to accept Chancellor Kohl's assurances, obviously we cannot, even for one second. As far as we were concerned, this was not rhetoric and not propaganda. We know the Arabs mean what they say.

I added that the Chancellor and the German people are proud of a heritage that includes Goethe and Heine. However, it was now unacceptable for the Germans to suddenly distance themselves from a legacy that also included Adolf Hitler and his unimaginably evil deeds. No, I emphasized, both facets must be taken into consideration; you cannot have one without the other. I explained that the Jewish people, and the world at large, remember Goethe and Heine, as well as Adolf Hitler.

I knew Chancellor Kohl did not like my remarks. He thought for a moment and replied, "Yes, Mr. Kent, I remember *Mein Kampf;* we all remember it well. However, let me assure you again that the Arabs do not really mean what they say." With that, he thanked all of us and left the room.

I strongly believe that the advertisement placed by survivors denouncing the proposed sale of arms to the Arabs by Germany was instrumental in preventing the sale from going forward. In its quiet way, this was surely a significant achievement of the American Gathering, and one that can be pointed to with great pride.

Another memorable occasion was a banquet held in the Waldorf Astoria in 1986. The grand ballroom of the hotel overflowed with 1,800 survivors, with not an inch of space to spare. The United States Armed Forces Band and Chorus and the Marine Color Guard participated in the event. It was extremely moving to hear beautiful Jewish songs being sung by the United States Armed Forces vocalist. "Guardian of Remembrance" awards were presented to Claude Lanzman for his memorable and moving motion picture "Shoah" and to Nathan Rappaport for his famous monument in Poland commemorating the Warsaw Ghetto Uprising. It was thrilling for me to make the presentation to my friend, Nathan Rappaport, an unassuming Holocaust survivor with immense talent.

One evening we were having dinner with Nathan at my home. He arrived with an unusual bouquet of flowers for Hannah, and we spent a most pleasant evening together. When dinner was over, Nathan declined my offer to take him home and insisted on calling a cab. When he was gone, Hannah said she thought something wasn't quite right, that she was worried about him. She thought he might be ill and she called in the morning to check on him. He assured her that he was feeling fine, but she was still uneasy. A few hours later, we learned that he had suddenly passed away.

Looking back on the evening we spent together, we remembered a comment he made: "I still have so much to do, but have so little time left." It was a premonition that became reality too soon. The same sentiment holds true for the American Gathering of Jewish Holocaust Survivors: "We still have so much to do, and so little time is left."

On Veterans Day 1984, the American Gathering and the United Jewish Appeal celebrated the 40th anniversary of the liberation of survivors. I was privileged to chair the event honoring the United States Armed Forces and presented an award to Lieutenant General James M. Gavin—aka Jumping Jim, commander of the 82nd Airborne Division—who accepted the tribute on behalf of the Armed Forces.

Yes, we at the American Gathering have unquestionably made history. Our work, however, is still not finished. There is one project in particular under our auspices which I consider one of the most far-reaching achievements of our organization. For years, we have been collecting names of Jewish Holocaust survivors living in the United States. This compilation, a Registry, is extremely meaningful and significant. In addition to the survivor's name it includes place of birth, town where he/she was living before the war, and where the person was during the war—each with a unique story.

This Benjamin and Vladka Meed Registry of Jewish Holocaust Survivors rightfully honors this extraordinary couple in recognition of their tireless efforts to memorialize the Holocaust and their dedication to compiling the detailed statistics. The Registry is on computer, contains over 150,000 names, and is constantly updated; it is a living historical document that is an integral part of the United States Holocaust Memorial Museum in Washington, D.C.

The presence of the American Gathering of Jewish Holo-

caust Survivors in American Jewish life has been invaluable. It
has served as a binding force for survivors and as a social, cultural and emotional influence. It has played a major role in laying the groundwork for historical documentation of the
Holocaust.

Holocaust and Jewish Resistance Summer Fellowship Teachers Program

In the early 1980s, after the successful assembly of more
than 20,000 Holocaust survivors at the American Gathering
event in Washington, D.C., a small group of us thought about
how best to continue and perpetuate the memory of the Holocaust for future generations.

Vladka Meed, a heroine of the Warsaw Ghetto Uprising who
was a messenger between the inhabitants of the ghetto and the
Aryan side, thought of a program for training teachers in the history of the Holocaust and Jewish resistance.

I enthusiastically offered her my support. It was brought to
fruition by active participants from three different organizations. The American Gathering of Jewish Holocaust Survivors
was represented by Vladka Meed and me. Vladka and Martin
Lapan also represented The Educators' Chapter of the Jewish
Labor Committee, and the American Federation of Teachers was
represented by Jeannette DiLorenzo, Ann Kessler, and Fred
Nauman. Our long-range goal was to include teachers from all
over the United States, but first we had to put together a pilot
program for teachers from New York State. We decided that for
optimum results we should bring the teachers to Israel for an intensive teaching program at two Israeli institutions, the Yad
Vashem Research and Documentation Center in Jerusalem and
the Study Center of the Ghetto Fighters' House at Kibbutz
Lohamei Haghetaot.

Yad Vashem houses the most knowledgeable historians and
experts in the study of the Holocaust, and so most of the trip was
spent in Jerusalem at Yad Vashem. We also felt the teachers
needed to spend time at the Ghetto Fighters House, because the

flavor of Israeli life was generally unknown to most of them—the majority were gentiles and had never been to Israel, and we thought living on a kibbutz for a few days would give them a taste, along with a little bit of history about the State of Israel.

When we proposed the first seminar in Israel, we received hundreds of applications, but we could select no more than twenty teachers. We carefully considered the best candidates: from public, private, and parochial schools, from middle school and high school levels. Those that were chosen did very well. It worked beautifully and the seminar was an outstanding success. Everyone on the Executive Committee was elated and immediately started to plan an expanded version for the following year. We decided that for practical purposes, the manageable number would be between forty and forty-five teachers—essentially one busload. It made it easier to accommodate all the teachers, made it easy to include excursions and trips, and it was just the right number to fill a classroom.

Our aim was, and still is, to attract the best teachers to Holocaust Studies and create master teachers to teach the teachers. We provide them with the best educators and resources in the field, including Yehudah Bauer, Israel Gutman, Sir Martin Gilbert, Michael Berenbaum, and Raul Hilberg, to name but a few. We give the teachers access to resources at Yad Vashem, the United States Holocaust Memorial Museum, the Museum of Jewish Heritage in New York, the Museum of the Diaspora in Tel Aviv, and Kibbutz Lohamei HaGhettaot—our teachers have a "passport" to Holocaust education resources around the world.

I also believed it was important for the teachers to go to the actual sites where the annihilation of the Jews took place—Auschwitz, Majdanek, and Treblinka. The contrast between Poland and Israel would speak volumes and the vivid comparison could achieve results in the classroom. To my way of thinking, it was an extremely effective tool for teaching seminar participants about the Holocaust.

Poland was also the country where the majority of European Jews lived before the war, so the teachers would also get a feel for the 1,000-year-old history of Jewish life in Poland, particularly in the *shtetl*. The Executive Committee approved the idea, so we included a trip to Poland in the seminar.

In the early 1980s, Poland was still Communist. The teachers' trip had to be properly coordinated with Polish authorities, and since it was my idea, and I had business experience with the Poles, the responsibility fell to me. Vladka Meed was in charge of the group, but I went to Poland before the teachers arrived to make sure that the arrangements were in order.

In the first year, I was also the person who accompanied the teachers to Auschwitz-Birkenau, and was able to provide them an eyewitness account of the atrocities committed there. After the visit to Auschwitz, I believe the teachers had a better understanding of what life was like in the concentration camps and why today Auschwitz is the word that epitomizes the worst evil in the history of mankind. That part of the trip left an indelible impression on them.

The committee realized that the trip to Poland was a vital component of the seminar and that we would probably have to extend the trip. We believed that three days was not enough time to digest the emotional impact of the sites, and it also put a physical strain on the teachers. We felt that the visual impact of the concentration camps should not be diluted with lengthy dissertations or lectures, particularly since the finest scholars in the world were waiting for them in Israel.

Eventually, we enrolled teachers from all fifty states, and almost 70 percent of them were gentiles. We didn't need affirmative action to see that in our seminars, all races were represented. The teachers were judged strictly on their own merits, not by race or religion. We based our decisions on the particular subjects they taught, the reasons they gave for wanting to attend, and their explanations of how they would use the knowledge they gained.

Those chosen were awarded fellowships covering approximately 50 percent of the expenses, and because they had to pay the rest out of their own pockets, we knew that those who applied were sincere. The subject matter and itinerary made it very clear that this seminar, though it involved world travel, was not a subsidized vacation junket.

We have essentially kept to the program as it was designed in those early days, with some accommodation for history and current events. Every year I am amazed when forty-five teachers, total strangers to each other, gather from all parts of the country to embark on this significant historic journey and at the end of the trip bond like family. Before we send them off, we bring them together for a reception not far from the airport to introduce them to each other, introduce ourselves, and give them a brief orientation. We call it "the send off."

I am thrilled whenever I can take that opportunity to explain how important it is for a survivor like me to be able to educate the new generations, our future leaders, about the importance of being just, moral, and prejudice-free. The most interesting part of "the send off" is the three-minute introduction given by each teacher. What I find fascinating are the personal reasons they give for joining the study group, more than the variety of their names and hometowns. In the last twenty years, I have heard some interesting reasons, and many of them came from people who had no Jewish students and no Jews living in their towns.

No matter how the participants present their reasons for joining the teachers program, there are a few characteristics in common. One in particular is the eagerness of every teacher to enhance and improve his or her skills by stressing the values that they feel are lacking in today's society. They want to teach their students morality, ethics, and tolerance, and how to use them in tandem with power and money—two roots of evil that must be tempered with good. They wanted their students to make the world a better place to live by giving them a solid foundation of understanding and tolerance. By the time they get back, they are fused like family with a mutual fervent purpose to teach youngsters about the tragedy of the Holocaust, and to impress upon them the oneness of mankind.

To keep that spirit alive, and to boost the enthusiasm and bonding the seminars generated, the executive committee decided to organize an annual alumni reunion in Washington, D.C., since it was both our nation's capital, and home to the respected U.S. Holocaust Memorial Museum. We hold these reunions during Presidents' Day Weekend, when the teachers have time off. These get-togethers have been very successful in refreshing motivation, in reporting new advances in education, in linking people, and in creating national networks where Holocaust education information is shared.

There are social gatherings in the early morning and late evening hours. During the day, there are work and study groups that discuss methodologies and report on cognitive results. We plan two festive dinners, with prominent keynote speakers, and we present awards to the teachers who have done outstanding work over the years. Sometimes there are personal milestones, too.

My granddaughter, my first grandchild, was born on January 1, 1989, just one month before the Teachers' Reunion. I had to chair one of these festive dinners, so I expressed my desire to bring this tiny infant to the dinner, since my daughter, Susie, was going to be there anyway. Of course, some of the more "proper" members of the executive committee were appalled at the thought of an infant disrupting the evening's proceedings, but I did it anyway.

I introduced my granddaughter in my opening remarks and said that this baby was the best proof that Hitler did not succeed. That night, though my granddaughter could not possibly realize it, she was responsible for the biggest round of applause at the event. The teachers loved it, and still ask how that little baby, now seventeen years old, is doing.

The Teachers Program we established is now part of the U.S. Holocaust Memorial Museum that sends one or two representatives to participate in the Teachers Summer Fellowship Program in Poland and Israel.

This is one project that gives me nothing but pleasure. I am proud of the tremendous success we have achieved in training 800 outstanding teachers who make a real difference in our world. The teachers program will always be near and dear to my heart, because the teachers who go through it use their knowledge to make sure, throughout the United States, that the memory of the Holocaust remains alive and that morality and ethics and tolerance are important.

We owe these teachers a debt of gratitude. They have stepped forward to make sure that future generations will never forget.

The Claims Conference

There are days I wish I'd never heard of the Claims Conference. Since I became involved in 1988, this organization has devoured exorbitant amounts of my time and energy. It is a source of gratification and despair, an emotional roller coaster ride that sometimes takes its toll. But think how much worse things would be for survivors without it!

Every year, around the winter holidays, the *New York Times* runs a series of articles under the slug "100 Neediest Cases," about people in the city who are desperately in need of help. One day in 1987, one of them happened to be a Holocaust survivor. When I read the story I went into shock, and had to read it again. And again. What I couldn't understand was why this survivor was in such dire poverty. So I investigated and discovered that the story was true and applied equally to thousands of survivors. Where was the safety net from the Jewish community? The issue ate at my soul.

Every Holocaust survivor I knew was doing well and living a comfortable life. I realized, then, how lucky we must be. I felt compelled to act and discussed the matter with my associates at the American Gathering of Jewish Holocaust Survivors and with Self-Help, one of the oldest Jewish organizations established in the 1930s to assist refugees from Nazi Europe and then, as time passed, the survivors. What they could do was insignificant and limited.

I was naïve when it came to Jewish politics, turf protection and especially allocations and fundraising. I assumed that the Jewish community could and should collect enough money to provide support to survivors in need.

Of course, I was wrong.

After doing my homework, I realized we needed to come up with a good plan, immediately if not sooner. With the American

Gathering, a very modest program was established through the
Self-Help network for the neediest survivors in the New York
metro area.

Together, the American Gathering newspaper, ran an article advising that some assistance was available to New York City
survivors in need. We were inundated with requests. Originally
we figured money collected from affluent survivors and social organizations would meet the demand, but we soon realized we
needed a special fund. As a gesture of goodwill, I made the first
donation, but that was just a drop in the bucket. The needs were
overwhelming, so Ben Meed, Sam Bloch, and I met with Ernest
Michel, then executive vice president of the UJA/Fed NY (now
vice president emeritus), which covers the greater metropolitan
area. Ernie, an Auschwitz survivor from Manheim, thought that
a small fundraiser would be supported by his organization. He
was wrong, and so we continued to muddle along, doing whatever we could in our own tiny way.

Then in 1987, a childhood friend of mine, a Lodzer living in
Israel, Noah Flug—who was aware of my quest for assistance to
needy survivors—told me about the Conference on Jewish Material Claims Against Germany. I'd never even heard of it.

Based on his information, I investigated and learned that
the Claims Conference was founded in 1952 as an umbrella organization, established for the well-being of Jewish Holocaust survivors with the sole purpose of handling their affairs. That year,
the Federal Republic of Germany, the State of Israel, and the
Claims Conference, headed by Nahum Goldmann, head of the
World Jewish Congress, signed the Luxembourg Agreement as
the basis for the German Federal Indemnification and Restitution Program for Holocaust survivors. This Agreement recognized Germany's responsibilities to Jewish individuals who
survived the war and to the Jewish community. (At the time, it
was West Germany, now it applies to all of Germany.)

This agreement was without precedent in international law
and diplomacy. It was the first time a sovereign state signed an
agreement with a non-governmental, non-profit organization to
make restitution payments to individuals around the world and
to Israel, a nation that did not exist when the crimes were com-

mitted. I was really surprised to see that there was not one survivor organization represented on the Claims Conference board—though the agency had been established only to meet survivors' needs and handle their affairs with foreign governments. This was particularly curious since the Claims Conference had been directly involved in negotiating pensions and settlements on behalf of Holocaust survivors for thirty five years.

When I discussed these things with Ben Meed and Sam Bloch, we decided that the American Gathering had to be members with standing and voice inside the Claims Conference. Along with our partner the Centre of Organizations of Holocaust Survivors in Israel, we "applied" for membership.

The Claims Conference notified me that our "application" would be heard in 1988 at a board meeting in Westchester County, New York, and that we and the Israeli survivors could advocate for our membership at that meeting. Flug and I looked forward to the meeting and expected a warm greeting and easy acceptance. We were both very, very wrong.

By the time the Board of Directors finally got around to considering our applications, Rabbi Israel Miller of Yeshiva University, then President of the Claims Conference, introduced Bernard Ferenz, a lawyer who heaped upon us legal reasons that he said prevented survivor organizations from sitting on the Claims Conference. Ferenz was one of the Allied prosecutors at the Nuremberg War Crimes Trials, and he was an excellent public speaker. A hush fell over the room as he began to recite the history of the Claims Conference and its accomplishments. Taking these points into consideration, he reached the conclusion that since the Claims Conference had done so well without survivors, he would not recommend, nor advise, that any new members be accepted. If they accepted the survivors, they would have to hear from other Jewish organizations, and they would be inundated with applications.

I could not believe my ears; I was completely stunned. Before I could fully digest what I heard, Rabbi Miller informed the Board of Directors that he agreed with Ferenz and recommended that the Holocaust survivors be denied membership in the Claims Conference. After a brief discussion, the Board of Directors, which had no survivors' organization represented, agreed with Ferenz and Miller against including Holocaust survivors in their membership.

I don't know how or why Miller concluded a few minutes later that survivors might perhaps be morally entitled to some voice in the Claims Conference. He offered us the role of advisors with no right to vote on any issues. Miller again emphasized what Ferenz had said, that we didn't belong at the table; they'd done well without us for forty years, didn't need us, and they didn't want anyone else to join their ranks. But we should accept the role of advisor and be happy that they would let us have that much.

I could barely contain myself. No matter how furious I was, I had to present my case in a most convincing manner, which, under the circumstances created by Miller and Ferenz, was almost impossible. I was ready to throw the table at them, but regardless of my feelings, I knew I had to control myself, and I did. In a quiet, cold, and firm voice, this is what I told them—in a more or less condensed version:

"I came here today fully expecting you to open up your arms and embrace us, asking, 'Where have you been for the last forty years? We missed you!' But I never expected the opposite. Despite the fact that your organization was created for and exists only because of survivors, and for the benefit of survivors, we stand rejected by the people who are supposed to help us the most. You do not want us in your midst, you do not want us as an equal participant.

"I want to thank you, ladies and gentlemen, for what you have done for survivors over the past forty years. However, I must point out that after the war we survivors were just skin and bones, and the ones who had some flesh on them were morally and spiritually broken from the experience of the Holocaust. We had to begin our lives again from scratch. We had to make a living, we tried to raise families.

"Above all, during those long years, we tried to forget the past and what happened to us. We did not want to have anything to do with the Germans and with Germany. I thank you for taking up our cause and creating this Claims Conference to protect our interests and the memory of the Holocaust.

"But I cannot express in words how much harm you have done right now by telling us point-blank that we are not needed, that we are unwanted and unnecessary. Ladies and gentlemen, I am flabbergasted and more than disappointed by your decision, and I will not accept it.

"Shame on you!"

I was angry; I was confounded. And that was just the tip of the iceberg of what I really felt and what I said. Noah said essentially the same thing. The reaction when we were done telling the Board of Directors and members of the Claims Conference exactly what we thought of them was interesting. There was a commotion, and the members started talking to each other. Noah and I were asked to leave the room. We couldn't wait to get out of there, but a few minutes later we were called back in. Rabbi Miller advised us that the vote to reject us had been rescinded and that in light of the moral and ethical issues involved, the Board of Directors had reversed their decision and allowed us to join on one condition: that the Israeli and American survivors would be represented by one membership.

One survivors' organization would have to suffice for the world's Holocaust survivors. I was fuming by then, and though Noah was willing to accept this, I was not. I would not accept membership based on conditions of exclusion rather than inclusion and asked Noah if he wanted to leave the room so we could discuss why I wanted to reject the proposal. He said he respected my judgment and to let them know what I had on my mind. So I did.

I glanced around the room and looked into the faces at the table. Slowly and calmly, with the anger coming through, I said, "Jewish agencies and many of you sitting around the table participate in a program that dispenses large buttons proclaiming 'We Are One,' meaning that the Jewish people are one people. Based on what I heard here today, that motto is purely hypocritical. I am suddenly finding out that you people are one, and we survivors are something else. You are really the Jewish anti-Semites.

"What right do you have to tell the survivors to combine forces so as to allow a single token survivor organization into your midst to clear your guilty consciences? To this, I say no. No, thank you, no. I already thanked you before for what you have done for survivors, and I still thank you. But I will not be a party to the immoral arrangement you are now proposing."

As I looked at the people in the room, I realized that I knew many of them from my Jewish communal work. As I continued to let them have it, my voice grew stronger, particularly when I emphasized that in the past we fought together for many years against the creation of despicable "numerus clausus"—the token Jew and quota systems.

"You tell me you are willing to take a token survivor into your midst. That to me is the same as an anti-Semite who allows the token Jew in medical school, in banking, in other industries, or at the social club. I will not accept this. I do not want to be a token survivor, just as I do not want to be a token Jew where I am not wanted.

"Now the Claims Conference wants to follow the example of the anti-Semites and accept one token survivor. You should be ashamed of yourselves! You have disgraced our fight for justice!"

As I spoke, my voice became angrier, but I did nothing to control the tone. My contempt for them was obvious. When I was done, bedlam broke out in the room. Miller pounded on the table to call for order while chastising me, and in a very angry voice told me that since I was an invited guest, I had no right to speak as I did, and that my statement was uncalled for.

I replied calmly, because at this point one of us had to stay calm, and it had to be me. I responded, "Since Noah Flug and I are invited guests and between us we represent and speak on behalf of virtually the entire Holocaust survivor population, therefore, my obligation as a member of the American Gathering is to represent the Holocaust survivors living in the United States and Noah Flug represents the Holocaust survivors living in Israel. It is my duty to state our case in the most proper and just manner possible. I had no choice but to voice my objection to accepting first the advisory position we were offered and then the token membership in the Claims Conference that would allow the initiation of a quota system among the Jews. This is anathema to me. I will not allow it, and I will not be a party to such an arrangement."

I asked everyone to remember that in our own lifetime, even in the United States, we had fought against such unfair practices. I added that although my brother, Leon, had been Phi Beta Kappa, he was not accepted into the medical school at Emory University because of the quota system. I was emphatic, and said that I refused to condone the fact that twenty-two non-survivor members of the Claims Conference, who supposedly represent only the survivors' interests and who represented the world Jewish community, would turn the survivors into their token Jews.

"No! No!" I proclaimed, loudly, proudly, and with heat. "I will not accept your condition. I will not tolerate a restricted quota system for survivors."

After my remarks, the meeting disintegrated since Miller could no longer keep order. He said that under the circumstances a vote could not be taken at the meeting and suggested that the ballots be cast via the mailbox, enabling those present to digest the points that had been raised.

The meeting took a great deal out of me, and it showed. As soon as I got home, Hannah asked me what went wrong. How could I explain to her, or to anyone, the humiliation, embarrassment, and indignity I experienced when the leaders of an organization established and functioning only for the specific purpose of helping survivors practically tossed us out the door.

It was not an auspicious beginning and was just a taste of what was to come.

It turned out that Noah Flug and I must have done something right on that stormy day in Westchester. It depends on who is sitting in judgment. The next day some of my friends wanted to know what had happened at "yesterday's meeting." They'd heard that Noah and I behaved abominably and created complete chaos, but when they heard our story, they supported my stance. Ultimately, the American Gathering and the Centre in Israel were granted full membership in the Claims Conference, with Miller insisting that I not be permitted to chair the American Gathering delegation, a condition I accepted. As far as I was concerned, the fight was not about me, but for the dignity and equality of all survivors.

Miller and his leadership slowly acknowledged that by adding the two survivor organizations, the power of the Claims Conference at the negotiating table was enhanced immensely, and added importance and influence to "his" organization. However, the two hard-won votes for the survivors' organizations count as only two among twenty-four, and we are constantly out-voted on important issues like allocations. Still, we keep fighting the good fight. Our mission is to see to it that the survivors themselves have more say-so in the distribution of the monies that came from their suffering and the deaths of their family members.

Today, the Claims Conference negotiating team consists exclusively of survivors, namely Noah Flug of Israel, Ben Helfgott of Britain, and myself. Ben Meed was also a member of the team prior to his untimely passing in 2006. Until recently, Dr. Israel Singer, a son of survivors, chaired these negotiations, and I now hold this position. I believe that most of the recent successes we have had in the German negotiations, particularly the inclusion of many additional concentration camps under the slave labor agreement, were achieved because of the survivors that comprised the negotiating committee.

Our participation as survivors in the negotiations for compensation to former slaves and forced laborers resulted in hundreds of millions of dollars being distributed to individual survivors. Though it was a significant achievement, we must always remember that it is the German government that stipulates specific criteria as to who receives payments—conditions by which the Claims Conference must abide in processing claims. Our job is to expand those criteria at the negotiating table. We do.

At first, Norbert Wollheim represented the American Gathering at the negotiation table. Before official sessions, we would discuss strategy and I participated in these meetings. But Miller, recognizing my abilities as a negotiator, soon asked me to go to Germany to represent the Claims Conference as a member of the team. I refused. I did not want to go to Germany. The only time I had gone back to Germany since the war was to visit Bergen-Belsen to say Kaddish at the mass grave where my wife's mother was buried.

Miller insisted that it was my obligation to go there and negotiate on behalf of survivors. He said he fully understood how difficult and painful it would be for me, and emphasized that I was going there to perform a sacred duty. "You are needed at the negotiating table," he insisted.

Despite my misgivings, I went. The first time was traumatic for me. To ease my anxiety, I made a decision that I would not speak German while in Germany and would stick to English.

To sit with the Germans in the same room, at the same table, and politely discuss matters connected to the Holocaust, was mentally exhausting and nerve-wracking. When I looked at them I sometimes saw them as the killers of so many of our brethren. What helped me overcome my initial reaction was that the German negotiating team was made up of people young enough not to have been part of the German war machine. Still, it was difficult to be polite when I vividly remembered their parents' and older siblings' cruelties. Yet I knew that if we wanted positive results, I had to put those unpleasant thoughts aside. I developed a split personality. Outwardly, I was calm, cool, and collected; inside, I was a seething, raging bundle of nerves, with the images of Auschwitz and my sister's eyes seared in my memory.

I do not regret my participation in the German negotiations, because I get personal satisfaction knowing I was able to contribute to the well-being of thousands of survivors, and that was because, once the Claims Conference accepted the two survivor groups into their ranks, we fought to institute radical changes. First, we objected to the language the Claims Conference and Germans used to describe survivors' compensation. The term *wiedergutmachung* was being used, and it means "to make good again." That was inappropriate and misleading. Germany cannot say that they were making things good again after murdering 6,000,000 and confiscating all Jewish properties. The word should never be used to describe money and properties returned to the Jews.

That was nothing compared to the real issue, the Luxembourg Agreement itself, the document signed in 1952 with the
Germans and representatives of the world Jewish community.

Long before Flug and I confronted Miller, Elie Wiesel wrote
something telling in *A Jew Today*. We quoted his statement in
the American Gathering commemorative book entitled, *From
Holocaust to New Life,* published in 1983.

"Do you know that not one survivor was asked to be a member of this special council in charge of the financial reparations
negotiations with West Germany—not one survivor was given a
chance to air his views on the distribution of funds—not one survivor sat on the international council of the famous Claims Conference?

"Others expressed themselves on behalf of the dead, not
they. Others managed their inheritance; they were not considered qualified, even to plead their own cause, in their own behalf."

Since the survivors were not a part of the original Agreement, and so many years had elapsed since 1952, the time had
come to make changes and modifications. When the Agreement
was signed, many survivors didn't apply for or even want German compensation. Now things had changed. Many survivors
were no longer self-sufficient and needed help economically or
medically or both. Their advancing age forced them to seek assistance, and not much was forthcoming from the local Jewish community. They were falling through the cracks, and for some
survivors conditions were deplorable, especially in Brooklyn,
Florida, Israel, and Eastern Europe.

Understandably, the 1952 Luxembourg Agreement signed
by Germany, Israel, and the Claims Conference was without precedent. It reflected the economic and political situation at that
time. Over the years, however, conditions had changed drastically. The Cold War was over and Germany had become, economically, the strongest nation in Europe.

I took part in practically all difficult negotiations to change
the qualifying criteria, to extend deadlines, and to get humanitarian assistance. These involved the German Finance Ministry
and the highest-ranking political leaders in Germany. A few of

the younger Germans on their team sympathized with our moral position, but at the Finance Ministry, the bottom line was always the bottom line: "How much will it cost?"

For me, the bottom line was morality and ethics, and the desperately needed help for the ailing survivors.

As leaders of a survivors group, we believe that as long as there is even one survivor who needs assistance, he or she must be helped. It was inconceivable to me that the perpetrators of crimes against humanity, namely the German guards and S.S. men in the concentration camps, had pensions and medical help from the German government, while those few who survived their brutality had no compensation and/or no medical assistance.

I did not keep detailed notes, so I cannot describe each and every meeting we had with the Germans. Still, some of them were unforgettable. We had one meeting around the time Daniel Goldhagen's book, *Hitler's Willing Executioners,* was published and translated into German. At this meeting, we were greeted by Ms. Irmgard Karwatzki, the Secretary of the *Bundestag* (German Parliament), the second most important position there. She announced that negotiations could not go forward since unfavorable economic circumstances now prevailed in Germany and there was no money in the budget to even discuss an increase in restitution funds. She also brought Professor Goldhagen into the equation and condemned him for portraying all Germans as willing executioners.

We were stunned by her remarks. It was ludicrous for us to have come all the way to Germany to hear that the negotiations were suspended. The Germans could have informed us beforehand, via faxes, telephone calls, telegrams, or express mail. Furthermore, Ms. Karwatzki should never, ever have brought up Professor Goldhagen's book in our discussions, when it was obvious the subject matter was so controversial.

After a long silence, I replied, "Madam Karwatzki, you are telling us something we already know. Since I and the other members of the delegation are no longer in concentration camps, all of us have access to newspapers, radio and television. This makes us fully aware of the economic situation in Germany, as well as that in Europe and the whole world.

"So let me tell you the things you failed to mention: I will say them for you. Since the fifties, the German work force has enjoyed the highest standard of living in Europe, including the highest salaries and the highest benefits. This very same work force, which, in a way, is referred to in Professor Goldhagen's book, currently receives the most generous pensions of any work force in any European country.

"Am I to understand that there is enough money for Germany to pay the highest salaries and pensions to the murderers, perpetrators, and bystanders, but that there is not enough money to even partially compensate the small percentage of those who were fortunate enough to survive the Holocaust?

"Let me tell you point blank that my heart does not bleed for the German pensioners; my heart bleeds for the survivors who are receiving no pensions at all, and no medical assistance. Apparently, you have chosen to reward the S.S. men and the guards for their crimes. If, as you claim, there are limited funds in the budget, one solution would be to reduce the German pensions by approximately one percent or so, and use the available funds to compensate survivors."

I told those present that by coincidence, when flying to Germany for the meeting, I was given a copy of a book whose one-word title seemed to signify the evil of the Holocaust. The name of the book was *Auschwitz* by Robert Jan Van Pelt and Devorah Dwork. When I read it, I noticed pages and pages of blueprints, a collection recently secured from Russian archives that clearly indicated how the concentration camps were conceived and built, all of it presented in the new material discovered by Van Pelt.

It was clear, I said, that individuals and industries, corporations, and small business were directly connected and involved in creating the means of mass destruction. I said to Madam Karwatzki, "Here are the blueprints, see for yourself how neatly and precisely they were drawn, and not just by Nazis." After a short pause, I continued. "If you will excuse me, Madam, since you told us to speak frankly, I will bring one more blueprint to your attention, and please forgive me for showing it to you."

I went around the table to show her a blueprint to prove to what extent German industries had taken part in the preparation of the camps. I pointed out politely the Special Barracks, opposite page 321, with a full description of what it was for—whorehouses—places for degrading Jewish women who were at the disposal of gentile inmates and Kapos. I told her that the SS pensions were morally reprehensible and that she must find a way to increase the budget for the survivors. She paled and silence reigned. A few moments later, we started negotiating and heard no more about budget shortfalls.

In 1998, there was a meeting that was presided over by Professor Dr. Rita Sussmuth, president of the *Bundestag*. I first met her in 1996 and I found it interesting that women held the two most important positions in the *Bundestag*. Professor Sussmuth was a warm and sincere person. While she was president of the 13th Bundestag, the front page of the annual listing of members and activities carried a dedication composed by her, which read: "Democracy is never perfect, never routine, never complete; rather it is a constant duty and responsibility, namely the practice of law and justice—solving together problems and conflicts step by step and strengthening each other's zest for life."

I conveyed this profound thought at our next meeting, and to the surprise of the other members of the Claims Conference delegation, I asked, "Madam Sussmuth, what do you do in the *Bundestag?*" and let the sentence hang in the air. Then I answered it myself. "Most of the time, like the U.S. Congress, you negotiate and discuss new laws. Many times you amend old laws. So why, in heaven's name, whenever we want to discuss changing the Luxembourg Agreement, which was written in 1952, it is suddenly considered taboo and a topic that nobody wants to pursue? Is that the democracy that you so eloquently describe in the introduction of the book dedicated to the 13th *Bundestag?*

"After all, the Agreement signed by the German government had no precedent. It was formulated under circumstances that never existed before and we hope will never exist again. Since the passage of this law, the situation has changed drastically and should be addressed.

"Yes, we have made inroads over the years to compensate some survivors, it was too little and very late—they should have been compensated long ago! The law needs drastic changing. By doing it piecemeal, more and more Holocaust survivors will die before they see any semblance of justice, or even a partial semblance of the justice they so richly deserve."

To everyone's surprise, Madam Sussmuth agreed with the points I'd made. Later, in New York, Ben Meed and I had a private meeting with her and we brought up the same subject. Though she personally agreed with us again, we are disappointed that we are still unsuccessful in substantially amending the Luxembourg Agreement.

We had one meeting in the German Chancellery presided over by Minister Friedrich Bohl, Chancellor Kohl's spokesman and right-hand man. He acknowledged the suffering the Jews had endured during the war and made a statement that emphasized the need for justice, assuring us that we would come to a speedy and amicable resolution to the challenges before us.

Picking up on Minister Bohl's comment, I said that in order to fully comprehend the tragic figure of 6,000,000, the number of Jews murdered during the Holocaust, this unbelievable amount needed to be translated into 6,000,000 individual stories. Since I was one of the few fortunate enough to survive the calamity that befell the innocent Jewish people of Europe, I offered my personal story in symbolic fashion. I told them that when I went to the Ghetto, the first page of my "passport" was blood-stained when the word Jüde was stamped on it. Another bloody stamp, Auschwitz, was imprinted on the second page of that "passport." Then, over six years, each new page bore a new bloody stamp: Gross-Rosen, Mertzbachtal, Flossenburg, and the names of other deadly places. In the end, my passport was covered in red, representing the blood of the 6,000,000 men, women, and children who were tortured and perished at the hands of the Germans.

I told the minister that my story is only one individual's story. Yet, I, a survivor of the Lodz Ghetto and Auschwitz, did not hold the minister responsible for the crimes committed by his parents. I let that sink in, and then added, "However, I, other survivors, and history will hold you responsible for what you will or will not do now."

I paused for a long time and then concluded, "I do not know, Minister Bohl, if you have children or not. But if, in five, ten, or fifteen years, they will come to you and ask, 'Daddy, did you do everything in your power to correct the wrongs of the past? You will have to look into their eyes, just as we are looking into each other's eyes today, and answer them honestly about whether you did or did not do the honorable, ethical thing when you had the opportunity to do so. Their judgment of you will be most severe if the answer is no." Silence prevailed. Later, that day, during a short break, Minister Bohl approached me in the hall and said, "Mr. Kent, I do indeed have children."

It was after this meeting, under the leadership of Minister Bohl and Chairman, Dr. Israel Singer, that the German government, for the first time, told the media that there were at least ten outstanding issues still to be resolved between the German government and the survivors. This was a real victory, because the Germans had never officially admitted that there were outstanding issues. To me, it meant the Luxembourg Agreement was amendable and would never be considered "closed" by the survivors. Minister Bohl added that it was Germany's intention to settle these matters within the shortest possible time.

Unfortunately, there is always a big difference between words and reality. Despite the genuine goodwill expressed by some German delegates, and the commendable intentions on the part of some people in the German government, over twenty years later a number of these issues are still unresolved and under negotiation.

We are in an ongoing process to bring them to a fair and equitable conclusion. For me, the frustration comes from the lack of concern for the morality surrounding the issues which remain unresolved.

Many survivors blame the Claims Conference for not exhibiting enough compassion or exerting the necessary resolve to finalize pending survivor issues once and for all. Some resent the fact that the Claims Conference has still not found acceptable solutions for many problems facing needy Holocaust survivors. Such immediacy is amplified by the advanced age of every survivor. Unfortunately, as much as the negotiating team of the Claims Conference constantly presses the German government to solve these critical issues, often our demands fall on deaf ears. The key issue for the Germans is always the bottom line, namely "how much is it going to cost?" The Germans fail to consider morality in the equation. Therefore, they are remiss in addressing and resolving urgent problems in a timely fashion while we are still alive.

Does the Claims Conference make mistakes? Yes, it does. I have yet to see an organization that does not. I realize occasionally there are times when the Claims Conference should act with more sensitivity toward the survivor community at large. Since I personally became involved with the Conference, I know, first-hand, that there is no other Jewish organization that moves more vigorously, or acts with as much compassion toward survivors as the Claims Conference. They are most assuredly at the forefront of every facet in the fight for survivors' rights, and they have made a positive difference in their lives. Since the survivors became direct participants in the negotiations in 1988, there have been significant achievements resulting in substantial additional compensation since we went to the table and fought the Germans. This is a partial list:

- More than 200,000 Eastern Europeans who were never given previous compensation each received a lump sum payment of 5,000 DM ($2,500.00); total about $1 billion.
- Approximately 50,000 survivors previously denied pensions are now receiving monthly stipends.
- Additional concentration camps were added to the existing lists to enable more survivors to qualify for compensation.
- Income limits for pensioners were increased from $21,000 per couple to $31,000 per couple (excludes Social Security benefits).
- Survivors living in Eastern Europe previously denied compensation are now receiving monthly pensions.
- Approximately 150,000 former slave laborers received a maxi-

mum lump sum payment of up to 15,000 DM ($7,500) per person; total about $1.4 billion.

- Former forced laborers received a maximum lump sum payment of up to 5,000 DM ($2,500) per person.
- Recovered Jewish property in Eastern Germany. Real estate is to be returned to survivors, heirs, or the Jewish community at large.

One of the most difficult problems facing me during the negotiations was balancing moral and ethical principles against the survivors' actual living conditions. There were tens of thousands of survivors reaching the end of their lives who were in desperate need of financial and medical help. They had neither received proper assistance from the perpetrators or adequate support from the Jewish community.

For historical accuracy, and because of the values instilled in me during my upbringing, I felt an obligation to present the issues with an emphasis on moral and ethical grounds. It is unfortunate that the financial requirements, the dire need of so many thousands of survivors, and the exploitation of these issues by the press and lawyers, placed an overwhelming weight on the financial issues instead of the moral ones.

For the first time since the mid '50s and the original agreements with Germany, in the 1990s, the Claims Conference found itself with a substantial amount of money—between $70,000,000 and $100,000,000—to distribute annually to the survivors for humanitarian and educational purposes. These funds were derived from the sale of unclaimed East German properties that belonged to the Jews and were confiscated by the Nazis and the Communists. This was the first time the Claims Conference had a vast amount of "unrestricted" money at its disposal that they could distribute without conditions or requirements imposed by foreign governments.

Though I was strongly opposed to it, the Claims Conference board voted to use 20 percent of available funds for Jewish education, Holocaust commemoration, and remembrance. It's not that I am against Jewish education, it is that I am first, and above all, committed to satisfying the humanitarian needs of the survivors. Jewish education should be primarily the responsibility of the Jewish community and 20 percent should not have been diverted from survivor needs.

Once the money became available, I noticed immediately that Jewish organizations suddenly wanted to be involved with the Claims Conference and partake in the distribution of the funds. When we added the additional income from other sources, like the Swiss Fund and ICHEIC (International Commission on Holocaust Era Insurance Claims) settlements—hundreds of millions of dollars—the demand for places at the table came as no surprise.

Because our efforts with the Germans were fairly successful, we survivors demanded more voice in the composition of the Claims Conference and in the allocations process. To achieve this goal, the American Gathering passed a resolution that said 51 percent of the votes should belong to Holocaust survivors. Of course, Miller and other members of the Board of Directors objected. They refused to increase the existing membership of twenty-four organizations by adding additional Holocaust survivor organizations.

A compromise was reached when the Board voted to add ten people "ad personam." We survivors thought we must play an active role in recommending and approving people who would become members of the Board. They would not represent specific organizations, but they would be allowed to vote. Of course, we wanted them all to be survivors, recommended by survivors. In the end, many of those appointed were not survivors, nor were they recommended or approved by the survivor organizations. Looking back, I can see how politics corrupted our aims.

After Israel Miller passed away, the by-laws were to be changed to distribute the responsibilities of the Claims Conference among four senior officers: the President, the Chairman of the Board, the Chairman of the Executive Board, and the Treasurer. They were to work as a team in consultation with each other. Moshe Sanbar, a survivor representative from Israel and Chairman of the Executive Board, and I realized that the existing by-laws gave too much power to the Chairman of the Board, and therefore we wanted to correct the situation immediately.

But Julius Berman, who succeeded Miller as Chairman of the Board, convinced us that would be too confusing to the other Board members to initiate a change in the by-laws so soon.

Sanbar and I wanted the newly established collective leadership to be acknowledged in a legal fashion. Therefore, in addition to giving us a verbal assurance that that would be the case, Berman (as well as Israel Singer) gave us a side letter saying we would be consulted before any actions were taken. Berman, an attorney, assured us that the side letter would have just as much validity as changing the by-laws of the Claims Conference, and as such, the by-laws need not be changed. After all he said, I am signing the letter so I am bound by it, but in actuality I never signed the by-laws. Thus, for practical purposes, now we are officially a leadership of four. I said I didn't need the letter, because I believed him, but Moshe Sanbar insisted on getting it.

MEMORANDUM
TO: Roman Kent
Moshe Sanbar
DATE: March 22, 2002

I understand that an issue has arisen concerning the element of consultation referred to in Article V, Section 3 of the proposed bylaws. Therefore I wish to reiterate my strong view that the four of us must work together with extensive consultation among us. The Treasurer and the Chairman of the Executive are a critical part of the process.

This system of consultation is the core of future operations of the Claims Conference. I believe that the Claims Conference will be stronger as a result, not weaker.
Signed:
Julius Berman

Sanbar was right. Berman soon appointed himself not only Chairman of the Allocations Committee (I agreed for him to hold this position for a period of one year), but also as Chairman of all other committees connected with allocations in general. This was not discussed by the leadership of the four, and as such, was never approved by us.

In actuality, it was my opinion that it was totally improper for one person to have absolute control over allocations involving such vast sums of money. I thought that the Chairmanship of the various allocation sub-committees should be headed by different people, some of whom should definitely be survivors. In truth, as time went by, I realized more and more that Berman had no problem ignoring the demands of the newly established leadership; I deeply resented his lack of communication and cooperation.

As I feared, a confrontation soon erupted at a meeting we had in Luxembourg, when I objected to some of the statements that Berman made. He contended that the by-laws gave him the right to make them, and then asked the secretary to read back the by-laws. I blew my top, and said, "The by-laws may be correct, but your verbal commitment to me, in addition to the side letter, are quite contrary to what you just said." I was disappointed, angry, and disgusted. I thought about my father, who taught me that one's word is one's bond.

Unfortunately, the confrontations continued, and with time the differences that existed in the leadership became even more pronounced and had a detrimental effect on our modus operandi. Of course, as long as we all had the same or similar opinions on an issue we could reach agreement. However, when there was a difference of opinion, Mr. Berman ignored our position and proceeded with his own.

My conflict with the Claims Conference also concerned fundamental philosophical differences concerning the definition of the rightful heirs to the sold property belonging to the victims. It was my contention, and that of the overwhelming majority of survivors, that the heirs to such unclaimed properties should be and must be the survivors, particularly those survivors in need. After all, society at large and the Jewish community in particular had heretofore denied them proper help. This difference was the main stumbling block between survivors representing the survivor organizations and the majority of the Claims Conference Board members who felt the true heirs to the property was the entire Jewish nation, though each one privately conceded that the money should be used primarily for needy survivors.

The Claims Conference reached an uneasy truce, guided by

the principle of 80/20: 80 percent of the unrestricted funds to be used for humanitarian purposes and 20 percent of the funds to be used for Jewish research and Holocaust education. I have great difficulty with this breakdown. I believe that as long as there are survivors who require medical and physical attention, the Claims Conference has no right to allocate significant amounts of money to research and educational purposes, except in special cases.

I am, and always will be, in favor of funding educational projects, and I personally devote my time and make financial contributions to many such undertakings. However, Claims Conference money, in my book, is sacred and should be used first and foremost for survivors in need.

I did agree to a few exceptions, such as for a small portion of the money to be put toward a specific and limited number of educational projects: to finance teaching programs to help teachers acquire accurate knowledge in Holocaust studies and to teach it properly; to support a few key museums and teaching centers that are involved in perpetuating the history of the Holocaust: Yad Vashem, the U.S. Holocaust Memorial Museum in Washington, D.C., Lohamei Haghetaot, and Beth Hatefutsoth, among others, and to save historical documents that will disintegrate if immediate steps are not taken to salvage them—if no other monies are available.

I am greatly criticized by the board members for my position opposing the 80/20 allocation breakdown. Nonetheless, I strongly believe it is the duty of the Claims Conference to assist the elderly survivors now in the final stage of life and unable to meet the challenges that confront them, instead of spending 20 percent of all available money for education. It is my opinion, and the opinion of most other survivors and educators as well, that a number of the educational projects are not properly scrutinized, some are completely unnecessary, and for many there is no great urgency.

I was frustrated and angered when, on a number of occasions, after I presented my views and each and every board member agreed with me, regrettably the overwhelming majority went on to say, "But." "But it is our obligation to perpetuate the mem-

ory of the Holocaust and to rebuild the Jewish culture." I pointed
out that that task is the obligation of the Jewish community at
large and is not to be financed primarily by Claims Conference
funds. To my chagrin, the 80/20 rule is still in effect today.

The old adage that "money is the root of all evil" is definitely
correct in this instance. When I first started to work with the
Claims Conference, there really was no great interest on the part
of any Jewish organization to participate. Those who were already members didn't care much either. However, when the survivors joined the organization and were instrumental in the
negotiations and brought in substantial amounts of money,
there was an instant change in attitude. They swarmed like bees
to nectar. The Claims Conference became a free-for-all.

In November 2003, Israel Singer, Julius Berman, Moshe
Sanbar, Gideon Taylor, our executive director, and I were in Israel for a Claims Conference meeting. At that time, in order to
determine the role of the Israeli government in the process of negotiations and distribution of funds, Benjamin Netanyahu, then
Minister of Finance, called a meeting of the five of us and four Israeli Ministers, including Natan Sharansky, Minister of Jerusalem and Diaspora Affairs, Health Minister Danny Naveh, Meir
Sheetrit, the Minister-Without-Portfolio, and Bibi himself.

The meeting began on a sour note when Sheetrit opened
with a harangue that accused us of giving Israel only crumbs
from the available funds and such distribution had to be rectified
without delay. I started to interrupt and said that Israel gets
about 55 to 60 percent of all Claims Conference money, hardly
crumbs.

My associates asked me to wait and listen to all of what
Sheetrit had to say. I agreed to remain silent but was not happy.
I knew that when a man starts by complaining that Israel gets
only a small portion of the funds, when I knew, and I am sure he
knew, that Israel gets 55 percent of all monies, it was better to
stop him before the situation got out of hand.

Sheetrit contended that as far as he was concerned, the
funds belonged to the Jewish people and the Israeli government
is the sole representative of the world Jewish community. Therefore, the Israeli government should have the principal voice, and

more than half of the representatives on the Claims Conference Board should come from the Israeli government.

When he finished, I interjected: "What's the sense of talking about percentages when we have basic philosophical differences? It is my contention, and that of my fellow survivors, that we survivors as a group care for and love Israel more than any other segment of Jewish society. However, the funds secured by the Claims Conference do not belong to the State of Israel; they belong to the survivors themselves. This is why the German government made an official declaration that the Claims Conference is the legal heir of the Jewish 'heirless' properties. Therefore, this issue must be settled before discussing anything else."

When Julius Berman asked Sheetrit who authorized him to make decisions in the name of survivors, Sheetrit replied, "We are democratically elected by the people of Israel to make decisions on behalf of the Jewish people of Israel, but who elected you to make decisions for the survivors?"

Although I completely disagreed with Sheetrit, I thought he certainly had a good point with regard to Berman. Survivors certainly did not elect Berman to be the Chairman of the Claims Conference. However, the real fireworks started with the arrival of Netanyahu, who came to the meeting a few minutes late, just after the above exchange. Netanyahu hardly settled into his seat (which happened to be right next to me) before he started shouting, "Unless you meet my two conditions, I will destroy the Claims Conference."

This bombshell created a momentary silence that was immediately broken by Netanyahu's follow-up threat, and it was nothing if it was not a threat. "And you know that when I say I will destroy you, I mean it. I will go after you and destroy you.

"Here are my two conditions: the Israeli government must take the leading role in all negotiations, and 50 percent of the Board is to be appointed by the Israeli government. The Israeli government will take the leading role in the distribution of all funds."

There was a deadly silence which permeated the room and, again, I stepped into the breach. I very calmly turned to

Netanyahu, looked directly at him, and said, "Bibi, I have known you since your tour of duty in the United States, so we go back a long time. I want to remind you of an old axiom that says that the one who does nothing is the only one who never makes a mistake.

"You are telling us that you want to be the key participant in the negotiations. If you insist on becoming a participant, you will be making a big mistake. You have no right to be a participant; Israel has no right to be a participant. The Claims Conference is an apolitical organization, and it is crucial that it remain an apolitical organization.

"Yes, it is true that we ask the United States government for support and also solicit some assistance from the Israeli government, but the moment any government becomes an official member of the Conference, its usefulness would be substantially, if not completely, diminished. This is definitely something we do not want. You have to understand that although we survivors love Israel, Israel cannot be a member of the Claims Conference. This is not a governmental undertaking, it is a survivor undertaking, in negotiations and in the distribution of funds. This is what it is all about!"

"As a rule, whenever we finish our negotiations in Berlin, we make two stops, one at the American Embassy and one at the Israeli Embassy. I must tell you that the American Ambassador, when he is there (or his associates, when he is not) receives us with his full attention and support, and follows up any of our requests. The Israeli Embassy, on the other hand, hardly gives us any time, is not interested in our conversations and does not follow up on our requests. I am ashamed to say it, but that's the truth."

Bibi thought for a moment and replied, "As far as the negotiations are concerned, Roman, you may be right. I might agree with you. But as far as allocation of the money is concerned, that is a different story."

However, to me, as well as to the other members of our delegation, it was clear that both the negotiation process and distribution of funds were solely the responsibility of the Claims Conference.

I left the meeting discouraged by the thought that it might

be impossible to reach a mutually satisfactory agreement with so many participating ministers having such opposing views. When it came to dealing with foreign governments I anticipated problems and frustration. This I could live with, because they were our adversaries. But I never thought that I should have serious problems and be greatly aggravated either by the Israeli government or by some Claims Conference members.

A perfect example occurred after a tough negotiation with the Germans involving the 2004 budget. After two years of difficult discussions, for the first time I had finally succeeded in securing six million Euros (approximately U.S. $8 million) for ailing survivors in financial need, earmarked specifically for homecare. Julius Berman, Chairman of the Allocations Committee, decided that these pre-designated funds should go through his committee, a group that meets only twice a year. I was fuming. After a strenuous fight with the German negotiating team, this money was obtained for a specific urgent purpose and Berman was, in essence, delaying its distribution. His insistence on controlling the funds by means of the Allocations Committee ignored the burning needs of the survivors.

Homecare for needy survivors was, and is, a vital primary project which I personally introduced and brought to the negotiating table with the Germans. It is particularly near and dear to my heart. In my view, at the present time this issue is of the greatest urgency for survivors and what is needed most for their well-being. This matter should be addressed without delay.

Having obtained an agreement with the Germans, my goal was to distribute the money as fast as possible to those who needed homecare. Besides, as a negotiator, one does not go back to the table to ask for additional allocations unless one has already fulfilled the negotiated obligation, i.e., spending the realized funds appropriately in a timely manner.

My insistence on the immediate dispatch of these funds, however, led to an ugly confrontation with Berman. Even with the support of Singer and Sanbar who fully understood the situation and were two of the four senior Claims Conference officers—myself being the third—and even though the money was approved by the Board to be forwarded as soon as possible, the direct intervention of Berman delayed the distribution of the funds for many months. He continued to insist that we follow the allocation process, the timing of which he fully controlled.

During my lifetime, I have always tried to treat unimportant events lightly and then forget them—or attempt to learn from them. But to delay distribution of funds to the elderly who are in such dire need indicated a complete lack of compassion and understanding by Berman regarding the plight of survivors. Therefore, to me, such action is unforgettable and unforgivable.

As time went by, the relationship between the leadership of the four became increasingly tense and uneasy, deteriorating more and more. To me, the main reason became increasingly obvious . . . Berman originally thought he would step into Rabbi Miller's shoes as President and exercise complete control. Now he was confronted with the fact that there was a leadership of four to contend with, and there was required a consensus of opinion or majority rule must prevail. This was not to his liking.

The real blow-up occurred in the Spring of 2005 during one of the meetings of the "four" when Berman angrily announced that he was revoking the agreement he had signed and would not live up to it anymore. Naturally, this outburst caught all of us by surprise. Thereafter, I discussed what had transpired with Moshe Sanbar who told me that under these circumstances he wanted nothing further to do with Berman's leadership position in the Claims Conference and would resign at the end of his term.

It was, and still is, my position that Berman had no legal right, and obviously no moral right, to unilaterally break the agreement that was in place. After all, it was at Berman's insistence that such a side letter was written in the first place, supposedly with the best of intentions, to create the basis for a harmonious working relationship among the leadership of the four as well as to formally acknowledge the collective leadership not specifically stated in the by-laws. It is obvious that unilateral cancellation of the basic agreement forming the leadership of four is unacceptable regardless of the reasons.

Shortly after the confrontation, Berman sent a letter to

Moshe, with a copy to me, and I quote from the beginning of the letter.

"June 5, 2005

Dear Moshe:

Gideon has informed me that, from a conversation he had with you a few days ago, he believes it is your understanding that my statement to the effect that, in light of Roman Kent's published article replete with repeated defamatory charges against me personally, I do not consider the letter that Sruli (Israel Singer) and I signed in 2002 to have any further validity, referred to you also. If that is your understanding, I apologize for the miscommunication. The rationale for my position did not spring from anything you did or said, and, consequently, I had no reason to suggest that the letter no longer has any validity vis-à-vis my relationship with you. I wanted to clarify that as quickly as I could; hence this letter. . . ."

The essence of Berman's letter was clear and obvious. It indicated that Berman was unilaterally nullifying only with me the agreement that established the basis for the working relationship in the Claims Conference. The reason for his decision was that he did not think favorably about an article I had written. In my opinion, the article I wrote stated the facts as I saw them; obviously, this is not the way Berman saw them.

To me, as well as to anyone reading his letter, it was clear that Berman wanted to make it known that he would not tolerate the actions of those who did not agree with him. He was telling Moshe in no uncertain terms that nullifying the agreement was a consequence for me, after I had the "impudence" to write something he did not like.

In effect, he was cautioning Moshe to behave or he would nullify the agreement as it pertained to him as well. Of course, such thinking is unacceptable since an agreement written to two parties cannot be partially nullified. Once you nullify part of the agreement, it is totally null and void. Above all, one cannot unilaterally nullify an agreement signed by two parties; both parties must agree. I tried my best, as did many others, to convince Moshe not to resign. I was upset not only because it would break up the leadership of the four consisting of two survivors and two non-survivors (as difficult as it was sometimes), but because in my view Moshe Sanbar was one of the best, if not the best, members of the Claims Conference board. He was truly an expert on financial matters, knowing them inside and out, and his input was invaluable.

I myself often entertain the thought of resigning from the Claims Conference, but I am constantly swayed by many survivors to remain and continue to fight for them. Being a survivor, as well as the Chairman of the American Gathering of Jewish Holocaust Survivors, I take my responsibilities seriously, and so I choose to stay on and do all that I can for my fellow survivors.

Much as I try, it is difficult for me to understand the motives which drive Julie Berman's behavior. For example, an illustration of his moral fiber is his insistence that each and every member of the Allocations Committee sign a Conflict of Interest form. Although admirable, I think there should be enough morality and ethics already instilled in each committee member voting for an allocation to know the difference between right and wrong.

Yet, as Chairman of the Board and Chairman of the Allocations Committee of the Claims Conference, Berman seeks personal glorification. One such instance occurred when he asked for his own name to be included on a permanent plaque presented at the dedication of a newly built addition to the Holocaust Museum in Yad Vashem. Traditionally, a plaque such as this contained only the name of the Claims Conference, and in very exceptional cases, the name of the President of the organization. Berman, however, was not, and is not, the President.

In my view, even though it may be legal, it speaks volumes about the Chairman of the Allocations Committee, asking for his name to appear on a plaque when it is totally contrary to previous precedence. It is also contrary to the Conflict of Interest form which each board member has to sign. How sad that a man who prides himself on the importance of precedence uses his position to bring about change in order to satisfy his need for grandeur and to feed his own ego.

The change in established procedure made waves when it became semi-public knowledge that Julie Berman had asked for his name to be included in the dedication on the plaque. That being the case the Museum decided to inscribe on the dedication plaque the names of all four individuals comprising the leadership group of the Claims Conference. When I learned about Berman's request for his name to be inscribed, I also learned that my name as one of the four people in the leadership group had also been included on the Yad Vashem dedication plaque.

Upon hearing this scenario, I wrote a letter to the Chairman of Yad Vashem asking that my name be removed. I believe that individual names should not appear on an inscription such as this, particularly mine, since I neither asked nor requested that my name be included. I thought there should be a general dedication that reads: "This is a gift from survivors." It was not our personal financial contribution that helped fund this new building—it was rather funds from the Claims Conference. Since Julie Berman requested that his own name be inscribed, which in my view is completely unethical and contrary to the spirit of the memo on "conflict of interest"; that is between him and his conscience; my conscience tells me otherwise.

It is interesting to note that on two occasions during "leadership meetings of the four" I asked Julie Berman about his request to have his name inscribed on the dedication plaque. On both occasions, he gave no answer and angrily ran out of the room slamming the door.

I believe that the Claims Conference's biggest fault lies in the fact that although it is composed of twenty-four key Jewish organizations, only two of them are actually survivor organizations. Though the Claims Conference purports to represent the well-being of the entire world community of survivors, survivors have nominal representation. In the voting process, survivors are constantly out-voted and thus unable to properly protect what justifiably belongs to them. Yet, it is the survivors themselves who give the Claims Conference authentic moral and ethical guidance. It is indeed sad that after all of these years an organization which was specifically established because of, and for the benefit of, survivors, for practical purposes is still controlled by non-survivors.

When I look back at the history of the Claims Conference, I

firmly believe that if survivors had been part of the Claims Conference from the beginning, many of the restrictions, clauses, loopholes, deadlines, and criteria would have been very different or non-existent, and would have benefited the survivors more directly. I learned, first-hand, that even with the best of intentions, no one can substitute for a Holocaust survivor in the negotiations with the German government.

As one who actively participates in those negotiations, I believe that survivor participation is mandatory, because only a survivor can make legitimate moral, ethical and medical demands. What we have accomplished since the survivors began directly participating in the Claims Conference and negotiations confirms that. I would be remiss, though, if I did not give credit where credit is due and acknowledge the contributions of the Claims Conference, which acted as an umbrella organization for the world's Jewish community and was instrumental in gaining the full support of the United States government.

Despite the *realpolink,* I say without hesitation that the Claims Conference as a whole was, and is, instrumental in achieving great success for the benefit of survivors, most noteworthy helping needy survivors today in the twilight of their lives. Sadly, such desperately needed assistance, particularly homecare, has not been forthcoming from any other source, including the Jewish community at large. Furthermore the Claims Conference has also ensured a documented historical imprint as to what occurred to the Jewish people during the Holocaust. I am truly pleased and honored that I have made a personal contribution to the process and have played a significant role in bringing about many positive accomplishments.

The German Foundation Initiative

The German Foundation Initiative, known as the slave labor and forced labor agreements, took place in the latter part of the 1990s. I was involved from its inception in intense negotiations with the German Government and German industry that lasted more than two years. It was not pretty, it was not easy, and the Germans didn't want to settle. It was a very unpleasant and frustrating time, designed by the Germans to cause maximum grief to the survivors.

Originally, the meetings were held in Bonn, the capital of Germany, and in Washington, D.C. When Berlin became the new capital of unified Germany, they held the meetings there. The active leadership position was taken by the United States government, with Deputy Secretary of the Treasury Stuart Eizenstat as a co-chairman of the negotiations, and with Count Otto Graf Lambsdorff representing the German government. The Jewish delegation consisted of three survivors: Ben Meed, Noah Flug, and me. Claims Conference staff was represented by the executive director, Gideon Taylor, Saul Kagan, former executive vice president of the Claims Conference, the late Karl Brozik, who headed up the German office of the Claims Conference, and Karen Heilig, an attorney with the Claims Conference. The Israeli delegation was chaired by Bobby Brown.

Israel Singer was chairman of the Jewish delegation. Representatives Stanley Chesley and Jean Geoppinger from the law firm of Waite, Schneider, Bayless & Chesley, who were our pro-bono legal advisors, accompanied us. Eastern European governments sent their own delegations and counsel to the table to represent the slave and forced laborers in their countries.

The Germans gave these negotiations an elaborate Madison Avenue-chic title: "The German Foundation Initiative: Remembrance, Responsibility and the Future." How ironic (or deliberately misleading) for the Germans to use the word "initiative" followed by "remembrance" and "responsibility." If the survivors of the Holocaust hadn't forced them to come to the table, if we hadn't taken the initiative, there would have been no German initiative, no remembrance, and certainly no responsibility for their heinous actions during the war. The German initiative was about sixty years late.

I believe that what prompted them to seek a settlement was their frustration with individual survivors who dragged them through expensive class-action suits, and applied political and economic pressure. The Americans handled the political pressure; the economic pressure came from Eastern Europe, because they wanted compensation for hundreds of thousands of their own citizens who were forced laborers during WWII. At the same time, German Big Business wanted to have good relationships with the Eastern Europeans in order to be able to expand their markets into Eastern Europe with little trouble. The Germans wanted to end the whole mess with as little responsibility, accountability, or decency as possible—they wanted full closure for their misdeeds during the Holocaust. Creating this Foundation was their easy way out.

It was evident, from sentiments expressed at our talks by representatives of German industry headed by Dr. Manfred Gentz of Chrysler/Mercedes-Benz, and Lambsdorff, that the Germans wanted these matters settled legally once and for all. That is called "legal peace."

It was also obvious, expressly stated and implied, that the Germans wanted to create good will between themselves, the Americans, and the Eastern European countries who were crawling out of communism.

The more involved I became, the more I realized that the German "initiative" had nothing to do with morality and humanitarianism; it was strictly business. For the Germans it meant legal closure and an end to what they considered nasty, annoying lawsuits; for the lawyers, it meant millions and millions of dollars in contingency fees. The lawyers were like vultures, sitting atop tree branches waiting for their spoils. And so we, the Holocaust survivors, had three adversaries to contend with: the Germans, the Eastern Europeans with their insistence on a larger share of money for the forced laborers, and the lawyers.

Still, I chose to participate in these negotiations in order to get some relief to needy survivors in Eastern Europe and other Holocaust survivors in the Diaspora—assistance which, for some reason, was not coming from the Jewish community at large. Sadly, not much had changed since 1947.

In addition to trying to get some relief, from a historical point of view, I felt that the negotiations would officially expose and acknowledge the evil acts perpetrated by the Germans against mankind. It would be an admission of guilt and proof of the direct, large-scale involvement of German industry. It would show beyond a shadow of a doubt that, yes, Hitler and the Nazis were responsible for the atrocities—as the Germans wanted the world to believe—but also that the entire German nation was complicit and culpable in carrying out crimes against humanity.

Because the American government and American lawyers were involved, the Germans wanted this to be a final legal settlement, a quitclaim, so to speak. The Germans didn't care about legal closure with any other country except the United States, which I found interesting, because it was clear to me that they feared only the American government and its legal system.

In most cases, a lawsuit involves a defendant and a plaintiff. The slave labor and forced labor negotiations were a three-ring circus. First came the German government with its lawyers and German industry with its lawyers; then came several Eastern European countries with their representatives and their lawyers; the third party was made up of representatives from Jewish organizations under the umbrella of the Claims Conference; and the fourth party, created by the U.S. judicial system, consisted of a horde of class-action lawyers, all looking to make money.

As the negotiations dragged on, it was obvious to all parties—each one of which wanted to claim the lion's share of the money (for the sake of "morality and ethics")—that the German government, and particularly the German industrialists (the same companies or their descendants that put Hitler into power) wanted to resolve the matter for peanuts. On the other hand, American lawyers demanded exorbitant amounts of money to justify their anticipated multi-billion-dollar settlements. For example, when the Germans offered $1 billion, the lawyers demanded $30 billion. Sadly, the only legitimate voice representing morality and ethics in these negotiations was the voice of the Holocaust survivors. No one else cared about humanity. What was of utmost importance to survivors on the negotiating team was safeguarding the memory of the Holocaust and not losing sight of the morality of our cause. It was one of the hardest things I ever had to do.

The negotiations were chaired on the American side by Stuart Eizenstat, Deputy Secretary of the Treasury. On the German side, Minister Bodo Hombach, who was later replaced by Lambsdorff, represented Chancellor Gerhard Schroeder.

My first private discussion with Minister Hombach took place in his office in Bonn. The original fifteen-minute appointment was extended to about two hours, as we touched upon general topics and various aspects of our negotiations. At one point he said, "I have a delicate question to ask. As you know, we are basically dealing with two different categories of people. There are former slave laborers who were in concentration camps and ghettos, consisting primarily of Jews, a few of whom survived. On the other hand, upon the insistence of German government and industry, we had to include the forced laborers, mainly Eastern European gentiles, mostly farmers, who, for practical purposes all survived the war. True, there were some gentiles incarcerated in concentration camps. This being the case, I want to have your input on how the gentiles incarcerated in concentration camps should be treated in relation to the Jewish concentration camp victims."

I told him that when it came to slave laborers, I made no distinction between Jews and gentiles who were concentration camp inmates; all of them were subjected to the inhuman conditions which prevailed there. But I also told him that one should not lose sight of the fact that all Jews, because they were Jews, were subjected to even more inhuman treatment, and almost all Jews perished in the concentration camps and ghettos.

"Only a small number of gentiles were sent to concentration camps. Also, for historical accuracy, note that some gentiles received favorable treatment in a number of concentration camps, compared to the Jews. Still, life in any concentration camp was so brutal that no words can possibly describe it. Therefore, without hesitation, I can say that in the concentration camps we, Jews and gentiles alike, were pretty much in the same boat."

When I finished, Minister Hombach sighed with relief and thanked me for expressing my thoughts so clearly. Over the next few months, I developed a good rapport with him and when he came to Washington with Dr. Rolf Breuer, president of the Deutsche Bank, for meetings with Jewish organizations and class-action lawyers, Ben Meed and I had a private meeting with them on behalf of survivors. We were the first meeting on their Washington agenda.

Dr. Breuer was flabbergasted by the American system of class-action lawyers and their contingency fees, which he said were running into "astronomical figures." Dr. Breuer's sincere opinion was that if the class-action lawyers were out of the picture, issues could be settled in no time to everybody's satisfaction. He also said that if it were not for the moral issue represented by survivors, German industry could litigate the case through the courts for five to fifteen years on legal grounds alone, at a relatively negligible cost. If the lawyers were allowed to drag the case out, the Jewish survivors who suffered the most would receive no recognition and no compensation during their lifetime.

I was very sorry when Minister Hombach was replaced by Lambsdorff. To my mind, Lambsdorff and his attitude brought a different and unwanted atmosphere to the negotiations, one that was antagonistic and confrontational. It didn't help my state of mind that Lambsdorff physically represented the harsh, callous image of a German-Prussian Army officer. When I closed my eyes, he sounded just like some of the Nazis who mistreated and tortured us during the war.

Lambsdorff's tactic was to accuse us, the Jews, of blackmailing German industry, and then he pleaded poverty on behalf of German corporations. He called in a well-known German historian, Professor Lutz Niethammer, to express his opinion and provide statistical information about slave labor in German industry during the Holocaust.

The way I understood Neithammer's testimony we, the Jewish slaves, should be thankful that industry employed us because it gave us a ninety-day grace period before we died through *Tod Durch Arbeit,* the bestial German-designed "Death Through Work" program. I really lost my temper then. I said that a man with such ideas and interpretations should not be a part of the discussion, and as for me, I did not want to be in the same room with him. I asked him to leave.

After the meeting, the professor tried to convince me that I misunderstood his remarks. If I agree that I might have misunderstood him at the meeting, his words of explanation were still too ambiguous for comfort. As far as I was concerned, the German policy of "Death Through Work" was the most brutal form of exploiting human beings.

Things were further complicated because the Jewish side and most of the class-action lawyers negotiated primarily on behalf of the slaves, while the Eastern European countries and their lawyers negotiated primarily for forced laborers. One exception was Michael Hausfeld, who had former slaves and forced laborers as clients. Ed Fagan was another who stood to gain millions of dollars in contingency fees.

The situation came to a head when it looked like the Germans were going to settle for a lump sum payment to be divided among the plaintiffs. The Eastern European governments and their lawyers wanted to distribute the same amount of money to forced laborers as the slaves were getting. They wanted no distinction between them.

It was, to me, imperative that a distinction be maintained. It was the slaves, the Jewish slaves, who were condemned to death and only about ten percent survived the inhuman conditions in the camps. Forced laborers did not experience the same harsh and severe treatment as Jews, and except for natural death, practically all of them survived. A ratio of compensation had to be established to reflect that reality. This caused a critical breach between the Jews and the Eastern Europeans that came to a head during a meeting at the U.S. Embassy in Berlin. I approached Stuart Eizenstat to see how it could be resolved.

I gave the matter a great deal of thought before discussing it in an open meeting. I thought it prudent that only delegates should meet face-to-face, without the lawyers present. I asked Stuart to start the proceedings that way, and the recommendation for lawyer-less meetings was presented. When he called the meeting to order, Eizenstat asked all lawyers and individuals who were not members of the negotiating delegations to leave the room. In looking around the room, I noticed attorney Michael Hausfeld still sitting with the Polish delegation.

I brought this to Stuart's attention and he asked Hausfeld to leave. Hausfeld then had a hushed discussion with the Polish delegation and when it was over, the head of the Polish contingent said that Hausfeld was now an official member of the delegation and therefore could remain in the room. This was an underhanded action on his part, but Stuart had no recourse, and Hausfeld stayed.

Then, when the meeting came to order, I said my piece:

"Ladies and Gentlemen. We, the Jews, were the main victims of the Nazi regime simply for being Jewish, as evidenced by the six million of us who perished. It is equally true that each of your countrymen also became victims of the Nazi regime, and millions of them perished as well.

"Thus, in a way, both of us were victims of the Nazis. I want to state clearly and emphatically that we, the Jewish survivors, will not be a party to a fight between us, both victims of Nazism, while the Germans throw some scraps [at us] with the intent to divide us, and then sit laughing on the sidelines as they watch us fight [over them].

"At this moment, I cannot say definitely what the situation is in Russia, Ukraine, and the other Eastern European countries. However, I can say what is happening in Poland, since I have received copies of articles appearing in Polish newspapers that are clearly anti-Semitic and contrary to the actual facts.

"You, the Polish delegation, must be aware of the articles accusing the Jews of grabbing billions of dollars in compensation from the Germans. Therefore, I address you, the Polish delegation, and ask how dare you let these lies be spread? It should be your moral obligation to defend the truth of the situation! You should be ashamed! You know that only approximately twenty-five percent of the settlement will be distributed to the Jews, while the balance will be divided among the gentiles.

"Furthermore, we, the Jewish side, stated that there must be no distinction between Polish and Jewish slave laborers or Polish and Jewish forced laborers. Also, it is we, the Jewish side, who spearheaded the fight for some semblance of justice for all. If we in this room do not harmoniously make the distinction between forced and slave labor, we are not worthy of being part of the negotiating team."

Israel Singer came to my defense and strongly supported the

distinction between "slave" and "forced" laborers. It was tentatively agreed that the distinction was accepted.

In a full session of negotiations that took place some time later, Hausfeld was sneaky and tried to equalize slave and forced labor by placing a slash between them in some of his documents. I told him in no uncertain terms that what he is trying to do is "clearly a disgrace to the memory of the Holocaust." He quietly accused me of not understanding English. "Mr. Kent, I don't think you fully understand the English language. That is not what I am saying here."

Just as quietly, I replied, "It is precisely because I understand the English language perfectly well that I repeat what I said before. You are a disgrace to the memory of the Holocaust. In addition, you have a conflict of interest by representing two kinds of clients, the slaves and the forced laborers. To the best of my knowledge, that's unethical. Doesn't your conscience bother you?"

Inevitably, there were fights between the lawyer-hordes and the Germans. At issue was the total cost of the settlement and the fixed assignment of money for each category and country. The survivors feared that such infighting would leave the impression that we, the Holocaust survivors, were only interested in money. I was just as convinced that most, if not all, the class-action lawyers were focused solely on the millions of dollars they would get in contingency fees. Their eyes reflected that "glitter of gold" greed. For them, it was a win-win situation that boiled down to how big their pots of gold would be.

In disgust, I put two non-negotiable conditions on the table. Without them I said the Holocaust survivors would never accept any agreement from the Germans. (1) The German government and German industry had to issue a full and sincere apology for their conduct during the Holocaust. (2) Slave labor and forced labor had to be referred to by name only, not labeled with numeric categories like Group A and/or Group B. Under no circumstances would we accept numeric designations to describe us.

The first condition was easily understood, but had to be digested and accepted by the Germans. Of course, the apology was not forthcoming without a major struggle—and a struggle it was.

Lambsdorff, in particular, objected strenuously. I was pressured to back off but I stood firm. After a while, I found myself repeating a mantra: "No apology, no agreement!"

The second condition was as firmly stipulated as the first. I explained that we had been numbers during the Holocaust and we would never be referred to as numbers again.

Most of the lawyers present at these meetings hardly ever uttered a word. They did not have to; their clock was running and with it, their fees were going up. Each hour earned them hundreds, if not thousands, of dollars. The longer it took, the more money they made.

The one calming force prevailing throughout these tedious, lengthy negotiations was Stuart Eizenstat. When presented with totally opposing points of view, he was always able to spin the issue to a more positive, less confrontational conclusion. I saw him blow his fuse once, and only once, during a closed session between the Germans and Jews. Lambsdorff and Gentz opened the meeting by telling us that they were presenting us with a take-it-or-leave-it offer, and that there would be no further negotiations. Stuart exploded. "We did not have to travel from the United States to Germany for negotiations when you are telling us that there will be no negotiations." The Germans were taken aback. They did not expect such an outburst from the always-calm Eizenstat. Gentz and Lambsdorff then had a tête-à-tête, and suddenly the negotiations continued.

At one meeting, Gentz raised a question about the taxes borne by German industry, since the internal German understanding called for industry and government to equally share the responsibility for the ten billion DM called for in the agreement. Gentz explained that for all intents and purposes, German industry agreed to pay a total of five billion DM, but since they also would have to pay German taxes, their share would turn out to be more than the agreed upon 50 percent. They wanted a refund linked to the overage percentage points.

Stuart couldn't believe what he was hearing. His jaw dropped, he just couldn't speak. Seeing that, I interjected. I told Gentz that he was absolutely right. He may indeed be paying more than the 50 percent stipulated in the agreement. Stuart's face registered puzzlement, since this was the first time I had ever agreed with Gentz on substance.

I then suggested to the Germans, "Since you want us to pay attention to the taxes you would pay over your 50 percent, we American survivors, who paid money into the Marshall Plan that rebuilt German industry, should be reimbursed for our contributions to it. Then we will see who comes out ahead." Stuart beamed, and that was the last we heard about a "tax" deduction.

When the negotiations became intolerable, when the Germans became really ugly, I consulted with Ben Meed and suggested that the survivors should boycott the next meeting in Germany. He agreed, we didn't go, and it worked. Lambsdorff called after the meeting we didn't attend to say he would be in New York and wanted a meeting. We told him to come to the American Gathering office, and since Israel Singer chaired the negotiating committee, we asked him to join us.

Lambsdorff had hardly sat down in his chair before he began waving his finger and accusing us of creating anti-Semitism—a good beginning. As hosts, neither Ben nor I could react the way we really wanted to. I quickly pointed out that the offensive tone of the articles and commentary in German media continuously reported that Jews were getting ten billion DM. Since this was not true, and was never denied or corrected by Lambsdorff, his accusations at the start of our meeting proved that anti-Semitism already existed in Germany, and it is he, not we, who perpetuated it. After all, Jews were getting only 25 percent of the negotiated settlement.

Lambsdorff also infuriated me with his "Draft Bill" for the German Foundation Initiative. After I read it, it took me quite a while to calm down. I wrote him a letter, but never received a response.

January 5, 2000
The Honorable Dr. Otto Graf Lambsdorff
Der Beauftragte des Bundeskanzlers
fur die Stiftungsinitiative Deutscher Unternehmen
c/o Auswartiges Amt
D-53001 Bonn, Germany

Dear Count Lambsdorff:

I have just received a Draft Bill on the establishment of a foundation "Remembrance, Responsibility, and the Future." I can express my thoughts about this proposal in just one word. OUTRAGEOUS!

I reach this conclusion because it is contrary to my understanding and contrary to the spirit of the negotiations we have had in the past. As a survivor, it is totally unacceptable to me, and I am sure that it is unacceptable to other survivors as well. In my humble opinion, this Draft Bill is practically an insult to the survivor community, and I would like to express my total outrage for such a proposal.

As you know, I am not a politician, therefore I use the language of a layperson when I state in my blunt fashion that a proposal such as this can never be accepted by us. In order to conform to the spirit of our meetings and our heartfelt intentions, it would be better to burn it and start from scratch.

Your comments will be greatly appreciated. I take this opportunity to wish you and your loved ones a very healthy and Happy New Year.

In the meantime, the propaganda wars surrounding the negotiations and the promise of money to come to hundreds of thousands of Eastern European survivors created such a furor that it became critical to finish the negotiations as quickly as possible, for all our sakes. Lambsdorff immediately tried to pack a new issue into the scope of the agreement—namely, the subject of German insurance companies who hadn't paid off policies to survivors and their heirs, an issue that was not discussed previously and had no business being included in the slave labor and forced labor agreement.

I did not take kindly to his proposal. As far as I was concerned, insurance and banking problems had nothing to do with slave labor and forced labor. I said that to include insurance companies in our agreement would be uncalled for and a mistake. The biggest problem was the German insurance company, Allianz.

An International Insurance Commission had been established—prior to the establishment of the Foundation Initiative (see chapter on ICHEIC)—to deal with unpaid beneficiaries of insurance policies. Allianz, the largest German insurance company, was a signatory. For all intents and purposes, Allianz had to adhere to the rules and regulations of the Insurance Commission and be held accountable to them, not to the slave labor and forced labor entity the Germans were creating which had nothing to do with insurance.

Unfortunately, I stood alone and did not prevail, largely because Lambsdorff loudly blackmailed the negotiators. He shouted, "If the German insurance company is not included in the agreement, then I cannot provide the ten billion DM to which the German government agreed." Sadly, his position was strongly supported by Stuart Eizenstat and by the lawyers.

Thus, with great fanfare in the Presidential Palace in Berlin on December 17, 1999, the agreement providing some measure of compensation to slave laborers and forced laborers was signed.

On this momentous occasion, German President Hans Rau said: "I know that for many it is not really money that matters. What they [survivors] want is for their suffering to be recognized as suffering, and for the injustices done to them to be named injustices. I pay tribute to all who were subjected to slave and forced labor under German rule and, in the name of the German people, beg forgiveness."

There, as I stood in the Presidential Palace, looking back at my life in the Ghetto and concentration camps, I felt compelled to reply to President Rau's statement. Hearing his acknowledgment of German guilt, his apology for past wrongs, I felt proud that it was my firm belief in justice and morality that was instrumental in achieving this historical announcement.

"From the very beginning, we, the survivors, fought for and stressed the moral issues and tragedies of the Holocaust, not only for us as Jews but for the world at large. Even today, the unimaginable damage caused by the Holocaust cannot be fully comprehended. One and a half million Jewish children were killed; no, not killed, brutally murdered.

Sixty years ago, I, too, was a child. I was one of the few who survived. Thus, the moral issues and historical justice are what we survivors fought for. The remarks that have been made here today, and the ones made by you, President Rau, justify the efforts we have made concerning morality, and morality only: Slach-Lanu, Forgive Us! Ki chatanu, For We Have Sinned!

That is what we and the world heard today. Let these words reverberate now and forever here and around the world so that another Holocaust can never happen again to us or to any other people.

I hope and pray that the victims of the Holocaust did not die in vain. If we can be a moral force, and by example make the world a better place to live, that would be the greatest legacy we survivors can leave for posterity."

I was asked to attend the signing of the agreement and represent the community of Jewish Holocaust survivors and it fell upon me to make a closing statement in their name. Until I spoke, there were only words of praise for establishing the German Foundation, so before I delivered my prepared remarks, I declared my intention to make comments that would be contrary from what had been heard from the speakers before me.

Berlin, July 17, 2000

"As I stand here today on German soil witnessing this historic moment, I, a survivor of the Lodz ghetto, Flossenburg and Auschwitz, find it surreal—and feel humble and full of humility. Surreal, because this seat of power was instrumental in initiating and overseeing the most destructive war known to mankind, World War II, as well as the genocide of the Jewish people—unparalleled in the annals of history. It also innovated the most hideous and brutal form of death known as Tod Durch Arbeit . . . death through work.

I feel humble, for how can I represent and speak in the name of Jewish survivors, when the list includes 6,000,000 innocent men, women, and children brutally murdered during the Holocaust?

Thus, as I stand here today, there are two very painful questions in my mind. Painful, yes it is painful. But in order to secure a peaceful future for mankind, we must honestly and truthfully acknowledge the past. Why did the Holocaust happen, and secondly, why did it take until the year 2000 to officially recognize the "death through work" bestiality and establish the Foundation?

Let me, a survivor, a slave laborer condemned to "death through work" by the Germans, share with you my simple explanations. Holocaust is the most tragic example of what can happen when prejudice and hate reign and people follow. By people, I do not mean just the Nazis, soldiers, or guards in the concentration camps. I mean the engineers, the draftsmen, the doctors, the chemists, the scientists, the businessmen, the politicians, and yes the lawyers who legalized it . . . all of whom devoted their energies to create the most efficient means of mass destruction of the Jewish community.

As to the Foundation, well, why call it "initiative" when in actuality the need for accountability for slave and forced labor, both Jewish and non-Jewish, was brought about by the recent demands of survivors linked with economic and legal issues. But to my way of thinking, it was possible to establish the Foundation because in a way Germany entered a new era . . . an era when the new generation born after the war realized the magnitude of the destruction brought forth by their forefathers and understood that places like Auschwitz, Treblinka and programs like "death through work" acquired a meaning of their own—since they represent evil, the worst that mankind can offer.

This Foundation, approved by approximately ninety percent of the Bundestag, is the conscience of the new generation. Yes, it was enacted sixty years late and is only a token gesture to financially compensate slave and forced labor. But it is the moral recognition for past wrongs, and we survivors take it as such.

I and the other survivors associated with the negotiations did not speak about money. How could we? The lives of one and a half million Jewish children are priceless. We will never equate morality and ethics in terms of dollars and cents. We only stress morality . . . This is our sacred duty.

We survivors cannot forgive nor forget. To forgive and forget can only be granted by the 6,000,000 who were murdered, and they are dead and their voices cannot be heard anymore. Thus, it is our destiny that we survivors and you the German nation must carry the burden of this terrible crime from now to eternity.

We did not come here to shed tears, nor did we come here to elicit pity or love. We came here to memorialize the ashes scattered throughout the concentration camps and ghettos; we came here knowing that these ashes, these bones of murdered Jews lying in their graves cannot and must not be forgotten, for if we were to forget, the conscience of mankind would then be buried with them.

For the past forty years, we survivors have been committed to preserve the memory and uniqueness of the Shoah, and we have achieved this by supporting museums, commemorations, and above all, educational programs. We survivors have realized that the story of Shoah must be told and re-told. Yes, the story has been told—but never well enough. How can one speak the unspeakable?

We survivors have also learned that the opposite of love is not hate, but indifference. How alone we were during the Holocaust! We must recognize that we cannot just be bystanders, for if we are, our morality and ethics will also be laid to rest and buried alongside the 6,000,000 victims of the Shoah.

I have hope that you, the new German generation, by this acknowledgment of your moral responsibility, will follow in our footsteps. If the Foundation is to have any meaning for the future, the terrible lesson of the Holocaust must be understood in your land and throughout the world so that the Holocaust can never happen again to us or to any other people."

When I completed my remarks, a great round of spontaneous applause brought me back to the paradox of the present reality and my wartime experiences. I was standing in a historic building that had been the headquarters of the *Reichsbank* (German Bank) during the war. This was the very same bank responsible for the gold transactions involving the gold teeth and miscellaneous jewelry of the victims, precious metals molded into gold ingots and used by the Germans to purchase military supplies.

I was utterly drained and soaked with perspiration when I was suddenly surrounded and embraced by a number of friends and dignitaries, members, of the delegation, and even the Germans. At that moment, I did not fully understand whether the outpouring of attention was because I happened to be the last speaker, or if it was due to the fact that my remarks made an emotional and meaningful impression on the audience. I hoped that it was the latter.

I felt we had accomplished the impossible. President Rau, in the Presidential Palace and the *Bundestag,* at long last acknowledged the moral and historical responsibility for the injustices that had been committed under German government and industry. Thus, the horrific crimes perpetrated against us were officially recognized and, more importantly, acknowledged as having been committed by the German people, not solely their Nazi rulers. This, I hope, once and for all, quiets those Germans who proclaim that they did nothing wrong . . . that it was only the Nazis.

After it was all over, I received a letter from our pro-bono attorney, Stanley Chesley. He wrote: "We were particularly moved when you so eloquently told Stuart Eizenstat, in response to his attempt to justify the use of the terms Category A and Category B, that 'we were numbers in the camps, and we will never be numbers or categories again.' "

My participation in the German Foundation Initiative was very difficult for me emotionally. What brought me some solace was that I knew that tens of thousands of survivors received a small form of justice, imperfect as it was, toward the end of their lives.

In the long run the "the pound of flesh," the millions of dollars taken by the class-action lawyers and the settlements so reluctantly paid by the German government and German industry, will become mere footnotes in history. What is important is that President Rau's apology and acceptance of responsibility for the German government, and the words inscribed by the *Bundestag* in the protocols, will live forever as a moral victory. With these admissions of guilt on behalf of the entire German population, history has been accurately documented.

This was my moral victory, but it didn't last long.

Before the Foundation could be activated, Michael Hausfeld and other class-action lawyers filed suit against Austria in a case that involved the German banks. Judge Judith Kram sided with the survivors and said that the Slave Labor and Forced Labor settlement had not taken the Austrian banks into account and refused to dismiss the suit before her. Since the Austrian banks were now German banks, this effectively prevented the legal peace we had promised the Germans in the settlement. Without legal peace our slave labor and forced labor agreements were dead. It took five months before the case was finally thrown out on appeal, and it delayed the distribution of funds to needy survivors.

I was standing in front of Judge Kram's courthouse the day the case was finally thrown out. It was just about one year after I had made my impassioned speech about morality and justice before President Rau in Berlin. Thinking how it was more about legal peace for the Germans than anything else, I estimated that in the year since the Berlin agreement, at least ten percent of the survivors had died. As I spoke to reporters gathered around me, tears came to my eyes, and I think my voice broke when I said:

"This moral gesture amounts to words and words only. This proves what morality means to them. For them it is strictly business, cold-blooded business."

ICHEIC

The International Commission on Holocaust Era Insurance Claims (ICHEIC) came into existence as several different factors came to a boiling point in the late 1990s. One of the main reasons was the arrogance and lack of feeling displayed by European insurance companies toward Holocaust survivors. They understood nothing, because they didn't want to.

Everything involving ICHEIC was, and continues to be, difficult. The negotiations themselves were complicated by the involvement of insurance companies from many countries, involving many currencies. Over the sixty years since the Holocaust, many of these companies had undergone mergers, acquisitions, nationalizations, and bankruptcies. In addition, since these companies had done business in different countries, a determination of their market share in each of those respective countries was necessary and difficult to obtain. If this were not complex enough, each company sought to utilize its country's privacy laws, laws they wanted to enforce to their own advantage. Everything varied, all of it made even more complicated by the loss and destruction of the hand-produced paper documents that were the sole record of the companies' business transactions.

These huge insurance companies have incredible economic and political influence in Europe and the United States. Before the war, the enormous European insurance companies held a great deal of authority, and now, with re-grouping, mergers, and acquisitions, they again became a major power in their own right. The best examples are Allianz in Germany and Generali in Italy.

Why did it take fifty years before these insurance issues surfaced? The great majority of Jewish policyholders perished during the Holocaust, and therefore there were no heirs or beneficiaries to claim the proceeds. The few who survived and lived through the Holocaust had very little, if any, documentation to prove the existence of the policies. The insurance companies were not about to search for them or provide documentation, and policyholders with documents were rare.

Individual survivors attempting to file claims found it extremely difficult to fight the enormous muscle of the insurance companies who refused to cooperate. They would not release their files or pay out the policies of insured individuals who had been gone for fifty years. Wrongly, insurance companies assumed that all unpaid policies and premiums belonged to them and considered them their rightful profit. They stonewalled and survivors could do nothing. Neither could heirs who had proof of policies that were in effect before the war began.

In some cases, when survivors knew the specifics and were able to furnish the exact information requested, including the policy number, the companies had the audacity to ask for death certificates before they would release payment. Imagine asking the relative of a person annihilated in the crematoria of Auschwitz, Treblinka, or Majdanek to provide documentation of death! The smug and ruthless attitudes of the insurance companies allowed them to avoid paying out policies for many Jews who had purchased policies but perished.

Slowly, but surely, resentment toward these insurance companies grew in response to their monumental injustice. This was particularly true in the United States where Insurance Commissioners in various states became personally involved because it looked like these companies were cheating their constituents.

Once exposed, it became clear to survivors and to the Insurance Commissioners that they were right, that the gigantic insurance companies operating in Europe and the United States were disregarding the claims completely and refusing to accept responsibility for non-payment. They were in breach of contract. In other words, these mega-corporations were committing insurance fraud involving hundreds of thousands of policies issued before the war. This gave the companies interest-free funds to play with for more than fifty years, and they wanted that to continue.

In our efforts, first we had to figure out what to do about the unwillingness of the companies to pay legitimate claims, especially when they knew full well that the surviving policyholders and their heirs could not produce death certificates. Then we had to determine what happened to the policies that were held by victims of the Holocaust who had no heirs. Did the money belong to the insurance company as a bonus for doing smart business with doomed Jews? Or did the money belong to the Holocaust survivors and the Jewish community?

The magnitude of these outstanding sums instantly attracted class-action lawyers who circled like sharks in a feeding frenzy. Of course, they claimed to have the well-being of survivors at heart. But this time, unlike the slave labor and forced labor agreement, it was not going to be easy for them to get a chunk of the money.

Insurance Commissioners in the United States had jurisdiction over the licensing of insurance companies who do business in the USA, and they were our backers. With them, we survivors found ourselves in a much stronger position to demand justice from these monolithic corporations that were bigger than some of the governments they insured.

Because they did business in the United States, these corporations were subject to the approval of the individual State Insurance Commissioners, whose sole purpose is to regulate the industry and prevent insurance fraud. Suddenly, insurance companies that had stonewalled for fifty years were expressing a willingness to investigate existing problems. They announced their intention to solve all pending cases, and to examine ways of correcting the injustices of the past, including the injustice of unpaid policies.

With these noble goals before them, the International Commission on Holocaust Era Insurance Claims (ICHEIC) was formed. The founding membership of the organization consisted of twelve Commissioners; six European insurance companies would each have one commissioner. Three State Insurance Commissioners would represent the fifty states and be the U.S. delegation. One commissioner would represent the Claims Conference, another would represent the World Jewish Restitution Organization (W.J.R.O.), and one commissioner would be present on behalf of the State of Israel. Each of the twelve commissioners could cast one vote.

For this Commission to have the clout, prestige, and respect it deserved, we needed a good chairman, a person of prominence, who had integrity, carried with him vast international experience, and had name-recognition in Europe and the U.S. We ran an intensive search for such a person and selected the former U.S. Secretary of State, Lawrence Eagleburger. He had all the necessary credentials and was fully aware that this was a massive injustice needing to be rectified. Reluctantly, he assumed the chairmanship.

Eagleburger was the best man for the job, a man who dealt with the toughest people on the other side of a negotiating table: Koreans, Vietnamese, the Chinese, and most Europeans. He had ample experience in handling huge corporations in Europe. With Larry at the helm, I hoped we could get matters resolved quickly and that justice was at hand. My hopes evaporated when it came time to draft the official Memorandum of Understanding (MOU) that would be the basis of the negotiations. The document had to be airtight, to the point, and provide enough leverage to give survivors their fair share. We finally hammered it out, and it did have some historic significance: it excluded class-action lawyers from the settlement, though some of them, like Edward Fagan, constantly tried to undermine our work.

Once we were established, the administration of President William Jefferson Clinton acknowledged that the Commission was the proper instrument for achieving overdue justice for survivors and the heirs of those destroyed in the Holocaust. That gave ICHEIC backing and legal standing.

You would think that professional representatives of the key insurance companies, all of whom signed the MOU, would make the work of ICHEIC straightforward and productive. The opposite was true. Because they had signed the agreement, they were now placing stumbling blocks in our path to stall and waste time. With each day that passed, another handful of survivors was dead, and there would be fewer people who could remember whether their families had policies.

Because the Commission was a volunteer organization, there was no ability to enforce rules or force mutual cooperation. From the outset, Eagleburger said he preferred to rule by consensus instead of casting ballots. In the long run, that proved an impossible task. Even Larry Eagleburger, who had conducted the most complex inter-governmental negotiations, could not foresee the problems this would cause.

What bound the insurance companies together was the fear that the American Insurance Commissioners would bar them from doing business in the United States. They preferred making a settlement approved by the U.S. government, instead of coping with swarms of class-action suits that would pop-up wherever Holocaust survivors lived. On the other hand, the insurance companies knew they could orchestrate and delay the lawsuits for years at relatively low cost. They hoped that eventually most cases would be dismissed, because the beneficiaries would be dead and there would be no heirs to make trouble. The problems were magnified by the fact that these numerous insurance companies from different countries were hiding behind each country's particular laws.

We also had legitimate obstacles to overcome. Fifty- or sixty-year-old insurance records would be extremely hard to find. To add to our woes, a great many companies were no longer in business; some had consolidated, and the ones in Eastern Europe were government-owned during the Communist era.

We soon confirmed that, relatively speaking, only a small number of survivors or their heirs were in a position to furnish the exact information required to file a claim—the name of the insurance company and the policy number. We decided that it was imperative that each insurance company publish a list of its policyholders, commencing a few years before the war. Such lists would at least enable survivors to locate the names of their families and provide them some form of assistance in making a proper claim. These lists would also be of historical value because they would provide us with diversified and unknown data about Jewish life in many European countries.

From day one, getting those lists from the insurance companies was a major stumbling block. We used contemporary records and looked for the pre-war files in order to reconstruct the number of policies held by Jews before the war, but we realized that we could never cover them all. After months of heated discussions, we were finally able to secure a limited number of names, about 60,000. To inform the public, ICHEIC spent close to $10,000,000 in advertising costs for outreach. We knew this was an exorbitant amount of money, but we had to start somewhere and proceeded with the small, partial list of policyholders. We knew much more could be accomplished if we had the complete list.

The insurance companies said they did not have the old records available. They insisted that their files were destroyed, moved and/or lost during the war. This was partially true, but the physical investigation of our Audit Committee proved that there were hundreds of thousands of names in the files, in addition to the ones already given to ICHEIC.

After we crunched what numbers we had, we could estimate the approximate total number of Jewish policies written, and an average value for each policy. We also determined that the average value of the Jewish policy was much higher than the average non-Jewish policy. In many countries, it was three times the average.

We also had to reach an agreement concerning the value of contemporary currency in relation to the currency in existence fifty-plus years earlier, dealing with a different currency for each European country. This was all complicated because what was good for one company in a particular country could adversely affect another company in a different country. This created situations where consensus was impossible. So, despite Chairman Eagleburger's best intentions to rule by consensus, he was occasionally forced to make unilateral decisions. Such decisions were resented by the insurance companies, by the regulators, and by us.

At first we were optimistic. We included observers from different governments, additional representatives from the insurance companies and their lawyers, and other interested parties approved by the chairman in our meetings. But it was really no wonder that Larry confided to me, more than once, that these were the most difficult negotiations he had ever encountered in his long and diversified career—including his stint as Secretary of State of the United States.

Since the insurance companies distrusted American lawyers (this was the only time during the negotiations that I fully agreed with the insurance companies), they insisted that the main operation of ICHEIC would be conducted outside the United States, that the organization would not be an American corporation. Meetings were held primarily in England, with the key operating staff of the Commission located there. We did have one full meeting in Israel, with everyone in attendance, as well as a number of meetings in the States.

The best aspect of working on the Commission was the opportunity to work with former Secretary of State Eagleburger. It was a privilege to get to know him personally and observe his many fine qualities. I am honored that he is now my good friend. He told me that one of the key reasons he undertook the chairmanship of ICHEIC was because he believed that the State Department did not act humanely during the Holocaust, and he wanted to seize the opportunity to participate in something that would bring some justice to survivors and/or their heirs. As he put it, it was "a small measure of justice" to rectify past wrongs.

As things began to move, Allianz decided it wanted to be part of the German Foundation and divorce itself from the Insurance Commission. When Allianz brought it up, their proposal was rejected outright because the German Foundation was established to deal with matters of slave labor and forced labor, while ICHEIC was organized for the distinct purpose of dealing with multinational insurance companies and insurance issues.

Allianz's demand, linked to that of Lambsdorff's at the German Foundation—to be included with all German insurance companies in the German Foundation—occupied a great deal of the Commission's time and money, and for almost two years, paralyzed most of our work. We were pressured by Ambassador Bindernagel, an observer on behalf of the United States government, and by Stuart Eizenstat, Deputy Secretary of the Treasury, to agree to allow the German insurance companies, Allianz in particular, to be subject to the rules of the German Foundation instead of ICHEIC. This was despite the fact that Allianz had signed the MOU and was a full-fledged member of the International Commission on Holocaust Era Insurance Claims. The German Foundation had its own rules and regulations, so we argued that it would be bad precedent for ICHEIC to concede this point as it would surely lead to conflicts of interest.

Eventually, mine was the sole voice against including Allianz in the Foundation. Whenever Eagelburger said, "The train already left the station, and we have to accommodate the German Foundation," I responded with, "The train may have left the station, but every train has a brake, and we can pull the brake to stop it. That is what we have to do. Allianz has no right to be included within the scope of the German Foundation. Allianz had signed the MOU with ICHEIC and we should not give in to their demands. Allianz should be subject to the MOU like all the other insurance companies that signed the document."

I won a delay in the decision until Stuart Eizenstat, by then Deputy Secretary of State, requested a closed meeting in Washington with Larry Eagleburger and a few members of the Commission to resolve the impasse. Stuart firmly and forcefully pressured Larry to allow the German insurance companies, including Allianz, to become part of the German Foundation.

Larry angrily told Stuart, "You have to say these things because you represent the State Department. I am now functioning in my capacity as Chairman of ICHEIC. At this point in time, I am not working for the State Department. Although I intend to cooperate with you fully whenever possible, I cannot blindly take the position of the State Department."

Stuart's response to that was blunt: "If the German insurance companies are not a part of the German Foundation Initiative, Lambsdorff will not cooperate, and you will scuttle the agreement we worked so hard to achieve."

That's when I interjected: "Stu, I and my associates do not want to scuttle the German Foundation, since it will bring some form of justice to hundreds of thousands of people, both Jews and gentiles. But neither do I and my colleagues want you to scuttle ICHEIC. I will do my best to see how we can arrive at an amicable solution, but I do not want you to scuttle the Commission; it is morally not right to do so. And Allianz should not be part of the German Foundation."

Eventually, despite my lonely crusade, Allianz and the other German insurance companies were included in the framework of the German Foundation. The economic and political forces won, and morality and justice were tossed in the trash. Again, Allianz was now, essentially, off the hook.

For the next year and a half we had nothing but grief and delays in negotiations between ICHEIC and the German Foundation. Larry Eagleburger privately said to me, and even repeated it in open meetings, many, many times: "Roman, I should have listened to you. Allianz should never be part of the German Foundation."

The operating costs of ICHEIC also became quite an issue. The main reason for some of the extra expenses was the lack of cooperation from all the insurance companies. Allianz was in the forefront with their "partner in crime," the German Foundation. They were followed by the lawyers who howled their criticism because they anxiously wanted a piece of the action and couldn't get it.

ICHEIC has exposed many shenanigans—illegal, immoral, and unethical actions committed by the insurance companies. Some of the insurance company representatives barely mask their contempt for the legitimate claimants. The best example of this heinous behavior was expressed by a managing director of Allianz, Herbert Hansmeyer, in an article in *Forbes* on May 14,

2001. Referring to the Commission and the Foundation, he said, "Ultimately it is an act of public appeasement. I cannot become very emotional about insurance claims that are 60 years old."

Of course, Hansmeyer denied the intent of his statement. *Forbes* is not a magazine known for sensationalism, and therefore its readers, including me, took Hansmeyer's disgusting statement at face value. His comments clearly showed that the insurance companies would do all they could to avoid making payments for the old policies issued to Holocaust survivors. It was because of Hansmeyer's negative attitude and constant procedural delays that the speed at which claims were processed was slower than anticipated and the costs of running ICHEIC were higher than expected.

The Commission was called upon to establish guidelines dictated by moral, rather than strictly economic issues, namely a relaxed standard of proof, but the insurance companies balked. The slow processing of claims caused a Congressional Hearing to be convened by the Committee of Government Reform on November 8, 2001. The hearing was ostensibly called to investigate complaints registered by a few survivors who could not get proper satisfaction from the insurance companies. But it was the political pressure exerted by lawyers and local politicians, particularly Congressman Henry A. Waxman of California, that made it happen.

Dan Burton, a Congressman from California, chaired the hearing, Congressman Waxman, who was nasty and arrogant, did most of the questioning. I found him particularly offensive when he questioned Eagleburger and made uncalled for insinuations. When I heard enough to make me sick, I interrupted the hearing:

"Mr. Congressman, I have to interrupt this hearing because I don't like what is going on. Sir, let me tell you clearly and emphatically ICHEIC is not the criminal, Larry Eagleburger is not the criminal. You have no right to talk to him like this! I was a participant at ICHEIC meetings. The only crime that Mr. Eagleburger is guilty of is wanting to see that justice prevails for survivors, and he fights for it. You should point your finger at the insurance companies. You should point your finger at the German Foundation. You should point your finger at Allianz, just like I did. They are the criminals, not Mr. Eagleburger. You have no right to speak to him that way.

"Ten million dollars was spent on advertising. You know what, sir? If all the companies, Allianz and the others, would send us the lists of unpaid policies, instead of $12 million dollars, then maybe $40 or $50 million dollars would be paid out. So why don't you pass a law that they [the companies] will be thrown out of the United States if they don't honor the policies? This you can do. But don't come here and talk this way to Mr. Eagleburger. I have too much respect for him."

Until then, Congressional hearings were something I watched on television. As a participant, the reality was very different. For the first time, I fully grasped how unfair congressional hearings could be. It offended my sense of justice that elected officials could conduct an investigation with impunity and make derogatory insinuations that were contrary to the facts. In my eyes, conducting hearings for political gain was not the true way to get justice. What I saw was a stage show for politicians, held to advance their own careers among their constituents. I know what people say about generalizations, but there it is: by and large, that's the unfortunate truth about our system.

The experience was much ado about nothing. The hearing was not followed up. It created a paper trail for some individuals to fall back on when needed. The hearing was called to investigate ICHEIC, particularly the modus operandi of processing claims and the expenses incurred. After the hearing, nothing really changed. The insurance companies and the German Foundation continued stonewalling. Eagleburger and ICHEIC were left to their own devices, as it tried to process claims as quickly as humanly possible.

To Eagleburger's credit, he persevered in going forward and at all times, he did his very best. ICHEIC continues its work, and a number of survivors and their heirs are beginning to receive monies against policies issued before the Holocaust. Monies from unredeemed policies will be distributed to needy survivors, instead of becoming extra profit for insurance companies. To date, ICHEIC has made settlement offers of close to $100 million.

At one of the very first meetings of ICHEIC, with support from then Insurance Commissioner Bill Nelson of Florida, now a senator from that state, I approached the insurance companies with what I thought might be a simple solution. I was so naïve! I suggested that instead of money, the insurance companies provide all living survivors with health care coverage. My proposal was rejected outright. Allianz was the insurance company I had in mind, because it is the largest and has experience in health issues. But the bottom line for Allianz was the bottom line. Morality, ethics, and responsibility were cast aside. Allianz and the other companies felt all the money belonged to them, and forcing them to return it was an insult to their integrity. Asking for free or low payment health insurance coverage was, in their opinion, adding insult to injury.

The majority of policyholders or their heirs are still waiting for proper settlement. The Generali Company is making some progress, while Allianz continues to drag its feet. Contrary to all accusations and innuendos, ICHEIC has accomplished a great deal. We have received over $250 million and over $100 million from Allianz and Generali, respectively. The first $130 million is being distributed to needy survivors, primarily those who require home care.

After years of struggle, fights and delays, we have forced the German insurance companies to make public the names of about 365,000 policyholders who were victims of the Holocaust. These are individuals who had life insurance policies, but whose records were previously sealed. The two largest German life insurance companies, Allianz and Victoria zuBerlin, made them public. They were compiled by comparing the names of about 550,000 German Jews with about 8,000,000 insurance policies that were sold before World War II. It was a long, tedious task and they fought us tooth and nail. But publishing these names will give relatives of the victims concrete evidence of life insurance coverage, so that many additional claims can be filed.

As a Commissioner in ICHEIC, my work was filled with frustration and disappointment, but it provided me with a sense of accomplishment. Before I started this work, I had no idea how rich and influential these mega-corporations were. I learned a lot as a member of the Insurance Commission. In Germany, Allianz has its fingers in almost every large industry, and did not hesitate to exert political pressure on all levels of all governments. As the saying goes, "They could buy, sell, and trade politicians, and still have enough clout left over for bad times."

Such concentration of economic power is unhealthy, but we see more of it daily as the influence of economic giants multiplies at a rapid pace. Through my association with ICHEIC, I watched them do it. In the eyes of these huge conglomerates, individuals have no identity, and morality, ethics, honesty, and integrity are replaced with greed and power.

I am grateful I was offered the opportunity to participate. The survivors got some benefits from it and I was able to meet many outstanding, dedicated individuals who wanted to make a difference. They helped accomplish the impossible and the work continues, bringing some measure of long overdue and muted justice to survivors.

Though there are many who deserve credit for pursuing this thankless task, I really feel I must name some outstanding individuals who sat at the table and fought for the right thing because it was the right thing to do:

Bobby Brown	Representative/State of Israel
Tom Gallagher	Florida/Dept. of Insurance
Karen Heilig	Claims Conference
Diane Koken	Pennsylvania/Dept. of Insurance
Neil Levin (died 9/11, WTC)	New York State/Dept. of Insurance
Harry Low	California/Dept. of Insurance
Zvi Ramot	WJRO
Audrey Samers	New York State/Dept. of Insurance
Moshe Sanbar	Claims Conference
Nathanial Shapo	Illinois/Dept. of Insurance
Israel Singer	WJRO/World Jewish Congress
Elan Steinberg	World Jewish Congress
Gideon Taylor	Claims Conference
Leslie Tick	California/Dept. of Insurance

Larry Eagleburger is the most outstanding of all, a giant among men and the one whose efforts brought closure to the insurance issue. I will always cherish his friendship!

There is one other individual without whom none of the negotiations would have been possible. Whether it was the Claims Conference, ICHEIC, or the German Foundation, this person played a significant role and pulled off major coups.

For many years, Dr. Israel Singer has been in the forefront of issues bringing moral and ethical justice to Holocaust survivors. Among the numerous positions he has held in various organizations, Dr. Singer is past Secretary General and past Chairman of Policy Council of the World Jewish Congress; he is also past President of the Claims Conference. Flamboyant, gregarious, and outspoken, he is a dynamic speaker, and can deliver a perfect oration on almost any subject without written notes, and mesmerize any audience. Even when I do not agree with what he says, it is always a pleasure for me to hear him speak.

As I write, the twenty class-action and individual suits brought by survivors in Florida, California, and Wisconsin against Generali were thrown out of court by U.S. District Court Judge Michael Mukasey. He ruled that the President and the Executive Branch had jurisdiction over Holocaust-era claims against foreign companies or governments. This happened because the year before, the U.S. Supreme Court struck down a California law that favored survivors because, ostensibly, it allowed individual states to meddle in foreign affairs.

This is not the only event that troubles me in this matter, however. I remember a particular day in Rome, where ICHEIC was having one of its first meetings. I saw Skadden Arps attorney Kenneth Bialkin, former president of the Conference of Presidents of Major American Jewish Organizations, in a hotel lobby and wondered out loud what he was doing there. I was stunned to find out he was lead counsel for Generali. I simply could not believe it. After all those years in America, I thought American Jews had finally gotten it right. I was very, very wrong.

As to the lawyers who were involved in representing the corporations and German government against survivors, I wrote a letter to the editor of the *Forward,* on June 15, 2001. I stand by what I said then:

> "It is no wonder that the German government, the German insurance companies and others hired a disproportionately large number of Jewish lawyers. It was a premeditated effort to convince the Jewish community and the negotiating team that the Jewish lawyers working for the other side would somehow be working on our behalf. In fact, it was just the opposite."

Because of the efforts of the vaunted Jewish lawyers representing the Germans, our negotiations for the just treatment of those injured by Axis governments and their companies became even more difficult. While the fact that they were Jews implied their efforts would benefit the Jewish community, in fact this was simply not the case. As a result, I firmly believe that we should not honor "respected" Jewish attorneys who represent multi-national corporations and governments involved in slave and forced-labor negotiations or ICHEIC cases. These lawyers represented such clients solely because it paid extremely well, not for any alleged moral high ground. They were hired as a public relations strategy to project equity and the appearance of penitence, all the while making it more difficult for survivors to obtain a semblance of justice.

For me, these cases were not just about money, but about ethics and morality. For this reason, I continue to believe that Jewish lawyers should not have represented these hugely profitable entities that derived benefit from Jewish blood. It just doesn't work for me.

When some of these Jewish lawyers afterward claimed that their efforts helped Holocaust survivors, they should have been disbarred for admitting to a legal conflict of interest or derided for the duplicity of such representations. When supposed Jewish leaders, acting in their professional capacities as attorneys, defend organizations involved in negotiations over restitution for what, to me, were essentially war crimes, I want to know if they are survivors' friends or adversaries.

After the long and tough negotiations, I had my answer.

They were not our friends. All those individuals could have recused themselves if they had cared more about morality than money—they would have had six million reasons to do so.

This search for justice from the insurance companies was a Pyrrhic victory. Though we eventually received a settlement, I was greatly disappointed that the insurance companies outright rejected my proposal to provide the health care coverage so badly needed by survivors. It would have been the right thing to do, particularly after their egregious behavior for so many years in not addressing the claims of survivors and their heirs.

Ultimately, history will acknowledge the positive role ICHEIC played, since it was the first time insurance companies were challenged and held accountable for misdeeds they committed during and after the Holocaust.

The Presidential Advisory Commission on Holocaust Assets in the U.S. (Presidential Commission)

I was astonished when President Clinton appointed me to the twenty-one-member Presidential Advisory Commission on Holocaust Assets in the U.S., chaired by Edgar M. Bronfman. It was truly flattering to be on a commission with so many prominent educators and politicians. The appointment, of course, depended on my security clearance, and I received a voluminous amount of paperwork and forms to complete. There were hundreds of questions, some of them of a very personal nature. I had to recall facts and incidents going back twenty-five years, and they especially wanted the names of specific countries I visited and the names of people I met. It was impossible to provide all of the requested information, so I called the person in charge and discovered that the government has an entire department that does background checks on potential candidates for presidential appointments.

I was scrutinized by the Police Department, the CIA, the FBI, and other agencies. I still wonder why such a detailed clearance was called for, since the Commission had nothing to do with security issues. To the best of my knowledge, we were dealing in historical facts pertaining to the U.S. government and the Armed Forces and their handling of Jewish assets during the Holocaust. I found it strange that the Presidential Commission, created to investigate wrongdoing, if any, of the U.S. government, was created by unanimous bipartisan support of Congress on June 23, 1998.

This twenty-one-member Commission was charged by statute with:

- conducting a thorough study and developing a historical record of the collection and disposition of the assets [of Holocaust victims] if such assets came into the possession or control of the Federal government, including the Board of Governors of the Federal Reserve System, and any Federal Reserve bank; and
- comprehensively reviewing existing research into the collection and disposition of assets of Holocaust victims—to the extent that such research concentrates on assets that came into the possession or control of private individuals, private entities, or non-Federal government entities within the United States.

In other words, President Clinton created a Commission and charged it to investigate America's conduct concerning the assets of Holocaust victims during and after the war. It is quite unique for any government to investigate, of its own free will, misdeeds it may have committed.

The United States is a leader in the international effort in this quest for truth, and the creation of the Commission on Holocaust Assets is certainly the best proof of that. The mandate was neither to restore or restitute assets to their rightful owners, but to depict and document the historical role of the U.S. government. The Commission was to submit recommendations to the President on how to right any wrongdoing, if any, but had no power to enforce them.

Some say it's easy for the Presidential Commission and its

staff to do Monday-morning quarterbacking, and were critical of the effort, but the Commission did indeed find many legitimate and bizarre things to report. While these incidents did take place, it is my firm conviction that there was never premeditation on the part of the United States government and its Armed Forces to conduct themselves in anything less than a proper manner. As far as I am concerned, the U.S. Armed Forces were primarily responsible for winning the war and they had neither the personnel or know-how to participate in proper distribution of the enormous quantity of assets that they uncovered and of which they took possession.

American Allied Forces discovered that the robbery, pilferage, and devastation attributed to the Germans were far greater than anticipated and unparalleled in history. They didn't know what to do with the huge amount of plunder; the scarcity of manpower and limited resources they had forced them to put a very low priority on seeking out and returning looted assets to the rightful owners. It was simpler, easier, and faster for them to follow the long-established international tradition of restoring properties to individual citizens by delegating the assignment to the country of origin. This process, however, was destined to failure because Eastern European countries did not recognize inherent rights to private property. Thus hundreds of thousands of legitimate claimants who had lost their property had no one from whom to seek redress.

As part of the distribution process, the U.S. government came up with the idea of designating successor organizations as the recipients of some of the heirless and unassignable property. These successor organizations would then sell the assets and use the proceeds to resettle the displaced victims of the war. In general, assets under U.S. control were first restituted to national governments. In the event they were not fully identifiable, they were handed to international relief or successor organizations. But when it came to the return of currency, no matter where the monies were seized, it was returned to the country of origin. The exception to this rule was that Bulgarian, Finnish, Hungarian, and Romanian currency was sent to the Soviet government in Moscow and not to each respective nation.

Political considerations soon came to the fore. The American people wanted their troops home as soon as possible. Searching for and distributing the looted assets of others were not the concerns of an American populace tired of war and desirous of seeing their fathers and brothers, husbands and sons. It became difficult, therefore, to delay their return from service. As a result, it is regrettable that the United States did not adequately help the victims. In addition, by establishing short deadlines and lengthy administrative procedures, the U.S. government made the process cumbersome and almost impossible for the victims to claim their assets. The report told the story.

Due to the lack of American personnel, the Americans gave the Germans permission to control and administer large portions of the assets, the equivalent of putting the fox in the henhouse. German citizens were retained as clerical personnel and as guards for the warehouses that contained the looted treasure of Europe, the very same Germans who had done the initial looting. Of course, the Germans then would proceed to sidestep and break every rule they could in order to profit from what they had stolen from the world. They did then, like they do now, delay and delay in order to prevent anything from being returned to its rightful owners, especially if those owners were Jews.

The procedure for filing claims became impossible to follow when the looted assets, commercial and private, were put under German control. Stealing Jewish property was one of the side benefits for the Holocaust and looting was a major tactic employed by German troops wherever they went. Now, as German civilians, they continued this process.

When I was in post-war Germany after May 1945, I noticed that the American forces that occupied Europe after the war were not the same troops who had liberated us from the camps. As I mentioned earlier, these occupiers did not have the same commitment to justice as the liberators, and some of them were even hostile to the Holocaust survivors, preferring to deal with their German hostesses. This, I felt, was because they hadn't seen, with their own eyes, the devastation of our people, and so most of them didn't care very much about victims and justice. I believe that if the liberators had been put in charge of the assets program, they would have been committed to returning them to their rightful owners. It also didn't help that the Armed Forces didn't have the right personnel to take inventory, create a catalogue, or maintain accurate records.

For example, the Jewish Cultural Reconstruction, Inc. (JCR)—a successor organization created to preserve cultural assets of Jewish people—transferred approximately 158,000 items to libraries in the U.S. during the years 1949 through 1952. Many valuable Jewish and secular books and manuscripts were sent to the most prestigious universities in the United States. The Library of Congress, for example, received approximately 6,000 books and periodicals, many of them rare.

As a result of our efforts, it was determined that the Library could indeed identify some 2500 items that were part of the JCR efforts and caused the Library to recognize the "unique provenance" of the JCR items and to create a "name" field within its computerized virtual library acknowledging this material. In addition, special exhibitions were created highlighting the efforts of the JCR that utilized some of the JCR items in the Library's collection.

An extreme example of what happened to loot under Allied control is the case of the "Hungarian Gold Train." In 1944 the Hungarian government appropriated the assets of its 800,000 Jews. To prevent these assets from falling into Soviet hands, twenty-four railroad cars were loaded with gold, jewelry, works of art, carpets, coin and stamp collections, and all sorts of household items, including antique furniture. Over the course of five months, the train took a circuitous route from Hungary to Austria, in the general direction of Switzerland. During its travels, the items on board were frequently rearranged, repacked, loaded and unloaded, and also looted by the Germans, Austrians, and Hungarians assigned to guard the train.

In mid-May 1945, the Third U.S. Infantry Division seized the train near Werfren, Austria. In July 1945, it finally arrived at the U.S. military warehouse in Salzburg, Austria. Only then were the American property control officers able to compile a general inventory and unload the goods in the Salzburg military government warehouse. Discovered among the valuables was a box that contained the lists of names of the people from whom some of the items were taken. The control officers ignored that information. To add to the confusion, the property control officers labeled the inventory with words that the train's contents were the property of an "enemy government."

Since the inventory had been designated as enemy property, it became eligible for requisition by high-ranking U.S. officials seeking to decorate their residences in now-occupied areas. The Office of Property Control for Land in Salzburg was quickly inundated with requests for furniture, carpets, art, silverware, etc., mandating on the requisition forms that "items are to be of the best quality and workmanship available."

Regrettably, a number of officers left for home without returning the items. As the administration and general staff of the warehouse changed frequently, in March 1946 the Chief of the Property Control Branch was forced to report "considerable doubt as to the present location of the furnishings on loan." As a result, in August 1946, the department issued a directive forbidding the requisitioning of property from the "Gold Train," because the contents of the train could not be the property of the U.S. Army and was subject to simultaneous diplomatic negotiations with Hungary.

In the beginning of 1946, a State Department official issued a stern warning: "Property is now located in large warehouse at Salzburg which is not and probably cannot be adequately guarded. Strongly recommend that unless property can be promptly placed in well-guarded bank vaults, it be transferred to Frankfurt. I have been informed that a certain amount of looting from warehouse has already taken place and do not see how further dissipation of property can be prevented under present conditions. Fact that no inventory exists makes almost impossible for control officers to know whether looting is taking place."

For almost sixty years, the "Gold Train" would remain as yet another example of the losses attributed to the Holocaust. Since those assets had been in U.S. hands at the time, a recently filed lawsuit was brought that was settled in 2005 in which the U.S.

government agreed to pay $25.5 million to survivors who lost
their property on that train.

Another instance involving the de facto looting of Holocaust
assets was a curious phenomenon concerning U.S. bank accounts. Unlike the laws in Switzerland, dormant accounts in
U.S. banks could not remain the property of the banks in question, but eventually had to escheat (be given) to the state in
which that particular bank was located.

The overwhelming majority of foreign assets were deposited
in New York State, so the Presidential Commission worked
closely with the Office of the Comptroller, Allan Hevesi. The
Commission requested the creation of a database to assist in un-
covering the accounts, and our efforts were fruitful. We matched
up almost 400,000 names with about 1,000,000 unclaimed property requests and in that way found a few beneficiaries.

One of the Commission's other responsibilities was to deal
with the community of art museums around the world. The museums made a commitment to provide the Commission with information about Holocaust-era works in their collections. In one
instance, the National Gallery of Art actually returned to a family a piece of art from its collection.

Though I had watched the Germans plunder and loot the
Jewish community of Lodz, and watched them take everything
they could from any Jew, right down to the rags on our backs and
the gold in our teeth, it was not until I joined the Presidential
Commission that I fully realized the extent of that aspect of the
Germans' criminal intent. It was the largest robbery in history,
and its magnitude exceeded even that of the Inquisition. The
German government and the German people successfully carried out the largest, formal, legalized thievery ever perpetrated
against mankind. Tens of thousands of German civilians participated in, and directly benefited from, this thievery when they
moved into confiscated Jewish homes, took over Jewish properties and businesses, and called them their own. I remember vividly how the local Germans took over our home in Lodz and how
they seized my father's factory.

So when Count Otto Graf Lambsdorff notes with pride how

many billions of dollars the Germans have paid in reparations to the Jewish people, I am struck by the irony of his remarks. Perhaps if his comments were more truthful and indicated that the Germans were returning not even one tenth of what they stole (a current Israeli study places the amount at over $350 billion), that would be more acceptable to me and the other Holocaust survivors. And then, of course, what possible price would they put on the lives of the six million, if any? Who can put a price on the lives of the one and a half million children and their potential? Without question, each and every human life is priceless, and Lambsdorff might benefit from a bit of humility.

I also learned something that was extremely positive. The greatness of America is that she was ready and willing to open a potentially painful investigation into her own history that could expose her to criticism for her conduct during and after the war. Although the Presidential Commission was not empowered to correct or undo any misdeeds of the American government, it did open our eyes to the transgressions and wrongdoings committed by our country. For the United States to establish such a Commission that will act as a prototype for the future, deserves a great deal of praise and must be considered a significant historical achievement.

Twenty-four

Reflections on the United Nations Commemoration for the Sixtieth Anniversary of the Liberation of Auschwitz

"We shall never forget."

January 18, 2005 . . . day designated by the United Nations to commemorate the 60th anniversary of the liberation of Auschwitz and the opening of the Auschwitz exhibit. On this auspicious occasion, I was privileged to represent the International Auschwitz Committee in the official opening ceremony alongside Secretary General Kofi Annan and Undersecretary-General Shashi Tharoor.

At noon I found myself in the office of the Secretary General, together with Kazimierz Albin, an Auschwitz survivor from Poland, Kurt Julius Goldstein, an Auschwitz survivor from Germany, and Christoph Heubner, Executive Vice President of the International Auschwitz Committee, where we were joined by an army of reporters and photographers. Needless to say, for me the occasion and setting were more than surreal.

Interestingly, my mind started to behave strangely that day. I began to merge the past, present, and future. One could say I was in somewhat of a trance-like state. I do recall hearing the voice of the Secretary General introducing his wife, who asked to be present at the opening ceremony to meet the three Auschwitz survivors. It then dawned on me why she had asked to be present.

I realized that she was the niece of Raoul Wallenberg, the Swedish diplomat who became a legend for saving thousands of Hungarian Jews during the war. Wallenberg was last seen in

January 1945, accompanied by a Russian officer on the way to Russian Headquarters. His disappearance is one of the most famous unsolved mysteries of the Holocaust era.

Half an hour later, we all departed for the exhibit floor to take part in the official opening. Following the introductory remarks of Undersecretary-General Tharoor, and still in a daze, I heard my name called. Without knowing how I got there, I found myself at the podium.

I wanted to speak of my great honor at being present at these ceremonies, but strangely enough, in my mind, the year was 1945 . . . and I was still in Auschwitz. Haltingly, I began my remarks:

> As a prisoner in Auschwitz, just attempting to stay alive in my hopeless day-to-day existence, I could never dream that sixty years later I would be standing here before you at the United Nations opening an exhibit about Auschwitz.

My heart was beating at an accelerated rate as I continued.

> What is Auschwitz? Surely, it is much more than a word. It is a symbol . . . a symbol of evil. Let me put it another way. When speaking about World War II, we soon realize that "Auschwitz" has acquired a meaning of its own. It represents, first and foremost, the most terrible form of evil; the worst that mankind can offer.
>
> No matter how much one studies, how many books one reads, how many survivors one talks to, or how many degrees one receives in the study of the Holocaust, the non-survivor can never even get a partial picture of the agony, brutality, and bestiality that occurred daily in the concentration camps. Auschwitz is the prime example. What happened there is totally inconceivable, beyond man's wildest imagination, and as such, it can only become an abstract for the non-survivor.

I closed my eyes, and suddenly my arrival at Auschwitz was clearly visible to me. I trembled and started to perspire profusely. It seemed as if it was happening right then, rather than more than sixty years prior. With difficulty, I continued.

How can one document the smell of burning flesh which filled the air? How can one describe the living skeletons, still alive but just skin and bones? How can one hear their voices, touch them, console them, give them medical assistance and nourishment? . . . Many of us came to Auschwitz not knowing each other in life, but many of us left together in the form of blue smoke emanating from the chimneys. The few of us who were fortunate enough to have survived can neither forgive nor forget.

It is often said that one picture is worth a thousand words. Yet, there is no picture that could possibly convey the look in the eyes of the tortured, or the feeling of hopelessness and despair we prisoners were forced to endure. Can a picture or written word ever truly depict the shameful enjoyment on the faces of the evil German perpetrators?

I went on with my remarks.

It is also our obligation to instill in our children what happens when prejudice and hatred are allowed to flourish. It is my conviction that only through education can such a calamity be prevented from ever happening again. We must teach our children tolerance and understanding at home and in school; for tolerance cannot be assumed . . . it has to be taught. We must instill in our children that hate is never right, and love is never wrong.

I desperately wanted to emphasize the past and tie it to the present. I thought about my early childhood. In my youth, I learned what it meant to be part of a family. I learned not only who I was, but more importantly that I was. I learned that I existed because others cared for me, loved me. My life had value. The memory of my family, of the love I came to know and practice, helped me to survive the Holocaust. No matter what happened in the concentration camps, no matter what the Germans did to me, they could not succeed in convincing me that we did not matter and that our lives were of no value. I continued.

Lately, the world was greatly distressed and saddened by the unfortunate events which took place in southeast Asia as a result of the horrific Tsunami that unexpectedly swept over numerous countries. The devastation and heartbreak caused by this overwhelming tragedy, in locations such as Thailand and Indonesia, become evident to us because of the in-depth reporting of the press and the vivid images appearing on our television screens. That comprehensive coverage has kept us informed and is indeed more than praiseworthy.

It is truly heartwarming to see how mankind has come to the aid of others when needed. People wanted to help alleviate the pain and suffering of the hundreds of thousands who were left hungry and homeless because of a catastrophe beyond anyone's control.

As a survivor standing here today commemorating the 60th anniversary of the liberation of Auschwitz, I cannot help but think back to the time of the Holocaust and question why the same response was not available to us in our time of need. After all, in Auschwitz alone, 10,000 human beings were killed daily; no, not killed, brutally murdered and burned to death.

At that time, why in heaven's name was there no widespread recognition of the brutal acts being perpetrated on a daily basis? The facts were known. With a proper immediate response, surely much of what transpired could have been prevented. What occurred during the Holocaust was not a result of Mother Nature, it was man's inhumanity to man at its highest level.

In a simplistic way, I can say in one word why the tragedy of Auschwitz happened . . . that word is "indifference." For the world knew, the facts were known, just as they were known about the atrocities in Darfur, Kosovo, Rwanda, etc., and yet the world did nothing.

I was jolted back to semi-reality by a loud round of applause and by the rapid succession of questions posed by reporters, not only about Auschwitz, but my experiences in the United States as well. Since I lived most of my life in America, I was pleased to answer these questions. My mind was racing as I attempted to respond.

Yes, I answered. My life in the United States has been truly blessed. I have known Presidents, high-ranking politicians, and world leaders. I have nothing but admiration and love for the U.S., a nation that took in two orphans whose only "role models" for the previous six years of their lives were members of the S.S. and concentration camp guards. This land provided us with a secure home, an education, and an opportunity to succeed.

In a sense, the United States became a surrogate parent to

my brother and me. We arrived with nothing but our will to live in freedom and security, and a fervent desire to rebuild our lives from the ashes. America did not disappoint us.

We eventually married and dared to bring children into the world, always encouraging them to get the best possible education encompassing moral and ethical values with compassion for all. Slowly we began to participate in all phases of American life, becoming over time an integral part of the economic, social, and political life of the nation.

Surviving the Holocaust, and living in the United States, taught me that we—each one of us—must be more than a bystander. It was the "bystanders" in the 1930s that, by their silence, permitted evil men to perpetrate their evil acts. It is our responsibility to describe that evil in order to assure that history does not repeat itself.

It is also my responsibility to thank the United States for what I have achieved and for the opportunity it affords all of us to enjoy the fruits of our labor. Doing business with Eastern European countries for many years, I could not help but see the differences, which readily enabled me to recognize the benefits and advantages of living in a democratic society such as the United States. How difficult it was for one to succeed under those other forms of government.

From what I observed, I believe that in the long run, the systems that were practiced in Eastern European countries had no chance of succeeding. There was no motivation for the people to work in a productive manner when they would not be properly compensated for their efforts. It is only human nature that we should care for ourselves and our families first, our extended families second, and for society at large third.

If the order is reversed, then there is no proper inducement for us to perform at the highest level. That is why I believe that the system as practiced in the United States is best suited to society at large.

As the reporters' questions continued, I felt it necessary to bemoan what I saw as a dissolution of the greatness of the country that had done so much for me. I proffered that in recent years the country that once welcomed those yearning to be free with open arms, now was more content to put the hands of those arms into our pockets, as personal and corporate greed have seemingly become the hallmarks of our nation. I feel that if the greed which exists today is permitted to continue unchecked, in the end it will destroy our sense of value, ethics, and morality. I would hate to see this happen.

The current super-colossal mergers in the United States and throughout the world that concentrate great economic power scare me—as it was a similar concentration of economic and political power that led to a world war and then to the death of so many. The greatness of our country was not based on the concentration of economic power in the hands of a few. Our economy was created, and then thrived, on the concept of having small, individual entrepreneurs flourish—because in their fulfillment was the fulfillment of every man's aspirations, the fulfillment of what became known as the American Dream. I fear that if this trend continues to grow we will lose our individuality and become only numbers in these massive organizations. Still, with my personal exposure to other governments, I realize how much we should cherish our own regardless of how imperfect it is.

The Enron debacle is a perfect example of that dream gone astray, as greed and decay in moral values become the hallmark of our modern society. Yet, Enron is not alone. There is Global Crossing, Tyco, WorldCom, and I could go on and on, all evidencing how our moral values have given way to Mammon's call and the glitter of gold.

By and large, the people wielding great economic power are the ones who benefit the most from our system. Yet most of them are the first to take unfair advantage of our valued democracy to the detriment of the masses. Such unhealthy trends can be visibly traced by those new words that periodically enter our vocabulary. Did our forefathers (or even our fathers) ever hear words such as golden parachute, poison pill, and greenmail, or expressions used by accountants and lawyers such as "aggressive and creative accounting" or "vigorous defense"?

Years ago, business dealings that are now camouflaged by these newly coined words would certainly have been called unethical or illegal, if not downright fraudulent. Yet, these acts are committed daily and defended by the ones who benefit most, earning for them millions of dollars annually.

When I was a child, politics was considered a most-respected vocation. This was followed by careers in medicine, teaching, and the legal and accounting professions. How do we regard these professions today? In the eyes of the public, lawyers are at the bottom of the list, followed by politicians.

How times have changed. Earlier I wrote about how when I and many of my friends were in the concentration camps starving from hunger, and stole some food from the Nazis to keep us alive another day, or two, or three, we did not call it stealing. Stealing, to us, was just something that one should not do, even under those extreme circumstances. We still harbored some morality, ethics, and dignity. Thus, we felt the need to find a new word for such acts of stealing, and chose to refer to it as "organizing." We knew deep down that it was stealing, even though it was totally justified. The word, however, cleared our consciences, since it masked its original meaning.

Today, too many individuals look to camouflage their unethical, immoral, or outright fraudulent deeds by coining new words to disguise their greed and corrupt activities. Many claim that a broader oversight is needed to correct the prevailing condition. I believe that it is rather the need for greater integrity and morality by all concerned that would be the most effective tool.

When I finally completed the interview with the reporters, I could actually feel my thought process slowing down, my arms and legs functioning at half-speed. I was dizzy. Reality was slowly returning to the present time and place. I realized that I was at the United Nations, and that after sixty years, they were finally acknowledging the past.

Maybe now we are experiencing an awakening, and maybe today the world is finally beginning to change for the better. By this commemoration, there is visible proof of compassion and involvement instead of indifference. This is progress! Thus, I want to hope against hope that there is a brighter future ahead for mankind. Perhaps we are finally realizing that we all live together on the same planet, and we are all one people.

Postscript

When a man reaches more than four score years, he is permitted to look back and present to others the lessons he has learned during his lifetime. I struggled for survival, recreated a family to help replace the dear ones needlessly lost during the war, succeeded in business, and served the Jewish people to rebuild a community that was almost entirely shattered. Yet understandably, it is necessary for one to reflect not only on the past, but also to look keenly toward the future.

Ordinarily, a memoir, like the life that has given rise to it, requires a conclusion. Over the past several years, I have experienced the loss of many dear friends and colleagues, those who have taken similar paths to mine, living the same history and engaging in the same causes. Thus, although blessed with family and friends, I find myself more alone these days, more solitary.

Naturally, as a person ages, life becomes more difficult, and day-to-day living makes more demands. One tends to do less and does it at a much slower pace. In spite of this, because of my good fortune and what fate has enabled me to achieve, I am at peace with myself and welcome the future.

I cannot give up fighting for justice because there is still so much to be accomplished. The battles I have fought on behalf of my fellow man continue. The struggles that have demanded my attention over the years endure. Therefore, I do not have the luxury of only reflecting on the past. I am driven to continue to persevere in assisting the needy survivors, perpetuating Holocaust remembrance and promote education to combat anti-Semitism, bigotry, and hatred wherever they may be.

Therefore, the most significant conclusion I can reach is that my life is still a "work in progress" and maybe, just maybe, I was spared for a reason. As Robert Frost said, "I have promises to keep, and miles to go before I sleep."

Selected Speeches

1996 Humanitarian Award Presented to Roman Kent Seventh Annual Interfaith Concert of Remembrance Cathedral of St. John The Divine November 16, 1996

Mr. Chairman, Honored Guests, Ladies and Gentlemen, and of course, Survivors . . .

It is indeed a great honor to speak here on the topic: "Survivers; 50 Years in America." It is also a great responsibility. In whose name do I speak? In whose name do I accept the award?

Do I speak, and more importantly do I have the right to speak, in the name of the six million who perished and never had the opportunity to be here, never had the opportunity to be heard. Yet I know that their voices should and must be heard . . . if not for their sake, then for the sake of the living and for the generations to come. And so it becomes my task as a survivor and that of every survivor to bear witness for both the dead and the living. This being the 50th anniversary of my arrival to America, and in memory of the six million who could not be here tonight, let me share with you on their behalf a few of my dreams and experiences.

In early childhood, I learned what it meant to be a part of a family. I learned not only who I was, but more importantly that I was. I learned that I existed because others cared for me, loved me. My life had value. The memory of my family, of the love I came to know and practice, helped me to survive the Holocaust. No matter what happened in the concentration camps, no matter what the Germans did to me, they could not succeed in convincing me that we did not matter and that our lives were of no value. The recent emphasis by politicians of so-called "family values" has been the cornerstone of Jewish life for centuries.

During the Holocaust, the tragedy of our existence was so great that the non-survivor can never comprehend or even get a partial picture of the agony, brutality, and bestiality that took place on a daily basis in the concentration camps. What happened there is inconceivable and beyond one's wildest imagination. Although it took only a few days to arrive at Auschwitz, the horrors I experienced there are enough to keep me awake until the end of time. It is my belief that the Holocaust could have been partially prevented and millions of victims saved. Unfortunately, the world's answer to the Holocaust was indifference . . . indifference and silence. It was this silence that sealed the fate of millions of Jewish men, women, and children.

Having spent all of my adult life here in America, I can firmly state that in spite of the fact that ours is still an imperfect country, it is the only place in the world which offers freedom and liberty to millions of oppressed people. And that is what I discovered firsthand when I came here with my brother fifty years ago aboard an army ship, the *Marine Perch*. In America, I found freedom, liberty, the chance to receive an education, and an opportunity to build a new life. For this, America, I will be everlastingly grateful to you.

It was here that we survivors began our gradual journey back to life. We came to America, our adopted country, with nothing but our will to live in freedom and the fervent desire to rebuild our lives from the ashes. We married and eventually dared to bring children into the world, always encouraging them to get the best possible education encompassing moral and ethical values with compassion for all. Slowly, we started to participate in all phases of American life and became an integral part of the economical, social and political structure. As for myself, I was greatly influenced by the profound remark made by President Kennedy ". . . ask not what your country can do for you, ask what you can do for your country." To paraphrase . . . ask not what humanity can do for you, ask what you can do for humanity. This axiom can and should be applied to our dealings with people the world over. In my endeavors, this thought was the guiding light that influenced my work.

Surviving the Holocaust and living in the United States

taught me that we, each one of us, cannot be just a bystander and that we must be actively involved in the unity and brotherhood of man. Just look around you . . . we are here together in this magnificent Cathedral . . . Christians, Jews, Moslems . . . white, black, oriental, all races and creeds.

The presence of all of us here this evening represents the solidarity of man standing together in peace and harmony. We are the proof that it can be done, that it must be done now and forever.

I have a dream I would like to share with you tonight.

I have a dream that one day. . . .

Hate will turn into love
Greed will change to sharing
Deception and corruption will give way to honesty
Headlines that trumpet drugs and murder will praise poetry
   and music
Force and violence will be settled with a handshake
Guns and bombs will turn into plows so that hunger
   disappears

And yes, I have a dream, a dream that one day. . . .

Wars will become peace

And then I have a very strange dream that one day, a day still in my lifetime, I will wake up and find that these dreams became a reality.

Thus, with my eyes still half closed and looking up to the skies, to the "Rebono Shel Olam," the Lord above, I hope and pray that all of us will never be a bystander and that we will get involved and stay involved so that justice and peace prevail and a tragedy like the Holocaust will never happen again to us or to any other people. And let us all say AMEN.

In such spirit, I humbly and respectfully accept this award.

Remarks by Roman Kent
Chairman, American Gathering of Jewish Holocaust Survivors
Vice President, Claims Conference, Berlin, German Foreign Ministry
Bundestag—July 17, 2000

As I stand here today on German soil witnessing this historic moment, I, a survivor of the Lodz Ghetto, Flossenburg, and Auschwitz, find it surreal and feel humble and full of humility.

Surreal because this seat of power was instrumental in initiating and overseeing the most destructive war known to mankind, World War II, as well as the genocide of the Jewish people unparalleled in the annals of history. It also innovated the most hideous and brutal form of death known as "Tod Durch Arbeit" . . . death through work.

I feel humble for how can I represent and speak in the name of Jewish survivors when the list includes six million innocent men, women, and children brutally murdered during the Holocaust.

Thus, as I stand here today, there are two very painful questions in my mind. Painful, yes it is painful. But in order to secure a peaceful future for mankind, we must honestly and truthfully acknowledge the past. Why did the Holocaust happen, and secondly, why did it take until the year 2000 to officially recognize the "death through work" bestiality and establish the German Foundation Initiative called "Remembrance, Responsibility, and the Future"?

Let me, a survivor, a slave laborer condemned to "death through work" by the Germans, share with you my simple explanations. Holocaust is the most tragic example of what can happen when prejudice and hate reign and people follow. By people,

I do not mean just the Nazis, soldiers, or guards in the concentration camps. I mean the engineers, the draftsmen, the doctors, the chemists, the scientists, the businessmen, the politicians, and yes, the lawyers that legalized it . . . all of whom devoted their energies to create the most efficient means of mass destruction of the Jewish community.

As to the Foundation, well, why call it "initiative" when in actuality the need for accountability for slave and forced labor, both Jewish and non-Jewish, was brought about by the recent demands of survivors linked with economic and legal issues. But to my way of thinking, it was possible to establish the Foundation because in a way Germany entered a new era . . . an era when the new generation born after the war realized the magnitude of the destruction brought forth by their forefathers and understood that places like Auschwitz, Treblinka, and "death through work" acquired a meaning of their own since they represent evil, the worst that mankind can offer.

This Foundation, approved by approximately 90 percent of the Bundestag, is the conscience of the new generation. Yes, it was enacted sixty years late and is only a token gesture to financially compensate the slave and forced labor. But it is the moral recognition for past wrongs, and we survivors take it as such.

I and the other survivors associated with the negotiations did not speak about money. How could we? The lives of one-and-a-half million Jewish children are priceless. We will never equate morality and ethics in terms of dollars and cents. We only stress morality . . . this is our sacred duty.

We survivors cannot forgive nor forget. To forgive and forget can only be granted by the six million who were murdered, and they are dead and their voices cannot be heard anymore. We the living survivors do not believe in collective responsibility; nor do we believe that the children should be responsible for the crimes of their fathers. Thus, it is our destiny that we survivors and you the German nation must carry the burden of this terrible crime from now to eternity.

We did not come here to shed tears, nor did we come here to elicit pity or love. We came here to memorialize the ashes scattered throughout the concentration camps and ghettos; we came here knowing that these ashes, these bones of murdered Jews lying in their graves cannot and must not be forgotten. For if we were to forget, the conscience of mankind would then be buried with them.

For the past forty years, we survivors have been committed to preserve the memory and uniqueness of the Shoah, and we have achieved this by supporting museums, commemorations, and above all through educational programs. We hope and pray that the victims of the Holocaust did not die in vain. We must be a moral force, and by example make the world a better place to live. That would be the greatest legacy we survivors can leave for posterity.

We survivors have realized that the story of Shoah must be told and retold. Yes, the story has been told—but not often enough. Forever would not be often enough. Yes, the story has been told—but never well enough. How can one speak the unspeakable?

We survivors have also learned that the opposite of love is not only hate but indifference. How alone we were during the Holocaust. We must recognize that we cannot just be bystanders, for if we are, our morality and ethics will also be laid to rest and buried alongside the six million victims of the Shoah.

I have hope that you, the new German generation, by this acknowledgment of your moral responsibility, will follow in our footsteps. If the Foundation is to have any meaning for the future, the terrible lesson of the Holocaust must be understood in your land and throughout the world so that the Holocaust can never happen again to us or to any other people.

Thank you.

I would like to expressly acknowledge our President, Bill Clinton, for the active role he took in these negotiations. As to Deputy Secretary of the Treasury Stuart Eizenstat, his role was invaluable, and without his wisdom and patience the negotiations would never have been brought to fruition. Stuart Eizenstat was ably assisted by Ambassador J.D. Bindenagle. We also appreciate the positive involvement of Chancellor Schroder. Last, but not least, I want to acknowledge my fellow survivors who participated in these difficult negotiations, namely Ben Meed, Noah Flug, Ben Helfgott, Karl Brozik, under the most able and devoted Chairmanship of Dr. Israel Singer . . . their moral strength and wisdom have been invaluable. The leadership of Rabbi Israel Miller, Gideon Taylor, and Saul Kagan is greatly acknowledged. Of course, the input of Stanley Chesley and his staff who worked tirelessly on a pro bono basis is greatly appreciated.

Remarks by Roman Kent
Acceptance of
Harvey Schulweis Award
JFR Dinner—December 11, 2000

Thank you, thank you for recognizing the importance of the humanitarian, interfaith work accomplished by the Jewish Foundation for the Righteous.

I humbly accept the honor bestowed upon me in the name of all supporters of the Jewish Foundation for the Righteous. It belongs to all of us. For if there is one group that fully appreciates the unique role the Righteous Gentiles played during the Holocaust it is the membership of our Foundation.

I will now attempt to answer the question why I, a Jewish Holocaust survivor, an individual who has witnessed the most hideous atrocities perpetrated by man, would be committed to an organization such as the Jewish Foundation for the Righteous.

My response could be best summed up in the widely known reflection of our sages . . . "He who saves but one life, is as if he saved a whole world." That alone, however, is just the beginning.

When we look back on the Holocaust, the Kingdom of Night, there are but a few holy gestures which somehow redeem our faith in humanity and mankind. Without hesitation, falling into this category are the courageous and heroic deeds of individuals who saved Jewish lives during the Holocaust.

To save innocent Jewish lives, the Righteous Gentiles endangered their own lives, and in most instances the lives of their families as well. Righteous Gentiles, the few among millions, showed the world that the answer to tyranny and indifference is involvement.

Their deeds should serve as an example of what could have been done, as in indictment of what was not done, and as a moral torch in a world of oppression and darkness. Their brave deeds

374

should be an inspiration for generations to come, and it is only fitting that their heroism should not diminish with the passage of time.

The Christian rescuers taught us that even in the hell known as the Holocaust one had the capacity to behave humanely if one only cared and had the courage to act accordingly. The Righteous Gentiles did just that, they are the perfect example. Indeed the Righteous Gentile exemplifies the oneness of all religions and races.

To help them in their old age, the Jewish Foundation for the Righteous provides financial support to over 1,700 needy Righteous Gentiles through the world. This beautiful banquet we are attending here tonight helps to keep the memory of the Righteous Gentiles' acts of valor and heroism alive for generations to come.

The least I can contribute today to that cause is to donate the monetary portion of the award to the Foundation.

May I add, if anyone present would like to become a part of the meaningful work of the JFR, your participation in this most worthy cause will be more than welcome.

The Folsbiene Yiddish Theatre Gala
Concert at Carnegie Hall
Remarks by Roman Kent—June 3, 2004

Throughout the centuries of our history, it is difficult to visualize Jewish survival without two forms of culture unique to Jewish life. Both were integral parts of Jewish culture, and as such, helped us to survive thousands of years of oppression and persecution.

One is books . . . our Torah, our book, is the most widely read book in Western civilization.

Just a step behind books is our music. The music of the Jewish people, the "Nefesh" . . . the soul of "Am Israel" of Jews wherever they are.

There is the happy and vibrant music associated with birth, bar/bat mitzvah, and weddings. Then there is the music of pain and sadness depicting pogroms, persecution, deportation, and loneliness in a strange land.

It is surreal to me on the evening of June 3, 2004, sixty years after the Holocaust that I, a graduate of the Lodz Ghetto with a master's degree from concentration camps Auschwitz, Gross-Rosen, and Flossenburg, am standing before a full house at world-renowned Carnegie Hall. How honored I am to be called upon to participate in The Folksbiene Yiddish Theatre program of Jewish music and songs that includes the legendary Neil Sedaka.

I couldn't help but compare The Folksbiene Yiddish Theatre sign of welcome to Carnegie Hall tonight with the one which greeted me in Auschwitz so many decades ago. I will never forget the bold, black letters at the Auschwitz gate which read "Arbeit Macht Frei" . . . "Work will make you free," which really meant "Tod Durch Arbeit" . . . death through work, with life expectancy of ninety days once you entered the gate.

And so, I was a witness to death; no, not just death, but the premeditated murder of innocent men, women, and children. Equally important, on June 3, 2004, I became a witness to the rebirth of Jewish life in America.

With my eyes half closed, but my mind wide open, I vividly remember that during the Holocaust another dimension was added to Jewish music . . . the sound of defiance. In the ghettos, in the forests, and in the concentration camps, Jewish artists composed music and performed concerts often at the peril of their own lives.

In the Lodz Ghetto, concerts were presented in cold, unheated, dark and dingy halls. The freezing musicians wore shabby gloves that partially exposed their fingertips so they could play their instruments. The beautiful sounds they created reached up to heaven and gave us, the starving and desperate ghetto inhabitants, the necessary spark and will to live another day . . . another day . . . and yet another day.

These Jewish artists, without guns at their disposal, are the unsung heroes of the Holocaust. Their music accomplished more than guns ever could, for they were the messengers of life rather than the gun-totting messengers of death.

It is amazing that some of us, the slave laborers condemned to death, did survive and are alive to witness today about two hundred young Jewish children on the Carnegie Hall stage singing Yiddish songs together with Neil Sedaka and the Klezmatics. Their presence and your support of The Folksbiene Yiddish Theatre is the proof of our survival and the Jewish tradition of continuity. For this I thank you from the bottom of my heart.

Reflections: "The Century That Was, Was . . ."

December 31, 1999

It was the best of times—

1999 — Life expectancy 76 years
1900 — 36 automobile fatalities

It was the worst of times—

1999 — 41,000 automobile fatalities
1900 — Life expectancy 47 years

It was the age of wisdom. What is better than wisdom? Woman.
   What is better than a good woman? Nothing.
It was the age of foolishness. I am not denying that women may
   be foolish, but God Almighty made them to match man!

It was the epic of belief . . . in the might of design, the
   usefulness of science and the goodness of man
It was the epic of incredibility . . . science fiction came to life

It was the season of light . . . both figuratively and literally
It was the season of darkness . . . the explosion of the A-Bomb

It was the spring of hope . . . penicillin, vaccinations,
   transplants, and Viagra
It was the winter of despair . . . the first time we had the means
   to destroy our little planet

We had everything before us; we had nothing before us
We were going directly to heaven or we were going directly the
   other way

378

Obviously, I took liberties with Dickens, but I must not over-look the tremendous achievements which were accomplished in the 20th century in practically all fields: medicine, physics, as-tronomy, communication, genetics, and the list could go on and on.

Therefore, I would like to characterize the 20th century as follows:

1. It is my strong conviction that the mind-boggling changes, particularly the scientific advances which took place in the sec-ond half of this century, have outpaced our ability to comprehend such rapid changes. We must now become specialists not just in one branch of science, but sub-specialists, comprehending a min-ute segment of the totality.

2. The second characteristic of the 20th century is what I call insecurity: political, economic, and social.

Political—We have had wars since the beginning of time, but never the means of complete annihilation.

Economic—Today we have a global rather than national econ-omy with complete disregard for individuals, states, and coun-tries.

Social—Since the time of Adam and Eve, the backbone of moral-ity and ethics was strong family ties. This unfortunately has greatly deteriorated and today these ideals are at their lowest level, providing little for new generations to look up to.

Let me add one more, a "catch-all" category . . . Indifference—to stand idly by, to see people suffer and to do nothing, or to do too little and/or too late. To put it another way, to love or hate and express it with words only is not enough, since I believe that the opposite of love is not hate, but indifference.

In spite of its shortcomings, I must emphasize that for me this century is ending on a positive note. On December 17, 1999 I witnessed a historical event that proved to me that everything is possible, and goodness will eventually prevail over evil. I, a survivor of the Holocaust and the Auschwitz Concentration Camp, was able to attend a news conference on that date held in Berlin at the Presidential Palace of German President Johannes Rau. I, a survivor of Auschwitz, listened to President Rau's plea: "I beg your forgiveness in the name of the German people. We will never forget your suffering."

And I, a survivor of the Holocaust, was able to reply to the President and the world at large: "The remarks made by you, President Rau, justify the efforts we (survivors) have placed on morality, and morality only. Forgive us for we have sinned. That is what we and the world heard today. Let these words reverberate now and forever here and throughout the world so that another Holocaust can never happen again to us or to any other people."

Finally, on a much brighter note, let me give you but a few examples of the adjustment in style and language we have seen in this century, many of them in our lifetime.

In the last century . . .

We got married first, and *then* lived together.
Closets were for clothes, not for "coming out of."
Bunnies were small rabbits, and rabbits were not
     Volkswagens.
"Making out" referred to how you did on your exam.
Grass was mowed, Coke was a cold drink, and Pot was
     something you cooked in.
Aids were helpers in the Principal's office.
For us, a chip meant a piece of wood.
Hardware meant hardware, and Software was not even a
     word.

No wonder I am so confused and am sending you such a convoluted message. I cannot blame it on my wife so I blame it on a century-long generation gap. But *I SURVIVED, WE ALL SURVIVED!* What better reason to celebrate. The best is yet to come. I wish you and your loved ones a very healthy and Happy New Year.

Remarks by Roman Kent at the
Bat Mitzvah of Emmalee Kent
May 6, 2006

Shabbat Shalom . . . Shabbat Shalom to one and all.

It is somewhat strange and awkward for me to be the one standing on "the bima" today to address Emmalee, her family and the congregation at large. For it is Emmalee's grandfather, my brother Leon, who should be standing before you on this happy occasion. That must be the reason why I sense his presence so strongly, and feel he is standing right here next to me, just as he had been by my side during the Holocaust.

Since our entire family had the misfortune of being part of the Holocaust, obviously my brother Leon became much closer to me than the average brother. One of the primary reasons I survived the dreadful ordeal was due to the fact that Leon was there for me to cling to during those horrific days in the ghetto, Auschwitz, and other concentration camps. Being together gave us an additional chance and helped us to survive. So when I was asked to speak here, I accepted the kind invitation on behalf of Leon, and thus, in a way, we are both standing before you witnessing the continuity of Jewish life.

A short while ago, Passover was celebrated in the homes of Jewish people throughout the world. This meaningful and joyous holiday commemorates the liberation of our ancestors that occurred about 5,000 years ago ending the merciless slavery they endured at the hands of the Egyptian Pharaohs. Sadly, history repeated itself when sixty years ago your own grandparents became slaves in the land of the Germans.

Understandably, these two events have become an integral part of our Jewish history. Yet, they are commemorated quite differently. The memory of the Holocaust is commemorated by the entire community at large, while Passover is celebrated in

381

the intimacy of the home in the midst of family and friends. The fondest memories from my childhood, and that of your grandfather, Leon, whom unfortunately you never had the pleasure of meeting and knowing, were the ones associated with "seders" when we sat around the dinner table surrounded by our loving family. I hope, Emmalee, such memories will be yours as well.

It may seem paradoxical when one considers the fact that Bar or Bat Mitzvah, which in effect relates to personal achievement and the individual recognition of a boy or girl becoming a full-fledged Jew, is acknowledged by a ceremony witnessed not just by family, but rather in full view and participation of the community. In essence, this is one of the few joyous events in Jewish life that occurs with full participation of family, friends, and the community at large.

For you, Emmalee, today is a day of transformation, a moment in time that symbolizes continuity of Jewish life and customs. According to our tradition, you are no more a child. You are a full-fledged Jewish woman, with all of the privileges and obligations this entails. On a personal note, I certainly can see you accepting all of the privileges; regarding the obligations, well, that is another story.

Adulthood comes upon us all of a sudden, but let me reassure you that no one is ever fully prepared for it. Even today, so many years after my own Bar Mitzvah, over sixty years after being admitted to the brotherhood of Jewish men, my wife and even some friends often remind me . . . "Roman, don't act like a child!" So, Emmalee, don't be afraid of suddenly entering this sacred world of adults. Just remember to behave like one, but never lose your youthful spirit and zest for life.

I, together with all those present today, heard you conducting the service in a most meaningful manner. To your credit, you accomplished this in spite of the numerous distractions which you had to overcome. I would be remiss not to mention a few additional disruptions you had to contend with, such as your parents and your older sister. In your eyes, I am sure all of them bothered you greatly, if not constantly. Yet, in a weak moment, you may admit that they were of great help.

I noticed how absorbed you were in conducting this service.

Therefore, you probably did not see the tears falling down the cheeks of your grandma, Hanki. If you did, I am sure you would ask yourself, "Why? Why should my grandma cry during this happy occasion? Did she suddenly remember all the things I did wrong in the past? There certainly could not be so many to make her cry. No, that could not be it." And you would be right.

Your grandma was indeed wiping away tears, but these were tears of happiness not of sorrow. We who lost most of our family during the Holocaust are overwhelmed with joy to see our family grow, and witness a granddaughter such as yourself become an "adult" member of the Jewish community.

With the celebration of your Bat Mitzvah, you are a full-fledged Jew. Now, however, you have an added obligation thrust upon . . . you are officially a "third generation" Holocaust survivor. Just like the family members who preceded you, it is your responsibility and obligation to see to it that the world never forgets what transpired during those dark days of our history; keep in mind that not only were we slaves in Eygpt thousands of years ago, but we were also slaves in our own "modern times" in the 20th century.

For us survivors, and hopefully for you, it is crucial that we remember the past, for without that, there is really no present or future. The chain, the link that binds us with the past, makes us guardians of the present and prepares us for the future.

For your grandmother, and for us as well, this simply means continuity. You are the visual proof that Jewish people live and Hitler did not succeed! You, dear Emmalee, represent the continuity which symbolizes and cements Jewish life, and strengthens our spirit and tradition.

Let me leave you with the following wish list . . .

Be a good person. This sentiment is expressed best in Yiddish, be a "mensch" . . . and as my son, Jeff, said, for only by being a good human being, can you be a good Jew.

Also, remember to laugh . . . laugh freely every day. More good things are accomplished with laughter than with any other state of mind.

And be happy. Happiness should be a sub-total of all you do. Be strong, yet weak when necessary. Be tough, yet full of compassion. Go forward, but know when to stop or retreat. Work hard, yet have fun while doing it. Have your own ideas, yet keep an open mind to the advice of others. And remember give of yourself, for it is more rewarding to give than to receive.

Enjoy this important day and remember it fondly. Going forward, be what you are . . . always be yourself and be proud of our heritage.

And finally, if I may be so bold on this meaningful occasion to add an 11th Commandment to the familiar Ten Commandments prominently displayed in Houses of Worship; I would say to you, Emmalee, and to each and every one . . . never, never be a bystander, for silence ultimately sanctions all crimes committed on the earth.

Mazel Tov!